David Hepworth has been writing, broa[...] music and media since the seventies. H[...] and editing of magazines such as *Smash Hits*, *Q*, *Mojo* and *The Word*.

He was one of the presenters of the BBC rock music programme *The Old Grey Whistle Test* and one of the anchors of the corporation's coverage of Live Aid in 1985. He has won the Editor of the Year and Writer of the Year awards from the Professional Publishers Association and the Mark Boxer Award from the British Society of Magazine Editors.

He lives in London, dividing his time between writing for a variety of newspapers and magazines, speaking at events, broadcasting work, podcasting at www.wordpodcast.co.uk and blogging at www.whatsheonaboutnow.blogspot.co.uk.

He says Chuck Berry's 'You Never Can Tell' is the best record ever made. 'This is not an opinion,' he says. 'It's a matter of fact.'

1971: Never A Dull Moment

'A trawl through the year in which albums took over from the pop single as the primary unit of consumption'   *Guardian*

'A richly entertaining reminder of when LPs ruled the world'   *Spectator*

'A witty, self-deprecating history of Hepworth's own *annus mirabilis*'   *The Times*

Uncommon People:
The Rise and Fall of the Rock Stars

'Hepworth is such an engaging writer'   *Irish Independent*

'Hepworth has acquired deep reservoirs of knowledge and a towering stack of anecdotes. He deploys his weaponry wisely and writes in an easy, fluid style'   *New Statesman*

'This book is a kind of elegy for a glorious but passing phase in entertainment history ... brim[s] with insight, humour and a certain genial astringency ... terrific'   *Mail on Sunday*

A Fabulous Creation:
How the LP Saved Our Lives

'Fascinating'   *The Week*

'A hugely entertaining study of the LP's golden age'   *The Times*

'Hepworth has more insider knowledge and knows more rock anecdotes than any man alive'   *The Herald*

Nothing is Real: The Beatles Were Underrated And Other Sweeping Statements About Pop

'This collection of Hepworth's journalism offers counterintuitive takes on everything from Sixties B-sides to wedding music' *GQ*

'A collection of essays that stretch and soar across a career spanning five decades' *Guardian*

'A collection [that] considers the real legacy of the Beatles, the importance of the drummer, the demise of the record shop – and much else besides' *Choice Magazine*

The Rock & Roll A Level: A Very Hard Pop Quiz

'The questions are as fascinating as the answers' *Choice*

'Unmissable for music enthusiasts . . . This isn't a book regaling you with facts and figures and chart positions, but a book for people who see real life through music' *Woman & Home*

'The broadcaster, radio commentator and *Radio Times* columnist combines general knowledge with anecdotes into a quiz book for pop lovers' *Radio Times*

Also by David Hepworth

1971 – Never a Dull Moment

Uncommon People – The Rise and Fall of the Rock Stars

Nothing is Real – The Beatles Were Underrated and Other Sweeping
Statements About Pop

A Fabulous Creation – How the LP Saved Our Lives

The Rock & Roll A Level – A Very Hard Pop Quiz

OVERPAID, OVERSEXED AND OVER THERE

HOW A FEW SKINNY BRITS WITH BAD TEETH ROCKED AMERICA

David Hepworth

BLACK SWAN

TRANSWORLD PUBLISHERS
Penguin Random House, One Embassy Gardens,
8 Viaduct Gardens, London SW11 7BW
www.penguin.co.uk

Transworld is part of the Penguin Random House group of companies
whose addresses can be found at global.penguinrandomhouse.com

Penguin
Random House
UK

First published in Great Britain in 2020 by Bantam Press
an imprint of Transworld Publishers
Black Swan edition published 2021

A CIP catalogue record for this book
is available from the British Library.

ISBN
9781784165031

Typeset in Minion by Jouve (UK), Milton Keynes.
Printed and bound in Great Britain by Clays Ltd, Elcograf S.p.A.

The authorized representative in the EEA is Penguin Random House Ireland,
Morrison Chambers, 32 Nassau Street, Dublin D02 YH68.

Penguin Random House is committed to a sustainable
future for our business, our readers and our planet. This book
is made from Forest Stewardship Council® certified paper.

This one's for my in-laws,
Tim Timmington and Annabel Rolls

CONTENTS

INTRO

They couldn't believe it.

The Beatles, who arrived in February 1964, couldn't believe that every time they spun the dial on the transistor radios they were gifted in New York there was yet another station playing their music.

When the Rolling Stones landed in New York in June of the same year they couldn't grasp that the temperature could climb as far as the high eighties.

When Eric Burdon of the Animals got there in late 1964 he was dazzled by the fact that American TVs came on straight away and didn't take an age to warm up as the ones at home did.

The following year, Graham Nash of the Hollies was similarly amazed to learn that if you didn't have time to go to a restaurant it was actually possible to have the restaurant send food to you.

Ozzy Osbourne of Black Sabbath couldn't get over being introduced to pizza, reporting excitedly back to his friends in Birmingham, 'There's a new food.'

Colin Blunstone of the Zombies was nineteen when he went on

his first US visit; his mother, unable to process the idea of a plane journey long enough to require the provision of meals, made him a packed lunch.

For Chris Dreja of the Yardbirds, gazing down from the eyrie of his New York hotel room, the cars on the street below appeared like boats.

For all these awestruck arrivals, everything about the United States seemed to have a dream-like quality.

The Americans who welcomed these immigrants when they arrived spoke their language but it was often difficult to work out the meaning of their welcome. Elton John, arriving in 1970, wondered why somebody had thought it a good idea to greet him at Los Angeles International airport with a red double-decker London bus.

In much the same way as the visitors had certain expectations of Americans, their welcoming parties often had a narrow notion of Englishness. Brian Jones of the Rolling Stones was met at JFK airport in New York by a photographer who insisted he pose with an Old English sheepdog because – well, the hair.

These people soon realized America was, in many ways, a harder land. Pink Floyd couldn't believe it when their agent suggested their manager ought to carry a gun.

Similarly the Beatles PR man Derek Taylor got a lift from the airport to the Indiana State Fair with a driver who apologized for taking him through a section of town he called 'Coonsville'.

Mike Pender of the Searchers saw the steam escaping from the grates on New York's streets and wondered from what diabolical underworld it could possibly have escaped.

Some arrivals took one look around them and decided they had finally arrived in their true home. Gazing up at the canyons of Manhattan, Rod Stewart resolved he would never see Orpington again.

They were deeply impressionable. Robert Plant was just twenty when he first went to Los Angeles and he later remembered 'all that English dourness swiftly disappeared into the powder-blue, post Summer of Love California sunshine'.

All these young men, and they were overwhelmingly young men, came from a country that at the time believed a taste for luxury or convenience was a harbinger of inevitable moral decline. Rick Wakeman, who went to the United States with Yes in the early seventies, could not believe they were staying in hotels with rooms that had actual bathrooms because 'we were used to bed and breakfast in the UK'.

They also came from a country not given to the advertising of feelings. John Peel, who first went in 1960, had never before heard a woman say 'fuck'.

The natives were refreshingly demonstrative in all kinds of ways. Jeff Lynne remembers the car load of American girls passing his band on Hollywood Boulevard, raising their shirts and showing their breasts. He remembers the band of Brummies looking at each other and saying, 'Good here, innit?'

It was all unimaginably thrilling. The time off was like an unsupervised school trip for horny young adults, financed from a bottomless exchequer. Even the work part, the bit that might be a chore back in the UK, was suddenly hugely exciting once you did it in the place you were soon referring to, to the considerable annoyance of your friends back in England, as 'Stateside'.

Ian Hunter of Mott the Hoople, one of the few of these adventurers actually to keep a diary, likened the experience of touring America to getting married every day.

These musicians' collective experience as part of what became known as the British Invasion changed them all as people. It also changed music. Furthermore, this apparently benign clash of cultures changed America as well. For the rest of us, who merely remained at home and read about it, well, it changed us too.

Once it had happened it seemed as though it had always been inevitable. Before it happened it had seemed as though it was impossible.

And the amazing thing was that when it happened, it happened so, so quickly.

Insufficient respect is paid by scholars of pop music to Germany's 'Iron Chancellor' of the nineteenth century, Otto von Bismarck. Asked near the end of his life in 1898 what he felt had been the most significant factor affecting modern history, he answered, 'The fact that the Americans speak the same language as the English.'

The Chancellor couldn't have been expected to see exactly how this factor would come to govern the outcome of two world wars involving the nation he represented. And it would clearly have been asking too much of him to foresee how this factor would play in another world where a shared language can similarly grease the wheels – the world of the popular song.

For the last hundred years, since the invention of radio and the talking pictures, two forms of entertainment have shaped the consciousness of much of the world: one has been pop music and the other has been the Hollywood movie. As Bismarck predicted, much of that shaping has taken place in English, whether in its original form or in its significantly different American incarnation.

Even at the time Bismarck spoke, in the era of horse-drawn transport and a pianoforte in every middle-class living room, there was already a brisk traffic in musical comedies and popular song between London and New York. In the nineteenth century the big hit operettas of Gilbert and Sullivan were regularly imported and often imitated on Broadway. However, the traffic wasn't all one-way, nor was it always of the kind you might expect.

The buttoned-up English had an unexpected reputation for craving novelty. Soon after the turn of the century the musical *In*

Dahomey, with its cast of African-Americans, toured Britain with great success. The Original Dixieland Jazz Band played 'Tiger Rag' at Buckingham Palace in 1919 in front of an audience that included King George V and Marshal Pétain of France. This was at a time when no similar invitation was forthcoming from the band's own President in the White House in Washington.

In the twenties and thirties, British entertainers Noël Coward and Gertrude Lawrence found Broadway audiences eager to lap up songs like 'The Stately Homes Of England', especially when delivered from the vicinity of an apparently authentic stiff upper lip.

This was broadly the way the trade worked for most of the twentieth century. Britain sent its quality of apparent classiness to its former colonies. In return, America sent sass.

This suited both countries. It was so widely accepted by both sides that the British were too cold-blooded to do the sexy stuff and the Americans too set against anything 'fancy' to do much that you would call classy, that it seemed this would be the way things would obtain throughout eternity.

This division of creative labour was further set in stone following the Second World War by the fact that, much as in the world of political power, American domination of the market for popular entertainment was achieved at the direct expense of Britain. They were now the rich cousins and we were the poor relations.

I was born in 1950 and as soon as I was exposed to popular entertainment I became aware of the clunkiness of the British version compared with the American. Whether in movies, TV or pop music it seemed that Americans spent more money, had access to better technology, were less troubled by inhibition and, most wounding of all, seemed to be using our own language better than we knew how to use it ourselves.

When rock and roll arrived from America in 1956 it hurt even more because now it was painfully clear that somebody like Elvis

Presley was about more than mere music. It wasn't just what he did. It was more what he was. One of the things he was most clearly was American. In fact it seemed that what he was could only be achieved by somebody who was American.

In 1961 I went to the cinema to see both Cliff Richard in *The Young Ones* and Elvis Presley in *Blue Hawaii*. It was obvious even to a pre-adolescent that while Elvis might have had some of his edge blunted by his army service he appeared to exist in a state of energetic grace that poor Cliff Richard could never possibly equal. And the reason Cliff could never equal it was because he was English.

This was the way the world still looked in 1962 and there was no reason to believe it wouldn't stay that way for ever more. Americans would be the producers. We would be their tame consumers.

Then, almost without warning, it changed.

Late in 1963, in a handful of weeks following the death of a President – a death that seemed to be felt every bit as much in Britain as it was in America, so much did we exist in their shadow at the time – things began to happen. The world was turned upside down. I was thirteen at the beginning of the year after when the Beatles went to America and I clearly remember everything changing in the most dramatic and joyous and heart-swelling way possible.

Like so many events in the career of the Beatles this was without precedent. No foreign entertainers had ever before run into such a tumultuous welcome, and certainly no mere Britishers had ever triggered such an outpouring of joy. In the weeks after that rapturous arrival we felt something we had never felt before. We felt accepted.

The seventh of February 1964 was the D-Day of what the Americans would come to call the British Invasion. This was an indication of how unusual it was for the recording stars of another country suddenly to become the biggest, most exciting names in the USA.

Within a few months the impossible had happened. Now the Americans seemed to be just as excited about Britishness as we had previously been about all things American.

It wasn't just a one-day affair. It wasn't just about one group. For a dizzy couple of years it was assumed that whichever group had most recently tumbled down the steps of a BOAC airliner and on to *The Ed Sullivan Show* was possessed of some special magic that Americans could not hope to match.

Such hysteria could not long endure, but even after the tide went out it left the British clearly established at the top table of the American music scene, and so it remained. America could no longer claim exclusive rights to rock and roll. Britain was now a permanent part of the picture. The end-of-the-decade extravaganzas of Monterey and Woodstock would have been incomplete without the Brits being represented. And they were not represented as junior partners. Had you been drawing up a pantheon of rock gods at the close of the 1960s you would probably have found the Brits outnumbering the Americans. This was a most significant transfer of what would now be called soft power.

Like everything to do with rock and roll it wasn't just about music. It wasn't just about how the musicians played it. It was also about how they dressed, how they photographed, how they spoke, how they joked and how they carried themselves. In that sense it was essentially about their Englishness.

Suddenly, Englishness – and the overwhelming majority of these performers were English – was nothing to be ashamed about. Obviously it was nothing to show off about either because showing off would be the antithesis of Englishness. The English temperament – in which feelings of inferiority are always at war with feelings of superiority, in which bone-deep understandings of the gradations of class may at any moment give way to insubordination from the most unlikely quarters, in which catastrophes are routinely described as 'a bit of a problem' and the phrase 'with respect' invariably denotes the exact opposite – was ideally suited to making a form of popular music that could never have come from any other country.

Although I played no part in this beyond watching the newsreels of departures and returns and combing the weekly papers for every crumb of information, it's something that I nonetheless take a certain pride in. During my lifetime there hasn't been a lot else to awaken national pride. We have grown accustomed to being schooled in the games we gave to the world by countries we formerly looked down on. British industries that were once the envy of the world have declined and disappeared. There have been false dawns when British films looked as though they were going to mean something in the USA but then quickly faded away. I remember somebody called Colin Welland standing up at the Oscars and warning, 'The British are coming', which was as good as a guarantee that they wouldn't be. Music, however, was different.

That's what made me want to write this book. I wanted to write about the way this generation of Englishmen heard what was essentially American music and then turned it round and sent it back with a twist, a twist that often said more about their Englishness than they knew. There's a term Americans use in baseball to indicate a pitch that comes at the batter in an unexpected way. They talk about 'putting some English on it'. That's what happened with American music. We sent it back with some English on it.

I also wanted to write about what America did to these people and what that generation of English musicians did to America. I wanted to try to make explicit many of the things we took for granted. I wanted to write about a time before the Gap, MTV, Virgin Atlantic and Google, when the cultures of different countries were distinct enough to clash as well as infect each other in all manner of unexpected ways.

After some scene-setting, this book begins with the British Invasion of 1964, which was led by the Beatles, and ends with the events of 1983 when, according to some accounts, a second British Invasion took place, this time spearheaded by Culture Club, pop video and a resurgent fashion industry. Obviously there are events that fall outside this time period, but by then breaking America was no longer the Great Adventure it had once been. Improved communications had shrunk the distance which formerly lent enchantment. The second invasion happened within living memory of the first so in that sense they fit together.

It seems particularly timely to do this in an era when digital communications have flattened the world, making New York, London and Los Angeles seem in so many ways the same, when more people than ever have travelled widely and use the same language, and when technology has equipped the youth of the world with exactly the same toys.

Furthermore, it seems timely when Britain is pitching itself out of Europe and being exhorted to punch above its weight economically and culturally, because (the people doing the exhorting imply) this is our national destiny. Politicians seeking to blow smoke up the national fundament often talk about the creative economy and our national virtues of inventiveness and irreverence. It seems this might be as good a time as any to look back on a brief period, possibly the last, when Global Britain meant something.

1

'One Yank and they're off'

I n the 1950s and 1960s British attitudes to America were shaped by two powerful forces: the first was Hollywood; the second was the memory of the war. As ever it was never easy to see where one ended and the other began, but what was certain was that both generated powerful feelings of superiority and inferiority.

The migration of an entire generation of young American males into the south-east of England in readiness for the invasion of Europe had brought actual British people closer to actual American people more so than any other event during their closely intertwined history. That closeness didn't always make for cordiality. By 1944 there were a million and a half US troops in the UK. This was a considerable weight of people to add to a population of forty-eight million.

It didn't help that so much of that weight was in testosterone.

An educational film shown to GIs at the time in the hope that they would get along with their hosts painted the natives of the UK as an easily satisfied, taciturn tribe who asked little more from life than a pint of warm mild and the odd game of shove-halfpenny, and who had few of the comforts the American soldiers enjoyed in what they airily referred to as 'back home'. Although the British public recognized that this massive introduction of fighting men and materiel, which had been magicked up over cigars and martinis by those two eminently clubbable transatlantic aristocrats Roosevelt and Churchill, was the only thing that might ultimately achieve victory over Germany, even the friendliest invasion could not be accomplished without a certain increase in tension. The arriving Americans found the British pale and defeated. The British thought the Americans far too full of themselves and too ready to look at their new surroundings and observe that they had something similar at home which was newer and bigger. They were also on average two inches taller than the British male and tended not to apologize for their presence. This meant it didn't take many of them to make a pub seem full. Faced with this, the British would go off with their half of mild into a dark corner, muttering that these interlopers were 'overpaid, oversexed and over here'.

For all their lighter, more stylish battledress and their ties tucked into their shirts, there is no empirical evidence that the American incomers had a greater sex drive than the Tommies in their scratchy blouson jackets and their hapless berets. Nonetheless the key brand value of these friendly invaders was undoubtedly sex. Their arrival in such numbers, with their patter, their free hosiery, their gleaming teeth and their inexhaustible supplies of American 'can-do', was for the British male a deeply emasculating experience. The prospect of her life being possibly cut short by a stray flying bomb had made the average young English woman far more likely to surrender her virtue in a bus shelter than had been the case previously, and suddenly the English boys were having to compete for that virtue with men who were better built, better dressed, better at expressing themselves and who had enough spare cash to be able to leave a ten-shilling note on a bar counter without thinking too much of it. One young man in the Home Guard at the time, probably guarding the local sewage works with nothing over his shoulder but a broom, later ruefully recalled, 'Never in history has there been such a conquest of women by men as was won by the American army in Britain in World War Two.'

For the wives, sisters and girlfriends of the British soldiers this influx of well-built young men with well-pressed uniforms recalled something else they associated with America. It was as though Hollywood had come to their local high street. Theirs was the generation who went to the pictures three times a week and now the race of supermen they had been used to seeing up on the screen was suddenly down here among them. These new men asking the girls to dance looked, sounded and behaved sufficiently like the lover they had gawped up at on the silver screen to make their dreams come temporarily true after a gruelling day in the munitions factory or washing hospital floors. Said one woman, 'It was as if the cinema had come to life. They were so handsome and well groomed and clean. And they smelled so nice. They used deodorants and aftershave – things unknown to 99 per cent of all British men.'

The precise amount of fraternization is impossible to quantify. What counted was the amount that people thought was going on. In such a febrile atmosphere jokes about utility knickers – 'one Yank and they're off' – were bound to take root. Much of this fraternization took place on military bases in the vicinity of hot music. In these far-off days this music would arrive in sudden, unsought blasts and had to be grasped as eagerly as life itself. Where was the hottest music from? Clearly, the hottest music came from America.

Although few said it aloud there was a tacit acceptance that

Americans had a near-monopoly of the sex appeal that would be the core currency of the second half of the twentieth century. British cinema had its idols, like Leslie Howard and Jessie Matthews, but they never had the lustre of their Hollywood counterparts. Where all Americans had a natural brashness, the British default position was cosy. This applied as much in music as it did in movies. In the inter-war period the two countries' organizations for musicians, the American Federation of Musicians and the British Musicians Union, did everything in their power to keep each other's players as far away from their shores as possible. This resulted in British bands favouring a comparatively polite form of dance music, exemplified by bands like the ones led by Geraldo and Henry Hall, who played for rich people dancing in the best hotels and were relayed to the rest of the country via the monopoly broadcaster the BBC.

However, there was always an appetite for something hotter. The British, in spite of a hard-won reputation for inhibition, were surprisingly in the market for the rawer varieties of popular music. The number of troops in Britain before D-Day stoked the ravenous appetite for proper American jazz and the good life that appeared to go with it. Young women in Britain, constrained by rationing and dulled by onerous factory work, vied for weekend invitations to go and hoof it with the GIs, who swung them about in the course of risqué, underwear-exposing dances like the Lindy Hop.

At the end of that war seventy thousand young British women went to the United States as GI brides. Instead of having its women carried off by its triumphant enemies at the end of hostilities, Britain suffered the indignity of having many of them carried off by its triumphant allies. Every English family in the late 1940s knew at least one local girl who had gone off to make a new life in the land of plenty and whose occasional parcels of precious luxuries were eagerly anticipated in a nation still in the depths of rationing. The soldiers and airmen returned with their brides to the land of chewing gum, blue jeans, supermarkets, outdoor everything, gasoline at twenty cents a gallon and seemingly endless possibilities. The old country meanwhile was supposed to scuttle back into its old routine, salving itself against the indignity of its clearly reduced status on the world stage with the appealing fictions of its own war films and the diluted version of American popular music that it was permitted by the BBC.

It was apparent to Lord Reith and to all the people who operated the levers of culture that Britain, like all European countries, was about to be deluged by the culture of the country whence their deliverance had come. It was the then Director-General of the BBC and his people who had attempted to stem the arrival of 'hot music' back in the thirties. Reith had even confided to his diaries that he envied the Nazis for the way they had suppressed this 'filthy product of modernity'. Unlike countries such as France, which feared for the disappearance of its own tongue beneath the onslaught of American films, TV and music, and imposed quotas on the amount of non-indigenous entertainment that was permitted into the country, British TV made the most of Bismarck's observation and the fact that the most expensive entertainment in the world was being churned out in a language it happened to speak.

The generation born during and soon after the war didn't think this was in any way alien. In fact they clamoured for it. They didn't resent the way the American entertainment industry failed to make the slightest allowance for the fact that its overseas audiences were not familiar with the lifestyles it chose to portray. In fact they grew up speaking two forms of the English language. One was the tongue they learned at their mother's knee. The other was the chipper, cheesy suburban argot of imported American sitcoms, all of them set in the sort of imagined anywhere where people actually did say, 'Gee, Mom' and 'Honey, I'm home', where people went on 'dates', where there were places like high schools and events like the prom for which their peers might borrow 'the car'.

In 1957 we had our first TV installed. In those days a new TV required installation. Two men in brown coats delivered it and stayed for the half hour it took to get it working. It took a while to warm up but when it finally did I sat enthralled on the floor and watched *I Married Joan*. This was a knock-off of *I Love Lucy* which starred former radio star Joan Davis as a suburban housewife who was always trying to keep from her husband the news that she had dented the car or hired a maid. This was the best the BBC could do. The big show later that evening was George Bernard Shaw's *Pygmalion*. This was a case of the BBC standing up for traditional British culture in the face of the competition from ITV, which had been launched two years earlier. To his dying day my grandfather referred to ITV as 'the soap programme' because in his mind it was linked with the American way of doing TV in which popular programmes would be sponsored by detergents. For him, the expression 'American-made' was synonymous with the cheap and meretricious. This was precisely what his grandson liked about it.

That summer of 1957 was the high-water mark of skiffle, which was the most uniquely English form of musical entertainment since the invention of the morris dance. In July that year, around about the time we were taking delivery of our TV, John Lennon met Paul McCartney at the Woolton village fete. Both boys, the former sixteen, the latter nearly two years younger, were in thrall to the American rock and roll that was figuring in the British pop charts at the time but was rarely heard on Lord Reith's radio. When the film *The Blackboard Jungle* was screened in British cinemas in 1955, the sound of 'Rock Around The Clock' amplified over cinema speakers had been so provoking to the young generation's ears that in some cases they had laid waste to their surroundings in a manner apparently unseen since the Gordon Riots. Anthony Sampson, reporting from the Lewisham Gaumont in September 1956 on a screening of the cash-in film named after the hit, noted how the mayhem stopped as soon as the music ceased and the plot took over. Some members of the audience came back five times just to experience the unaccustomed rush of hearing a rock and roll record played loud, and to chorus hip catchphrases like 'see you later, Alligator' along with the actors.

On that July day in 1957, John Lennon performed Gene Vincent's 'Be-Bop-A-Lula', and during a break McCartney impressed the older boy with his mastery of Eddie Cochran's tricky 'Twenty Flight Rock', but the music that Lennon's group the Quarrymen played, with their acoustic guitars and tea-chest bass, was essentially skiffle, a hot reworking of American folk songs performed on home-made instruments which was often played for dancing. One of the reasons British groups of the 1950s couldn't make the sound of American rock and roll is that they simply couldn't get access to the tools with which it had been made.

That wasn't just down to lack of funds. It was also the fact that imports of any expensive luxury goods were tightly controlled in those years after the war when the British economy was trying to find its feet. The British government introduced an embargo on a range of American-made pleasure machines and therefore would-be rock guitar players had to make do with Scandinavian and German copies which simply didn't sound right. The first Fender Stratocaster didn't come to Britain until 1959, when Hank Marvin persuaded Cliff Richard that they should get a mail order catalogue and send away for one. For most people the attraction of skiffle was that you could make a virtue out of a limitation by using whatever instruments were at hand. Whereas American rock and roll was made in the garage, England's poor relation was made in the shed.

All national modesty aside, skiffle was an early example of the British knack for taking something from America and accidentally giving it a quality that the original didn't possess. Skiffle took the work songs of rural America – songs in many cases birthed in the misery and cruelty of the American frontier, songs that described poverty, prejudice and justice dispensed under the nearest tree – and rendered them somehow cheerful. Its key practitioner was Lonnie Donegan, a Scots-Irishman who initially performed his American folk songs in the course of a novelty interlude in the middle of an agonizingly authentic revivalist jazz set by Ken Colyer's band. This quickly proved more popular than the jazz group itself and Donegan's flair for showmanship and disdain for notions of authenticity did the rest. His hit song 'Rock Island Line' began with a spoken recitative in which he pretended to be an engine driver attempting to smuggle pig iron past the authorities on the Illinois Railroad. Amazingly, it was also a hit in America.

Because it appealed to English self-effacement, skiffle proved to be England's secret door into rock and roll. Skiffle was not born of showbiz. It didn't have the same smell. It sprang up instead in scout huts, church halls, college common rooms and on protest marches. Skiffle was all about collaboration rather than individual brilliance. Skiffle groups presented themselves as workmen more than entertainers – hence 'the Quarrymen', a standard artisanal way of naming what was essentially a hopped-up folk group. Because so many skiffle favourites were about work rather than women, about rights rather than romance, it further provided a way in which singers with English accents could adopt an American way of singing without feeling like utter frauds or ten-bob Lotharios.

This ultimately is what made British rock in the sixties so different from the American variety. All the acts that made up the British Invasion of the United States in the mid-sixties had learned how to play 'Last Train To San Fernando' or 'John Henry' and therefore there remained in their music a quality of rootsiness that never went away. They carried that with them as they began to electrify and morphed into rock and roll groups – or, as they were more usually termed in the early sixties, 'beat groups'. By then the expression 'rock'n'roll' had the wrong kind of associations for people like me, who were growing up in the fifties.

In the wake of the success in America of 'Rock Island Line', Lonnie Donegan actually went there to play, in 1957. This was pretty much unheard of for an English musician at the time. As far as the American entertainment industry was concerned there was no more likelihood of America looking to the United Kingdom for a guitar strummer than of its national leagues searching in the same place for a baseball pitcher. Donegan played some big venues. He even played Madison Square Garden, the arena that would in time become the benchmark for British acts trying to measure their success in 'breaking America'. But Donegan never made that claim for he knew the truth that had led him there. He had only been in Madison Square Garden to play a few numbers between two 'sets' by the real headliners of the evening, the Harlem Globetrotters.

From the vantage point of today's media-saturated landscape it's difficult to convey adequately just how constrained access to music was in the UK in these days. The most seismic American records could only be heard by pressing a cheap radio to your ear late at night and hearing Fats Domino or Chuck Berry amid the swirling aural fog between you and the distant transmitter used by Radio Luxembourg.

The BBC, an organization that was obsessed with being able to control the music it featured, preferred skiffle to rock and roll on the grounds that it seemed far more wholesome. The big rock and roll hits of Elvis Presley, Jerry Lee Lewis and Little Richard were rarely heard on British radio. That only increased their appeal. Music was just music but a record was an event. American records were the most dramatic sort of event. There was a drama about them that you couldn't help be swept up by. This continued even into the late 1950s when Elvis Presley had gone into the army, Little Richard had gone into the Church and Jerry Lee Lewis had gone into disgrace. America still had a sound to it, and that sound called to the youth of England in a way few home-grown records did. On the rare occasions when the unpasteurized sound of American records like the Everly Brothers' 'Cathy's Clown' or 'New Orleans' by Gary U.S. Bonds or even 'The Twist' by Chubby Checker pierced the frowsy air of the standard British living room in 1960, they arrived like visitations from a world immeasurably more vibrant than the one in which they had landed.

For generations of English adolescents who had felt that the most they could expect from life was a kiss from pursed lips this represented the sudden shock of someone unexpectedly placing a hand on their crotch. This was the sound of America.

2

'England? Is that in France?'

I n 1960 a twenty-one-year-old Englishman, privately educated, of solid upper middle-class stock but with little discernible ambition, was sent by his father to Dallas, Texas to learn the cotton trade. The Englishman came from the north-west of England, a region that had known close economic links with the southern states of America since the eighteenth century. Although the young man indulged his father's earnest wish to see him take an interest in the family business, his true purpose was to use the opportunity of a prolonged visit to the home of blues and country to learn more about the American vernacular music he loved so much. Like many of the generation who came of age in the 1950s the young man had been shaped by exposure to the competing pulls of obligatory military service and skiffle. The abolition of the former at the end of 1960 was the one factor that made it possible for many of the young men who played the latter to at least toy with

11

the idea of turning their strumming into a job. Had National Service continued in the UK, as it did in neighbouring nations like France, the events described in this book would never have occurred.

On his arrival in Houston by ship the young man attempted to map this vast, unfamiliar land by imposing on it the people and places he had come to know through the skiffle hits of Lonnie Donegan. What he had found intoxicating in the music of Donegan was the sense of space, and he fully expected the people he met to be similarly outgoing. In fact the young man found that his curiosity about anything to do with the United States was not reciprocated by the locals. Most of the people he met had little sense of a world beyond their part of Texas. For them, any countries that had the misfortune to lie beyond the US belonged strictly in the realm of the theoretical.

This didn't apply to everyone. During the 1960 election campaign the young man had a brief conversation with one of the candidates, John F. Kennedy. At the time the emergence of Kennedy, with his luminous handsomeness, his magazine-quality wife and his willingness to be photographed with his shirt off, seemed to clinch the argument about American vigour versus European fatigue. The young Englishman was impressed that Kennedy, who had lived in England when his father was ambassador, knew more about Britain than most of the people he met in Dallas. He certainly knew more than the young man's boss, who had greeted him with the words 'England? Is that in France?'

After his period in the cotton trade came to an end he remained in the country, selling insurance to people who found that his private-school English lent him a certain authority, and taking every opportunity to talk his way into a job as a presenter on the radio. The young man, who was in the process of changing his name from John Ravenscroft to John Peel, happened to be in Dallas on 22 November 1963 when the same John F. Kennedy he had talked to in 1960 was assassinated. He even talked his way into the Lee Harvey Oswald press conference as the representative of the newspaper of his hometown, Liverpool. This is not as unlikely as it may seem. The media world was at the time dominated by newspapers associated with big cities and many of them retained correspondents overseas. At the time of the press conference Liverpool was known abroad, if it was known at all, for shipping. Within a few months it would be known for something else entirely.

In 1960, Dallas and Liverpool seemed to belong to different universes. While the former was aggressively future-facing the latter was unapologetically backward-looking. While the former was one of the brash, sprawling American cities that had been expanding at what seemed like an unsustainable pace in the 1950s as Americans abandoned the old big cities of the north-east in search of a suburban place in the sun, Liverpool still looked like the cramped, grimy city the Victorians had built and the Luftwaffe had knocked about a bit. Dallas was go-getting, nakedly ambitious, openly acquisitive, busy installing air conditioning and demanding that the things it wanted had to be delivered today. Liverpool, on the other hand, was content with its lot, didn't have much in the way of ambition, and concealed any resentment about its lot behind a wall of self-lacerating humour. More people were killed in Dallas every year than in the whole of England, let alone in Liverpool. The two cities ostensibly spoke the same language but would have had some difficulty understanding each other's lives.

This was largely because they were entirely at variance. In 1960, British kids looked to America for the future that seemed to be taking an age to arrive in their own land. They gawped at TV programmes like *77 Sunset Strip*. Programmes like these didn't have to be particularly good in order to please a young British audience because they simply ate up with a spoon the premise of the good life implicit in its opening titles alone. Each episode began with one of the sharply suited detectives with gleaming teeth step-ping out of his office and looking up to check that the sky above Hollywood was still cloudless before getting into the Thunderbird that had been delivered round the front by car-hop Edd 'Kookie' Byrnes. The latter, who was a teen idol even in Britain for a few months on the back of the show, always ran a comb through his quiff before sending the T-Bird on its way by goosing one of its tail fins. Cars, a basic necessity for teenagers growing up in the United States, were to their British counterparts as distant as private jets. One of the most profoundly appealing things about the new music coming from America was that there they actually sang about the Hot Rod Lincoln, the forty miles of bad road or the race between the Jaguar (exotically pronounced 'Jag-wah') and the Ford Thun-derbird. This was the key feature of the American dream that played in the head of every English teenager stranded in the back of the family Anglia on the way to the seaside in the pouring rain. Cars provided American kids with a measure of freedom not avail-able to their British contemporaries. Mom and Dad might be home watching Lucy. Junior, on the other hand, was out in the borrowed passion wagon, hoping that under the cover of Wolfman Jack's vul-pine patter he might get a girl to slide on over on the bench seat and allow him to run a hand up her skirt. What did the British get for their part but a song about seven little girls sitting in the back seat kissing and a-hugging with Fred? This was not the same thing at all.

In the late 1950s a third of radio listening in the United States was done in the car. The vehicle, either your own or the one you borrowed from your parents, was a mobile boudoir, a travelling frat house. It was where you escaped to, where you lived your real life. Hence American disc jockeys would naturally position them-selves as co-conspirators on your climb to Inspiration Point, exulting in their role as jive-talking panders whose music was chosen to help you get your way. At a time when the only pop station in Britain insisted you eat up half an hour of the Tottenham Citadel Salvation Army Band before you be allowed an entire half hour of Keith Fordyce's Record Hop, Brucie Morrow was all the way over there at WINS in New York opening the fader with the words 'This is your cousin Brucie, and for all you cousins everywhere I have what you want: the music, the magic and the message.' Whatever strange tongue this was, one thing was clear: America spoke it and we didn't.

In 1960, Dallas and Liverpool even listened to different music. The rock and roll stars of the late fifties had left the stage for one reason or another and American music seemed to have no leader. Rock and roll seemed to have been and gone, much as calypso had done before it. The music that had made those artists famous, however, was being belatedly reworked by the British bands who had started with skiffle before graduating to electrification. By the end of 1960 there were reckoned to be more than two hundred of these groups in and around Liverpool. It's highly likely that every single one of them knew how to play 'Roll Over Beethoven'.

One of these acts called themselves the Beatles, and in December 1960 they had just come back from three months in Hamburg where they had learned that they must entertain or perish. Formerly the skiffle group the Quarrymen, they had adopted their painful, punning name in honour of a Texan group, Buddy Holly's Crickets. By the middle of 1963, to everyone's surprise but that of their naive manager Brian Epstein, they were causing such a sensation in England that even American TV stations, amused at this outbreak of hysteria in the land of the stiff upper lip, began to take notice. Mainstream media interest was piqued by three elements: the screaming, the hair and their appearance on a Royal Command Performance, which clearly meant they had the approval of the Establishment. The London bureau of CBS television even prepared a report about the 'Beatlemania' phenomenon. It was soundtracked with the sound of 'She Loves You', the Beatles' biggest hit in the UK. This report was slated to be shown twice on 22 November 1963. The morning showing went ahead but the plan for the evening repeat had to be shelved. This was because Friday the 22nd was the day John F. Kennedy was shot.

The news reached the UK early that evening. The Beatles were playing Stockton-on-Tees, a chemical town in the industrial northeast of England. The news came through as they were playing the first of their usual two shows. There was no TV backstage at the Globe Theatre in Stockton so the story was broken to them in stages. First there had been a shooting. Then the President had been hit. It was more than an hour later when his death was announced. When John Lennon told a girl from one of the other acts on the bill that Kennedy had been shot she assumed it was just his usual black humour. Although ITV shelved its entertainment programmes for the evening, the second show, in which the Beatles were supported by the Kestrels, the Vernons Girls and Peter Jay and the Jaywalkers, went on as usual. The BBC, blindsided by the fact that much of their management was at an awards ceremony in the West End, blundered badly, allowing a Harry Worth comedy and the Scottish drama *Dr Finlay's Casebook* to go out as usual until somebody realized the gravity of the situation and they switched into solemn tribute mode.

On the same day their second LP, *With The Beatles*, was released. Their new single, 'I Want To Hold Your Hand', was just a week behind it. If you were to isolate one week when Beatlemania truly crested in Britain it would probably turn out to be the week that JFK was shot. The *Record Mirror* announced that this single had advance orders from the shops of three-quarters of a million, which was even more than 'She Loves You'. These were sales figures that would have been notable even in the United States and here they were coming from a country you could fit into Texas three times. The American trade paper *Billboard*, taking a polite interest for form's sake and holding hard to some outdated certainties, described it as 'a driving rocker with surf on the Thames sound'.

John F. Kennedy was the first political star to be made by television. Even after over two years in the White House he had very few political achievements to his name. His age at the time, the manner of his death and the glamour of his wife meant that he passed into the collective memory as a bigger star than he was as a politician. He was by no means a rock and roll President but he was the first President the rock and roll generation really noticed. Just three days after his death his widow gave an interview to the journalist Theodore White during which she made a point of telling a story about his love for popular music. This aside would echo down the years. At night, she said, before they went to sleep, Jack liked to play records. His favourite was the cast recording of a Broadway show and the line she particularly remembered was 'don't let it be forgot that once there was a spot that for one brief shining moment was known as Camelot'. In a hundred years' time political historians will still refer to the short Kennedy era as Camelot, purely because of something his widow, grief-stricken but media-savvy, said to a journalist.

At the beginning of 1963 the Lerner and Loewe musical *Camelot* had completed a three-year run on Broadway. Its stars were two British performers, Richard Burton and Julie Andrews. As it closed another hit musical opened, this time one that was not merely set in England but also invented in England. Lionel Bart's *Oliver!* was to run for over a year. At the time, instances of British entertainment successes achieving any kind of equivalent traction in the United States were rare. This was purely a reflection of where the economic power lay. Although even the least distinguished American sitcoms and cowboy series would find some place on British

TV, the traffic never flowed in the opposite direction. American TV had no need for *The Good Old Days* or *The Bob Monkhouse Hour*. The subject of *The Black and White Minstrel Show* would not even have been broached.

The same 'not for export' stamp applied even more emphatically to British rock and roll. To most Americans this seemed to be a contradiction in terms. In 1962 two British records, Acker Bilk's 'Stranger On The Shore' and the Tornados' 'Telstar', had actually gone to the top of the American charts, but since both seemed to be instrumental one-offs there was no sense of their representing a British Invasion of any kind.

If Americans looked to Britain for anything it was eccentricity. This seemed a quality associated in the American mind with class. For instance, one of the best-known faces on American TV in the 1950s was that of the boss of the soft drinks firm Schweppes. He was a former naval man still known as Commander Whitehead, who fronted the company's advertising in the United States with his distinctive officers' mess English and impeccably clipped beard. The Commander made such a name for himself in the United States that the Queen gave him an award for services to export. When he came to Dallas, the president of the Neiman Marcus department store announced he would throw a party for bearded men only. He was forced to cancel it because he discovered that there weren't actually any bearded men in Dallas. As Lawrence Wright reminds us in his memoir of growing up in the city in the fifties and sixties, 'America was a conformist society'.

Kennedy's assassination happened just before the Thanksgiving holiday, which then led into Christmas and New Year. During that seasonal lockdown American families spent most of their time together. There followed a long period of buttoned-up national mourning. The comedy pastiche of the First Family, which had been number one on the LP charts up until the shooting, disappeared from view to be replaced by solemn reverence for all things Kennedy. The pressing plants couldn't keep up with the demand for LPs of the late President's speeches. The one British record in the Hot 100 just a couple of weeks before Christmas 1963 was 'You Don't Have To Be A Baby To Cry' by the Caravelles. Americans who were teenagers at the time remember spending most of their days sitting indoors looking at each other.

When Brian Epstein first met the Beatles he had told them that they would one day be bigger than Elvis. This would have been a preposterous thing to say if the person saying it had been a show business professional. Coming from the manager of a provincial record shop with no experience of the higher reaches of what passed for a music business in Britain, it was laughable. At the time the idea of the Beatles' music ever being heard by American ears was far-fetched. Most British acts never got their records released in the USA. Even the American arm of the English record company that was having such success with the Beatles didn't believe that it would ever happen for them in the USA and allowed their first British hits to be picked up by independents.

The people who resisted the Beatles were the people who ought to have recognized their quality. Here there was an element of nativist prejudice at work. Bruce Morrow, one of the DJs who ruled the airwaves of the East Coast, was more honest than most. 'I think most of us had the feeling of "How dare these Brits, these upstarts, take the American forms of rock'n'roll and do what they did to it?" I think it took over three meetings for us to realize that there was something more to this than protecting the American rock'n'roll industry and community.' In 1963 the American music industry was as receptive to the message that their music was about to be revolutionized by foreigners as the people running the Premier League today would be to being told that the next big world club side would be run out of Detroit. The American people who allegedly knew rock and roll thought the Beatles were overblown. The hipsters simply couldn't hear it.

Ironically, the people who got it were the squares. The people who had never pretended to understand rock and roll – in fact hadn't understood it when they booked Elvis Presley, hadn't had much sympathy for it when they interviewed Little Richard, and were probably the first in the queue when it came to pointing out that it would never replace real music – these were the people who could nonetheless smell a phenomenon when they saw one, and they correctly figured that between the hair and the screams and the opportunity for jokes about creepie-crawlies there might be enough going on around this Beatles thing to give their ratings a bump or to give them an edge over their competing columnists as they came out of the Christmas break; furthermore, people were looking for something new for the New Year and maybe Americans wanted to cast aside their mourning, and at least the kids could have a little fun. And so it proved. The Beatles might have been the earliest rumbling of a youth-quake but their entry into the United States would be plotted over steaks and cigars in Delmonico's and in the cocktail bar of the Regency on Park Avenue. They would be ushered into America by the gatekeepers and power brokers themselves. They would start not in the streets but at the very top. Brian Epstein had always said they would not come to America unless it was trailing clouds of glory. Which is exactly what happened.

Of course that's not the story they told. Epstein always said he found the Beatles after a man called Raymond Jones came into his shop asking after them, which wasn't true. Ed Sullivan, the lantern-jawed eminence whose Sunday night show was the place where America came to be entertained and to learn what was supposed to be entertaining, had his own personal myth about how he came to 'discover' the Beatles. He said that he and his wife happened to be at Heathrow when the Beatles were returning from Scandinavia and, noting the screaming, dispatched a minion to find out what the fuss was about. In fact Sullivan used a British agent called Peter Prichard to keep him apprized of which British acts he should be booking. It was Prichard, a man who in a long career handled the bookings of such comedians as Bob Monkhouse, who told Sullivan that he should make room for these four young men from Liverpool. When Sullivan, who wasn't about to have his opinion in any way prejudiced by actually listening to them, growled 'What's the angle?', Prichard, who knew how to make an elevator pitch, was ready with his answer: 'They're the only one of the long-haired groups to play for the Queen.'

Sullivan was instantly sold. The idea that these four scraps had appeared 'by royal command' was even more thrilling in a country where the British royal family have their biggest fans, a country where state occasions tend to be starchier and even the glamorous young President they were in the middle of mourning had been entertained by the cellist Pablo Casals rather than Paul Anka. Prichard's line worked to satisfy Sullivan. He had found a way to fit them into his idea of England. Sullivan was happy. He, and not his competitors, would give this neatly turned-out bunch of counter-jumpers the chance of a lifetime.

The rest of the media marched in lockstep with Sullivan. In January 1964 *Life* magazine, which at the time went into eight million American homes, devoted three spreads to a feature announcing 'Here Come Those Beatles'. This story set the template for numberless articles that would be printed in the days ahead as American journalism tried to reduce the Beatles phenomenon to its key elements: they come from Liverpool, they have funny hair, the girls scream, the royal family like them, and it's our turn next.

Before confirming the booking Sullivan had checked with his friend Walter Cronkite, the august anchor of the CBS evening news. They both knew there was some group that was creating a lot of fuss and that their name had something to do with insects. 'Tell me about them, those bugs or whatever they call themselves,' said Sullivan. Cronkite knew about them also through his two teenage daughters who were visibly palpitating as they watched 'I Want To Hold Your Hand' – the first Beatles record to be given the benefit of a release by a major label in the United States – do what Brian Epstein had always said it would do, which was not so much climb the American chart as vault to its top in the same way as King Kong had conquered the Empire State Building.

It was Cronkite who, only a few weeks before, had taken a phone call live on air, replaced the receiver, taken off his glasses and then told the American people that their President was dead. The week of Kennedy's funeral was the first time in world history when a major historical event had been carried live into the world's living rooms. The man from *The Times* said then, 'No man, living or dead, had ever been given such concentrated exposure.'

That would remain the case until 7 February 1964.

3

'Close your eyes and I'll kiss you'

I t was towards midday New York Eastern Standard Time on 7 February 1964 as Paul McCartney looked down through the window beside his seat in first class on the Boeing 707 serving Pan Am flight 101 and the Beatles' plane descended towards Long Island and JFK airport. It was a windy winter's day and all he could see below were houses and highways, both occupying more space than they would have been permitted on the crowded island from which he and his party had taken off. He was looking down at a city that seemed to be made up entirely of suburbs. Those suburbs didn't have the same features as they would have had if they were clustering around English towns. Instead they had car ports, basketball hoops, barbecue equipment in the yard and wide driveways separating each house from the one next door.

This particular way of coming to New York, which was still only a few years old, was nothing like as spirit-lifting and strange as the heart-stopping vista of the towers and canyons of downtown Manhattan that had greeted visiting entertainers of an earlier age as Cunard liners like the *Mauretania* and, later, the *Queen Mary* steamed into New York harbour. Nevertheless McCartney was filled with the same mixture of awe and apprehension as the young Charlie Chaplin had been on his arrival in New York in 1910. Chaplin had gone there, as any ambitious young entertainer from Britain would, because he felt he had gone as far as he could on the London stage and needed new worlds to conquer. Nobody noted his entry into New York at the time. He cowered in his rented room, fearful that he was simply too small, too timorous, too English for a city so vast, so brash, so noisy in its heedlessness. Thanks to the movies, which were silent, and the First World War, Chaplin swiftly became so famous that everybody forgot his Englishness. His fellow English entertainers didn't and scores of them would follow in Chaplin's footsteps over the next fifty years, their hearts full of hope. Most would sooner or later be forced to beat inglorious retreats.

First of all they had to decide the manner of their arrival. Was America likely to take most notice of somebody who had clearly made a name elsewhere or did they prefer people who landed with becoming modesty? When Noël Coward came for his first time in 1921 he was determined to make a splash, spending £100 he could ill afford to make sure that he arrived in the city on the *Aquitania* in the hope this would earn him star treatment on arrival. In those days the shipboard photographers and correspondents wielded considerable power over who did or didn't get in the papers. Coward was among the latter group. Three months later he slunk back on a free passage to Liverpool, having learned bitter lessons about how cruel a place New York could be to anyone who makes the double mistake of being an alien and not a famous one at that.

The stars of British show business looked to America with fear and trepidation. Even the most established among them approached the gatekeepers of America on bended knee. They did so because these people, like all their compatriots, wielded their power without apology. They were not in the business of letting anyone down easily. They would not sweeten a rejection with the words 'if it were up to me' as their London counterparts might. Only four years before McCartney gazed out of that Boeing window Britain's biggest rock star Cliff Richard had been compelled to begin his inaugural appearance on *The Ed Sullivan Show*, which was the one and only key to the American living room and the nation's heart, with the whiskery vaudeville song 'Where Did You Get That Hat?'. Cliff was forced into this abrupt addition to his repertoire for no other reason than that Sullivan happened to like it. Like most American impresarios of the time, and in truth like the bulk of his viewers, Sullivan considered America the one, the only true reality. The other pages in the atlas were little more than a source of comic relief. France was a reliable provider of swarthy balladeers, if you wanted tumblers or jugglers there was no beating the Germans, Italy could generally be relied on for a talking mouse, while entertainers hailing from that rainy island off the coast of northern Europe were naturally expected to be able to turn their hand to a music hall favourite as easily as they could remember the words to the national anthem. Cliff Richard's career in the USA never entirely recovered from that indignity. He settled instead for being a star in the Commonwealth and nowhere else.

Thanks to the headlines they had generated in the UK papers in the previous year of Beatlemania, and thanks also to the breathtaking naivety of their young manager Brian Epstein, Paul McCartney and the Beatles were arriving with greater expectations than Cliff Richard, though even they couldn't be sure. Epstein had decreed that they would not visit America until they had a number one record. Anybody who knew anything about the American entertainment business and about the supplicant role Britain played in it would have written off such promises as proof of the fact that this pampered son of a provincial furniture retailer didn't have so much a management interest in this group as a crippling crush on them.

A year earlier, when the Beatles were having their first number one records in the United Kingdom, Epstein had experienced difficulty getting anyone in the United States to take his calls. Thanks to the speed of the Beatles' ascent in the months since then he and his group were now in such demand that some businessmen had booked seats behind him on Pan Am 101 in the hope of getting to speak to him.

It wasn't his first visit. He had made sure of that. For somebody like Epstein, star-struck, theatre-obsessed, Jewish and gay, New York pulsed like a distant star. He had visited New York the previous November to finalize arrangements for the Beatles' appearance, staying at the Regency on Park Avenue with Billy J. Kramer. Kramer was a management client but Epstein also knew that in those days, when nobody talked openly about homosexuality, some of the prominent but impeccably discreet gays in the business would say nothing but would nonetheless be awarding him points for arriving accompanied by such noteworthy arm candy. The first night in the city they dined with Lionel Bart, the writer of *Oliver!*. The second night Epstein dined with Geoffrey Ellis, an older man who had fled the north-west of England to pursue both his business and personal romantic interests in the USA.

For the handful of young British men who had the opportunity to go there, America was a deeply arousing prospect. To go there as a celebrity, as someone who was sought out, someone for whom all doors would potentially be open, made the boy who had been bullied at school, busted out of the army and patronized at RADA suddenly feel like Nero. Epstein was the first of the Beatles party to test the limits of his entitlement. He was never one for doing this the safe way. Ellis was asked by Epstein whether he could fix him up with a companion in New York, preferably the kind of rough trade that was his personal taste. Reasoning that it would be better to do this through the right channels than have Epstein arrested behind some bushes in Central Park, Ellis arranged for a presentable young man to be waiting for him at his hotel when he returned. The following morning he asked Epstein how it had gone and was taken aback by his laconic response: 'He didn't really satisfy me, so I went out later and had a good time in the park.'

Paul McCartney, only twenty-one but already one of the most famous people in the world, reflected on the year that had just passed as the plane continued its descent. It was just a year since the Beatles had released their first number one record 'Please Please Me' in the UK. Capitol Records, the EMI-owned label which had the golden benefit of first refusal on all Beatles records in the United States, refused. They passed on the next one too, 'From Me To You'. As if to prove that this was not merely an oversight but more akin to a deliberate act of self-sabotage, rooted in their conviction that Britain had no business with rock and roll music, they then crowningly passed on 'She Loves You'. This came out in Britain in the summer of 1963, broke all sales records and heralded the beginning of Beatlemania.

By December, when Capitol finally gave in and deigned to release the Beatles' latest single 'I Want To Hold Your Hand', there was such pent-up demand in America that Brian Epstein was able to visit the Beatles in their suite at Paris's Hôtel George Cinq in January 1964 and read to them a telegram from the United States confirming that 'I Want To Hold Your Hand' was now number one in the *Cashbox* chart. This meant that when they went there for the first time the following month it would be as conquering heroes rather than audition fodder. They would not be required to perform 'Where Did You Get That Hat?'.

The story that Epstein would only agree to the Beatles going to

America once they had a number one was another of the tales cooked up after the event to invest the key players with uncanny foresight. In fact he had already been persuaded by an American promoter called Sid Bernstein, who had contacted Epstein as soon as the Beatles began to happen in the UK and told him he was prepared to put them on at Carnegie Hall if Epstein was prepared to commit. It had taken some persuading but eventually Epstein had agreed that they would play Carnegie Hall on 12 February. This was Lincoln's birthday and hence the kids would be off school.

In fact things had been running so heavily in his favour that Epstein had been able to dictate his own terms to Ed Sullivan. He demanded – and got – top billing. In exchange for this he agreed the Beatles would also appear the following week in a Sullivan show to be broadcast from Miami. That way he was assured that the network had just as much riding on the success of the first show as his clients did. In exchange for this they would get $3,500 per appearance plus flights and hotel costs.

With such a premium plug spot lined up it was finally possible for Epstein to lean on Capitol and demand that they support the release of 'I Want To Hold Your Hand' with a ground game such as the American record business had never seen. This included the drastic measure of issuing all their sales staff with Beatles wigs. 'Until further notice,' the memo accompanying them ordered, 'you and your sales and promotion staff are to wear the wig during the business day.' By the time 'I Want To Hold Your Hand' had been declared the fastest-selling single in the history of Capitol it was being pursued up the charts by 'She Loves You' and 'Please Please Me', both of which had been licensed to small labels in the winter of Capitol's lordly disdain.

In a matter of weeks the prospect of the Beatles taking America by storm had gone from the never-gonna-happen column to the surest of sure things. In November 1963 at the Regency, Epstein had given an interview to the *New Yorker* that quoted him borrowing a metaphor from cricket which would be unlikely to land with its readers but was certainly true. When the Beatles come to America, he promised, 'they will hit everyone for six'. It now appeared entirely possible that this could be the case. Phil Spector, one of the few people in the American record business who had seen the Beatlemania phenomenon on its home ground, was convinced of it. That's why he had sent his group the Ronettes back home after their tour of Britain with the Rolling Stones while he himself hung about in London purely in order to be able to travel with them, be photographed with them, and ultimately disembark from the same plane with the Beatles, as though they were somehow in his personal gift.

Seated with Paul in the first-class section were the rest of the group. They were all more thrilled about this visit than anything else that had happened during their career. Only one of them had ever visited the country before. During a brief break in September 1963, George had flown off to see his sister Louise in Benton, Illinois, and bought some Bobby Bland records and a new guitar, neither of which could be obtained in England at the time. In this average American town George visited a drive-in movie, bought T-bone steaks for the barbecue and gawped at the waitresses on roller skates. It was the last time any Beatle would get to taste such thrilling yet mundane pleasures away from the cameras.

Ringo, who had named himself after a character in a cowboy film, was a member of the generation of English rockers who were infatuated with everything American. When it appeared that his previous group Rory Storm and the Hurricanes were not going to provide him with a future he had gone, as a nineteen-year-old, to the United States Consulate in Liverpool and enquired about emigrating to Houston, Texas. This was a city he knew only through the liner notes of a favourite blues album. He even wrote off for details of employment opportunities. It was clear to him: it was better to be a manual worker in the USA than a drummer in the UK.

John Lennon, the group's de facto leader and guiding spirit, was sitting alongside, his style somewhat cramped by the presence of Cynthia, the young woman he'd secretly wedded in 1962 and with whom he had fathered a child. The press had slowly cottoned on to the fact that Lennon was married and the American visit would mark her official coming-out, even though Lennon was certainly not going to let her get in his light, not at this point in his life when he was finally going to get the glory he sought in the country from which he had acquired the lion's share of his attitudes since 1956. Even if there was no guarantee that this would turn out to be more than just a few glorious days in the sun, Lennon was determined that nothing was going to spoil this undreamt-of opportunity to bring it all back home.

At the same time, what was nagging at them all was that this visit was ripe with opportunities for embarrassment, that if there was a chance of it going wrong in some way it would go wrong and that when they went back home they would be able to hear clearly the snickering at their backs – the almost instinctive reaction the British reserve for those who have committed the cardinal sin in their eyes of going to America and getting above themselves.

As the plane came in to land and the ground rushed up to meet them, Paul McCartney looked out of the window and thought to himself, 'Why should they need us? They've got lots of groups of their own.'

He was right to think that he could be engaged in a farcical game of carrying coals to Newcastle, but America at the time didn't really have lots of groups. Although the biggest hit on the American charts in the year just past had been the Beach Boys' 'Surfin' USA', most of America's groups were either instrumentalists like the

Surfaris or vocal groups like the Chiffons. They rarely sang and played at the same time; they tended to do one or the other. The American pop scene was overwhelmingly dominated by solo performers, a disproportionate number of whom seemed to be called Bobby. There was Bobby Vee, Bobby Rydell, Bobby Vinton, Bobby Goldsboro and even Bobby Darin. Together they formed a cohort which Jerry Lee Lewis, himself somewhat sidelined by the new world the Beatles ushered in, would derisively refer to as 'the Bobbies'. The Bobbies were just the first artists to feel the impact of this changing of the guard presaged by the Beatles. Lewis saw their commercial demise in almost biblical terms. 'Cut 'em down like wheat before a sickle,' he cackled.

What Paul McCartney wasn't to realize at that time was that it would be the things the Beatles gave no thought to that were to endear them to America.

As their plane taxied towards its stand they could hear above the whine of the engines a familiar noise. This was the screaming of thousands of Long Island girls who had found some way to get out of school on a Friday afternoon and come to the airport to welcome them. In this they had been aided by the record company, that was not satisfied simply to let hysteria run its natural course: swiftly transitioning from active hostility to passionate support in a way that only a record company can, they had had no hesitation in making sure that those who didn't have home-made banners of welcome were provided with a manufactured one.

The girls were excited but not remotely as excited as the Beatles, who couldn't believe they were here and couldn't believe the fuss. They dealt with it because dealing with it was what they did. They were taken inside and exposed to an assault from the local press. When are you going to get a haircut? Why don't you sing? How long will it last? They reacted to this broadside in a way that nobody had ever done before. They gave better than they got. They seemed to understand the importance of keeping the ball in the air. They talked about the importance of 'having a laugh'. It was clear they had charm, a quality nobody in pop had bothered to exude before. And there was something extra. Michael Braun, an American journalist who had spent time with them in the UK, said they seemed to be 'a new kind of people'. Braun had it right. They were smart without being conspicuously educated. They were English but their Englishness was overlaid with Liverpudlian. When the Beatles had arrived in London, one of the truly novel things about them was not so much that they came from Liverpool as the fact they made no effort to hide it. This was unusual enough in England. In America it was without precedent.

They didn't sing at the airport, as the reporters had requested, but in many respects they did their act. Their act was something they never gave any conscious thought to. The key feature of this act was, that they were a group. They all stood behind the microphones. They shared the questions equally. They looked like one another but they were also distinct. They took the opportunity to tease each other, but as soon as there was the minutest threat from the outside they imperceptibly closed ranks. And because they were a group they also brought with them the key defining element of their Englishness, which was their profound belief that humour is not light relief, but a guarantee of sanity. What that press conference at the airport clearly established was that music was only part of what the Beatles were all about. What they were bringing from Britain was not just a different haircut, not just a different way of playing music, not just some fresh slang, but also a new way to walk, a new way to talk, a new way to be.

Two days later, introducing them in front of what was reckoned to be the largest TV audience ever assembled, Ed Sullivan closed the sale. He said that even veteran newsmen agreed that New York had never seen anything like the phenomenon of the Beatles and that New York City had never seen anything like the impact these four had had. This is something big cities, which take pride in remaining unimpressed, almost never say. Then Sullivan brought the Beatles on. They began with 'All My Loving', one of those effortlessly lovely, heart-lifting songs that they were peeling off at the time as though from a bottomless wallet stuffed with fifties. This was the perfect introduction to what was to follow. That Sunday, 9 February, at just after eight in the evening Eastern Standard Time, American youth finally put the death of a President behind them as Paul approached the microphone and sang, 'Close your eyes and I'll kiss you . . .' America took one look and decided to fall in love.

4

'The effect of the hair'

On the Monday morning following the Beatles' two appearances on *The Ed Sullivan Show*, in the course of which they had played five songs, the verdict came in. And the verdict that mattered most was the one provided by the overnight Nielsen ratings which measured TV audiences. These had the previous night's show, which had also featured Tessie O'Shea and the Broadway cast of *Oliver!* – including future Monkee Davy Jones – achieving a score of 44.6. At the time this was the highest rating in American TV history. It meant that just under seventy-four million Americans, a number significantly greater than the entire population of the United Kingdom, had tuned in to watch an act they had never previously seen and a few weeks earlier had not heard of. In those far-off, one-TV-to-a house, pre-remote control days, tuning in didn't merely mean being in the same room while the programme whispered and flickered in the background.

It meant entire extended families gathering in one room, whole neighbourhoods leaning in and listening and watching and wondering.

Even for the days when it was possible for an entire continent to be drawn together by a single television event, the reach of this particular edition of *The Ed Sullivan Show* was quite exceptional. Future action movie star Mark Hamill watched it in Annandale, Virginia, would-be rocker Tom Petty in Gainesville, Florida, drama-obsessed cheerleader Meryl Streep in her parents' comfortable home in New Jersey, comedy fiend David Letterman in a modest single-storey house in a suburb of Indianapolis. Even Jimmy James, a guitarist who was not yet known as Jimi Hendrix, settled down to watch it at the home of the Isley Brothers, for whom he was working at the time. As all these people watched they were simultaneously exposed to the commercial messages of the show's sponsors, headache pill Anacin and dough conglomerate Pillsbury. Whatever these companies had paid for their slots they had surely got value for money. Whoever was going to sponsor next week's show, which would also feature the Beatles, would in all probability be paying even more.

The bet Sullivan had made in booking them had paid off. Its chance of success had been made more likely by sudden unanimity of sentiment towards the Beatles right across the entertainment and media business. It was probably helped by the five million 'The Beatles Are Coming!' stickers Capitol had paid for and plastered over every available surface in the New York area. In the car on the way in from the airport the Beatles had punched the buttons on the radio and couldn't believe how many stations there were and how often they heard themselves. At the hotel they were given Pepsi-Cola-branded transistor radios. These had earphones which enabled them to wander round their suite enjoying the intoxicating novelty of listening to more than one station. The success of Sullivan's booking was further sealed by the way the mainstream media pitched in to multiply the actual hysteria on the ground ('How many had been at JFK? 3,000? 5,000? Make it 15,000!'). The details didn't matter.

The cultural critics of America's newspapers and magazines, the phrase-mongers, opinion formers and pipe suckers who preferred to think it was their national duty to fight the good fight in defence of the Great American Songbook, combed their thesauruses for the clinching entomological pun, wondered what the twelve hours just past had told them about the flower of American maidenhood and used all their lordly powers to cut this excitement down to size. Still, for all their Manhattan sophistication, none of them managed to leave so much as a dent on the juggernaut of charm that had rolled into town the previous week, subdued an entire city within twenty-four hours and was now responsible for gridlock surrounding the Plaza Hotel.

Much of the energy of these wordsmiths was spent on scratching around for ways to describe the Beatles' hairstyles. Rarely in the short history of tonsorial commentary have so many ill-chosen words been fired in the direction of such an essentially uncomplicated look, a look whose key defining feature was that, set against the prevailing style favoured by the US male at the time, it appeared so natural and relaxed. Nevertheless they tried. The *New Yorker* characterized the Beatles hairstyle as 'dishmop'. *Time* magazine likened their head shapes to mushrooms. When it came to specifics they were all over the place but the old men in their button-back chairs in studies overlooking Central Park all agreed on one thing: it was long, shockingly long, so long as possibly to constitute a threat to good order and the American Way.

This being the United States it wasn't long before the psychologists weighed in. One Joyce Brothers wrote a column explaining 'why they go wild over the Beatles'. To be fair it took a woman to point out that there was an attractively feminine side to their performances. She noted how the girls in the audience screamed when

Paul and George closed on the same microphone and shook their heads. When they did this their hair did something hair had never previously been seen to do in the entire history of American popular entertainment. It moved.

The fuss about the Beatles' hair, which in truth wasn't a great deal longer than the average, served only to illustrate how many years it had been since America looked at itself in the mirror. The length of their hair wasn't the issue. The way they wore it was.

The prevailing American hairstyles of the post-war years, which had been beamed into Europe's living rooms via TV sitcoms, had valued control at all costs. This applied equally to men and women. American women would visit the salon once a week to have their hair 'set' so that it might maintain its shape throughout the following weekend. Men, many of whom had formed their idea of an acceptable hairstyle in the armed services, would have their hair cut every three weeks for fear that anyone should suggest it was anything that could be described as 'scruffy'. The same conventions were imposed on the rest of the world by Hollywood. In those movie epics popular at the time which were set in the ancient world the hair of heroes such as Kirk Douglas as Spartacus was kept under such firm hold that even a duel to the death in the Circus Maximus would be unlikely to disarrange a single strand. Leading ladies such as Gina Lollobrigida's Queen of Sheba had clearly spent an inordinate amount of time under whatever passed for a drier back in those biblical days. As Sibbie O'Sullivan writes in her memoir of being a teenage fan at the time, 'if teenage girls screamed when the Beatles shook their heads they could have simply been responding to seeing hair actually move, given how flat-topped, greased up or encased in military grade hairspray American hair had become by 1964'.

None of this was taking place in a vacuum. By 1964 the British hairdresser Vidal Sassoon had already built a reputation for his revolutionary approach to cutting the hair of fashionable women. Sassoon, who took his inspiration from modern architecture, moved the emphasis from the dressing of hair to the drama of its cutting, ideally in ways that complemented the bone structure of his client. After Sassoon, women could wash their hair, let it dry, and the severity of the cut would take care of the rest. 'You could even,' recalled one early client wonderingly, as though lucky enough to have been present at the invention of sex, 'run your hands through it.'

This sensuality was a galaxy away from small-town America where it was believed that hair, like the emotions, was best kept under tight control. Bruce Springsteen of Freehold, New Jersey, who was fourteen at the time, recalled just how much was at stake when people talked about hair. 'It is almost impossible to explain today the effect of the hair. In 1964 Freehold was redneck ugly. If you were going to grow your hair you ran the risk of having to get into a fight to earn your right to do so.'

This had already been an issue before the Beatles came along. Back in May 1963, *Life* magazine had carried a story about hair length and young boys. This had been occasioned by photographs of the two-year-old John Kennedy, the son of the President, with hair which strayed slightly over his ears. The writer told a personal story of how her own young son preferred to wear his hair at the same modest length. She added, controversially, that she had been prepared to support him no matter how much the barber argued that he should be 'given a butch' (a butch was the kind of crop favoured by the nation's heroes of the time, the astronauts). However, even she was forced to give in when a delegation of mothers came to see her and begged her to cut her son's hair because they were worried about the effect his hair length was having on their own sons.

In December 1964, after almost a full year of American Beatlemania, a Connecticut schoolboy called Edward Kores was involved in a dispute with the education authorities at state level. He had been sent home from school because of his bangs (the American term for hair combed forward into a fringe rather than to the side). He had been dismissed even though, in the words of the *New York Times*, 'unlike the British singing group' he had his hair short at the sides and back. His school had still objected to the style. His parents supported the boy, arguing that the school had infringed his constitutional rights.

Whereas similar squabbles in the UK would rarely amount to much more than a few headteachers being quoted in the *Daily Mirror* and an opportunistic would-be pop star called David Jones popping up on the BBC's current affairs programme *Tonight*, announcing himself as being from the Society for the Prevention of Cruelty to Long-Haired Men, in America the same argument would soon be about the nature of the republic and would involve the enlistment of the Founding Fathers on both sides of the argument. Such disputes didn't readily go away. Fully two years after the Beatles' arrival members of a Dallas rock band called Sounds Unlimited actually sued their school in federal court over the length of their hair. They eventually took their case to the Supreme Court. The school in this case prevailed. Two members of the band cut their hair and joined the US Marines.

It is only overstating the case slightly to say that in pop music, hair is everything. The Beatles understood this. One of the first things John Lennon said to Ringo Starr when the latter agreed to join the band was 'the sideburns will have to go'. The manner in which they choose to wear their hair is one of the few things artists can agree on early in their career, and this usually happens long before they sign a contract or see the inside of a recording studio. The look is who they are. Once they've arrived at a look they are unlikely to depart from it. Long before Elvis Presley had made a record he was known around Memphis for the care with which he swept back his hair and the trouble he went to to dye it to achieve the Tony Curtis shade he favoured. Artists like Little Richard were 50 per cent hair, often literally. The Ronettes sported the towering beehives of girls who wished to be taken as slightly older and possibly a tad sluttier than they really were.

In the year 1964 it was impossible for anybody to talk about the Beatles without mentioning their hair. It appeared to be, much as it was with Samson, the source of their strength. That snap decision John and Paul had taken during a short holiday in Paris in 1961 to abandon the last vestiges of their swept-back rocker pompadours and instead to embrace the choirboy style favoured by the Parisians of the *nouvelle vague* was, it turned out, the most consequential creative decision they ever took. In Liverpool it instantly defined them against the competition. In America it defined them against the adults of an entire continent and invited its youth to join them in this great revolution of the head.

The morning after the Beatles appeared on *The Ed Sullivan Show* many young Americans, like Tom Petty, began their long march to guitar ownership. Far more of them were like Paul Middleton of Vancouver Island. Paul was fifteen at the time. On the Monday following the show his school had declared a Camera Day in the course of which students would be encouraged to take candid snaps of each other for the high school yearbook. Because he and some friends of both sexes had watched the Beatles together they decided between them that their best response was in their own hands. They agreed that the following morning they would get up, wash their hair and wear it to school in its natural state without fixatives of any kind. This daring act of solidarity was within both their reach and their budget. It was also difficult to imagine that anyone could possibly object. They were wrong about that. Within an hour of arriving at school Paul and his friends had all been sent home with instructions to 'do' their hair and in future not to be subversive.

Long before the battle lines were drawn over the Vietnam War, sexual liberation or recreational drugs, the struggle between the generations was waged around hair. That week in February proved to be the week when the fuse was lit. Within a year of the Beatles' appearance on *The Ed Sullivan Show* no less than 41 per cent of the American population would be under the age of twenty-one. They were now the driving wheel of what nobody had yet got around to calling 'the culture'. The first people to recognize this were the people with something to sell. There wasn't a sector of American commerce that wasn't thinking about the Beatles and there wasn't a businessman in the United States who didn't think he could turn this no doubt short-lived mania into money. It was around this time that Bob Dylan was beginning to sing a new song called 'The Times They Are A-Changin''. Everybody picked out the line that went 'your sons and your daughters are beyond your command'. It was a thought nobody seemed to have expressed before.

In fact it was the daughters who were going to be the first beyond command, and where the Beatles were concerned the daughters mattered more than the sons. It had been much the same with Elvis Presley. Girls made Elvis, and girls would make the Beatles too. Boys need permission to fall in love with a band. Girls just need a moment. It was the girls who had trooped out to JFK. It was the girls who waved the signs at the Plaza Hotel. It was the girls who instantly chose their favourite. It was the girls who embraced this new sensation. It was the girls who rode it for all it was worth. These four unlikely young men, whom two years earlier they would have passed in the street without a second thought, now provided permission for them to gather together, feel their collective power and simply to experience the rush of being part of the noise, the sound that announced that they were at last coming out of the fall-out shelter of the last few years. They could emerge from under the kitchen table ready to cast aside the penny loafers, the pleated skirts, the winged spectacles of the era of Eisenhower, because their time was most assuredly now and the Beatles belonged to them and they belonged to the Beatles.

It was the girls who spent their time picking up signals just from looking at the Beatles. For the whole period they were in the United States they were directly under the fiercest variety of the female gaze. It was a different experience for both parties. This was the first time these girls had harboured feelings for any fantasy figures who weren't American and they couldn't help reflecting on the ways in which it opened up different bits of themselves. The novelist Jane Smiley, then a fourteen-year-old high school girl in St Louis, Missouri, watched them on *Ed Sullivan* and was struck by the fact that 'there was a kind of neatness and panache about them that American singers didn't have and that seemed characteristically English. When the music stopped, they bowed suddenly, like toy soldiers, and that seemed alien and desirable, too.'

There was also the question of their physique. When the Beatles flew down to Miami for a few days' rest and recreation, during their visit they appeared before the press wearing shorts and towelling tops. In these they couldn't help but appear faintly camp. They were presumably adopted to avoid drawing attention to the fact that next to the local sun worshippers and the average American outdoor type the Beatles appeared somewhat weedy. Like most of the British Invasion bands the Beatles were slight and lived their lives far away from sunshine. Sibbie O'Sullivan saw them with the eyes of a fifteen-year-old American girl. What struck her was 'their lack of muscles, their thin arms and, compared to American examples, their sunken chests'.

The fact that this did not alter her devotion to them one whit says much about the many things that were beginning to thaw, the plates that were beginning to shift, the aesthetics that were beginning to change in the wake of that Sunday evening television appearance.

The writer Ray Connolly, then recently graduated from a British university, was in New York in the summer of 1963 when 'She Loves You' came on the radio for the first time. At first American friends just thought it was quaint. By the time he got back to London in the autumn they were the ones who seemed quaint.

A girl from Liverpool said to him, 'Don't the Americans seem old-fashioned now?'

'I said, "Yes, they do." The change had come that quickly.'

5

'All the heaviness of our hearts'

I n the fortnight that the Beatles spent in the United States, during which time they played on Ed Sullivan's show twice, performed at Carnegie Hall in New York, and in Washington DC endured a humiliating evening at the British Embassy – the one place where they really ought to have been most feted – the media back in the UK did everything they could to keep the home fires burning.

The story they found themselves writing was one no British paper had been called upon to write before. The visit had obviously been a success. The *Sunday Times* in London quoted the *New York Times* saying they were 'the most successful British export since the bowler' (a curious parallel, particularly when examples such as Charlie Chaplin and Alfred Hitchcock were so near at hand). More sober observers reported back that the city of New York had seen nothing to match the public enthusiasm on display since the war

44

hero General MacArthur returned from Korea. But British fans didn't have to take the reporters' word for it. They could see it with their own eyes.

On the eve of the Beatles' departure to the States, Granada TV, which had been the first broadcaster to bring the Beatles to the public and considered them one of their own regional assets, had presciently commissioned the largely unknown American documentarians the Maysles brothers to shoot and edit an instant documentary about the band's visit. The brothers got the call just two hours before the band were due to land and immediately headed out to the airport. They didn't know what they would find. Recalling the events forty years later, Albert Maysles said, 'Nobody could be sure whether there were going to be five people or five thousand people there.' It turned out there were more than that. The phone call from Granada didn't just give a fresh impetus to the Maysles' joint career. It also led to their unwittingly stumbling upon an entirely new form, which is still being emulated over fifty years later, a form which transformed our expectations of popular entertainment by taking the audience somewhere they had never been before: behind the scenes. Here were such riches that the Maysles had no need of a script. All the brothers had to do was load their cameras and point.

The resulting *Yeah! Yeah! Yeah! The Beatles in New York* was edited at breakneck speed so that it could be shown on ITV on 12 February, the day the Beatles played Carnegie Hall. Viewer reaction at home was so positive it was shown again the following evening. This film meant the Beatles' visit was no longer simply a pop music event. It now seemed to add up to something more than that. People watching in their home country, particularly young people, experienced a feeling of validation which was without precedent. For the first time they were watching people like themselves, people with similar haircuts, similar accents and a similar tendency to seek the funny in everything, being warmly embraced by a foreign country; and not just any foreign country but America. Had an instant polling of the national mood been possible in mid-February 1964 it would no doubt have recorded a noticeable uptick in British self-esteem, all the more remarkable for being attributable to the very young people who a few weeks earlier had been responsible for the country going to the dogs. It captured everyone. Even Pathé News, whose narrator Bob Danvers-Walker still delivered the script in the stentorian tones of Empire, reported 'John, Paul, George and Ringo have found new worlds to conquer' and assured the viewing audience that the Beatles were 'the top musical phenomenon of the century'.

Everybody on the business side knew that their reception in America changed everything; what nobody quite realized was by just how much it changed everything. If the Beatles' British success was going to be replicated in the USA it wouldn't so much double the arithmetic of the calculations as change the mathematics entirely. This was now the big time, and the big time would require that things be done in a wholly different way. In some cases it was already too late. As the Beatles flew back to London on 22 February, understandably intoxicated by their preposterous success, it was only just beginning to dawn on their painfully inexperienced manager that he might already have been guilty of selling the biggest entertainment phenomenon of the age at a knock-down price.

Brian Epstein had been besieged by offers. While in New York he had even resisted Sid Bernstein's urging for them to seize the moment and prolong the visit to play Madison Square Garden while they could. Bernstein envisaged charging a dollar a head. Some natural cautiousness had held Epstein back. Had the plan gone further the Beatles themselves would also have pointed out that they simply didn't have the artillery to play music in a space that big. It would be another year before Epstein would book them into venues which even began to be commensurate with the scale of the demand. This was not in itself harmful. There would be other opportunities.

Far more serious was the mistake Epstein had made in leaving the negotiation of the contracts to produce officially licensed Beatles merchandise, a business which was if anything more lucrative than the business of recorded music, to his solicitor. This man ended up giving away 90 per cent of the profits to a bunch of naive businessmen who would have been deliriously happy with 10 per cent. It was only when a representative of this business met Epstein in New York and presented him with a cheque for $10,000 that he realized he had already given away nine times that much. The implications were chilling. Even if the Beatles' career were ultimately not to amount to anything more than one golden day in the sun it was still only breakfast time.

In February 1964 the department stores and malls of America had not yet begun seriously stocking up on plastic Beatles guitars, Beatles pennants, Beatles ballpoint pens, Beatles dolls, Beatles wigs, Beatles lunch-boxes and Beatles pillow cases. Not surprising, then, that much of Epstein's miscalculation arose from a failure to comprehend the sheer scale of the market. When somebody offered Epstein $100,000 to sell Beatles T-shirts his English sense of scale and innate modesty led him to think they couldn't possibly make that kind of money back. Three days later it turned out that the company had already sold a million shirts and they were just getting started. Clearly when American youth spent, it spent on a scale nothing in Britain had prepared him for. Epstein hadn't been swindled. He'd simply been caught between his own ignorance of what he was dealing with and the American readiness to make a bet. In the week the Beatles were in New York the *Wall Street Journal* predicted that in 1964 American teenagers would spend $50 million on plastic tat. This was probably an underestimate. This is what

Epstein was thinking about on the journey home. While they were in the air on their way back to London following their triumph the Beatles probably lost another million dollars. And they weren't yet aware of this fact. What would they say when they were?

There was no sign that their British fans had felt in any way neglected during their two-week absence. Significant crowds at Heathrow welcomed them back. The *Daily Mirror* printed a special edition with a wrap-round you could post in your front window, the kind of thing they'd only previously done for a royal wedding. At Heathrow the Beatles went straight into a press conference which was filmed and shown on that afternoon's BBC sports programme *Grandstand*. Because in 1964 there was no youth-specific radio or targeted TV programme the broadcasters were compelled to put the Beatles on the biggest shows. In that way their adventures in America became part of the national narrative. There wasn't a newspaper, magazine or TV programme that didn't have some kind of Beatles angle. The day after their return they appeared on ATV's *Big Night Out* with Billy Dainty and Lionel Blair. Here hosts Mike and Bernie Winters played customs officers welcoming them back and opening their suitcases to reveal the piles of dollars inside. Epstein must have watched this with a particularly wan smile.

There was no respite from their work load. The intensity only increased. The following day they went into the studios at Abbey Road where they recorded 'And I Love Her', 'I Should Have Known Better' and their next single, 'Can't Buy Me Love'. The week after that they were on a train in the West Country, to shoot their first film. Every day seemed to bring forth something they had never done before. Quite a few days brought forth something which nobody had ever done before.

The whole nation felt part of their success. At the time, one of the staples of British newspaper coverage was the 'brain drain'. The term was used to describe what seemed to be an inevitable story of British scientists tempted overseas by the prospect of greater funding for their research and a better lifestyle for their families. *Record Mirror* borrowed the idea for their front-page story. They said that their readers should be worried by the 'rave drain', raising the spectre that British pop stars might be similarly tempted away to the States and could be lost to their British fans. There had never been a time in the past when the British music papers could even joke about such an eventuality. What's more, the story continued, it turned out that the Beatles' visit had been such a success that the American agency of Dave Clark, whose group had just finished a run at number one with 'Glad All Over', had demanded that he should immediately fly out to do press and promotion in anticipation of returning with his group to tour in the summer.

The Dave Clark Five were the second group of the British Invasion. By some measures they were the second most successful. The cloth they were cut from, however, could not have been more different. This much was apparent from their name, which made it clear who was in charge. They were also actual Londoners rather than people who'd come to the capital to seek their fortune. They came from relatively poor areas of north London but were big on pulling themselves up by their boot-straps. This was evident from the fact they had met up at a gym. None of the other groups of the 1960s would have known what a gym was, let alone met at one. Clark's clean-cut good looks got him work as a film extra so he knew a bit about showbiz. He put together the group and they were soon packing them in on Saturday nights at the Tottenham Royal where they impressed the crowds with their well-drilled professionalism and their American sound. Unlike almost every other English band of the time, the Dave Clark Five featured a saxophone. They had also played a lot of American army and air force bases where on the jukeboxes they would hear the latest dance craze records from America, rehearse their own versions and then return with them the following week.

The really impressive thing about Clark is that when he took his band to the record companies he had a product to sell, not a favour to ask. With £300 he had been given for rolling a car on a film set he actually paid for the band to make their first record. He then leased it to EMI, where he immediately made three times as much as he would have made if he'd had a standard record contract. This became even more impressive when he began to have huge hits like 'Glad All Over'. That had followed 'I Want To Hold Your Hand' to the top of the British charts, which inevitably meant the headlines misleadingly said they had 'toppled' the Beatles. When they were asked on the TV news how they felt about this, Dave had his soundbite ready: 'As the record says, glad all over.' The Beatles would never have allowed anything so glib to sully their lips.

The week the Beatles returned from the USA they held three of the top ten places on the *Cashbox* Top 100. Below them Dusty Springfield, the Swinging Blue Jeans and the Searchers were among the fastest-rising hits. So were the Dave Clark Five with 'Glad All Over'. By the time the *Record Mirror* story appeared, Clark's plans to go to the States and do a bit of promotion had been torn up as British agents were scrambling their acts on to planes to respond to this sudden demand. There had already been acts lining up to get in through whatever door the Beatles managed to prise open. Now that it was off its hinges even people who hadn't been thinking about going to America suddenly realized it ought to be an urgent priority. Few yet had the confidence that all this madness might turn into a career and not be just a once-in-a-lifetime lark. Clark's boys had been more cautious than most. It was only Ed Sullivan's offer to Clark for them to be the first

British act on his show after the Beatles that prompted them to turn pro. The first completely professional engagement the Dave Clark Five undertook was on 8 March. That was when they head-lined the biggest TV show in the world. As singer Mike Smith later recalled, he left his job on the Friday, on the Saturday he took his first ever plane journey, on Saturday night he stayed in his first hotel, and on the Sunday he sang 'Glad All Over' in front of seventy million people.

They went down very well. Sullivan was so pleased with their performance that he offered them the same deal as the Beatles, insisting they stay and do the following Sunday's show as well. Clark, who managed the group himself, said they couldn't because they had a sold-out show to play back in the UK. Sullivan said he would buy that show out if they would only stay. Clark bridled at spending the week hanging around in New York. Sullivan asked him where he would prefer to spend it. Plucking from his memory the name of a holiday destination he had seen on a poster coming in from the airport, Clark suggested Montego Bay. Hence, this group from Tottenham who had only just left their day jobs back in cold, rainy Britain spent a week in Jamaica lying back and enjoying such sun as they had never known in their lives, all courtesy of Ed Sullivan.

The standard rule in show business is it pays to be first. However, there are exceptions to this rule. On the basis of the example of the Dave Clark Five in 1964 it would be perfectly possible to argue that it's even better to be second. Clark and his band made themselves available at a time when the Beatles were busy mak-ing their first film and grabbing what rest and recreation they could. The Dave Clark Five's post-Montego Bay appearance on *The Ed Sullivan Show* would turn out to be the second of no fewer than eighteen times they were featured, which was a show record. By the spring they were touring the country on a private plane they had hired from the Rockefellers. Clark, who was untroubled by modesty from an early age, proudly pointed out that it said 'DC5' on the nose. They didn't just stick to the eastern seaboard either. They ventured into the Midwest, playing Ohio, Missouri and Chicago. They even ventured into the South with shows in Memphis and Arkansas. The whole of America heard the sound of the Dave Clark Five's marching feet.

The Dave Clark Five seemed built for America. They already had the stamp of the military about them, from the gleam of the buttons on their blazers to the barrack-room shine of their shoes; it was in their music too – tunes like 'Glad All Over', 'Bits and Pieces' and 'Catch Us If You Can', each built inexorably to a regimental-sounding percussion break. This kind of thing was catnip to adolescent boys, those not-quite men who feel most comfortable in that liminal space between drill and dancing and in all cases prefer something they can act out with each other. 'Glad All Over' was the record that attracted the boys who couldn't dance on to the dance floor, and there were plenty of those. It's no surprise that Dave Clark's records live on in the twenty-first century as popular run-out music at sporting events.

Clark retained the rights to those records, which is something nobody else had the foresight to do. The idea of the Tottenham Sound, in reference to their home area of north London, never fooled anybody outside the USA. Their records were actually cooked up in an independent studio in Holland Park and engineered by Adrian Kerridge. He drove the faders into the red in order to achieve their machine-like sound. Their records sounded, if anything, American. If they had been recording in the company-supervised studios of Abbey Road or West Hampstead some white-coated guardian of technical standards would have stepped in to prevent them doing just that.

In Britain, although they had big hits, there never seemed to be a lot of love for the Dave Clark Five. There was something about

Clark in particular that the British would never quite warm to, but it certainly didn't hold them back in America. Their British peers were slightly resentful of the Dave Clark Five in a way they were never resentful of the Beatles. They didn't feel they belonged in the same fraternity. However, even from early on they admired the speed with which Dave Clark had positioned his band on the shoulders of the Beatles. They were making hay while others were stuck back in Blighty. As the Stones manager Andrew Loog Oldham said, Mick and Keith may have sniggered at Clark's white polo necks and robotic rhythms, but 'we didn't laugh at his business acumen and ability to get it right in America'.

Dave Clark made hay. Lots of it. In 1964 alone, a year in which his group had begun as a semi-pro act, Clark released no fewer than seven singles and four LPs in the USA. That second album, which came out just three months after the first one, was frenetically christened *The Dave Clark Five Return!* as though bringing to an end a period of unbearable separation. In the same year they played the biggest venues in fifty American cities. They put out another LP to mark this event, calling it, with startling obviousness, *American Tour*. A further LP in the same year was called *Coast To Coast* in direct recognition of the country where they increasingly went to work. There was nothing of that troubling tone-of-voice business with the Dave Clark Five. Nothing ambiguous. Nothing fancy. Fancy is the worst thing you can be in the United States. 'Fancy' is the word America saves for those things of which a true republican could never approve. The Dave Clark Five seemed to speak America's language.

Many of the Dave Clark LPs were never released in the UK. The American market was already adjusting to different versions of the records that came out across the pond. Much of this was a question of accounting. American LPs were always shorter than the UK versions because whereas British record companies had an agreement with the music publishers that meant they paid a flat rate regardless of how many tunes were involved, American companies were forced to pay per song. Therefore they responded by making the LPs of even the Beatles shorter, weaker, and usually changing their names. *With The Beatles* was reborn as *Meet The Beatles*. This might not have pleased the Beatles but it didn't cause Dave Clark to lose much sleep because he knew you had to feed the beast while the beast still had an appetite.

Once it was plain that they were thinking about the American market first and everything else was an afterthought, the Dave Clark Five slipped from the reckoning at home. If you had done an interim accounting at the end of 1964 you would have been tempted to declare the Dave Clark Five the leading beneficiary of the British Invasion on the basis of the energy with which they attacked the market, the amount of cash Clark sucked out of it in a short time and, thanks to the fact he wasn't sharing any of it with a manager, how much he personally managed to hang on to. That was how he was looked at in the UK, with grudging respect for how ahead of the game he was. He made a million and invested it, first securing the rights to all his old band's material, and then later, when nobody else was far-sighted enough to see that it might have some long-term value, buying up all the footage of TV programmes like *Ready Steady Go!*. This meant that if anybody could be said to own the sixties, it was Dave Clark.

Two weeks after the Dave Clark Five did their second appearance on *The Ed Sullivan Show* it was the turn of the Searchers, whose version of Sonny Bono's 'Needles and Pins' was in the US singles chart. Later in the spring Sullivan hosted Gerry and the Pacemakers, Dusty Springfield and Billy J. Kramer. By then the Beatles held the first five places in the *Cashbox* chart and *Billboard* was announcing the imminent arrival of a group called the Rolling Stones, whose 'Not Fade Away', the advert breathlessly announced, was already top five in the UK, and also Chad & Jeremy, who were presented in bowler hats and pin-stripe suits to stress the fact that they purveyed 'the Oxford sound'.

Dusty Springfield had been in the United States ahead of the Beatles as a member of the Springfields, who had gone to Nashville in order to make a country-flavoured record for the American market. It was while she was in New York on that trip that she heard the Exciters' 'Tell Him' coming out of a record shop and decided that henceforth she should make r&b-flavoured pop songs. At the height of Beatlemania her 'I Only Want To Be With You' got as high as number 12 in the United States. She made the usual TV appearances but it was difficult for female performers to achieve the same traction as the groups. Cilla Black, Sandie Shaw and Lulu were all popular performers at home but couldn't get arrested in the USA during the British Invasion. Somebody even got the nineteen-year-old Elkie Brooks a slot on the same New York show as the Animals in 1964 but she had to get her parents to pay both the air fare and her hotel costs in order to take advantage of the offer.

Six months before all this England had been, for most young Americans, a faraway country of which they knew nothing. By the spring of 1964, as the Beatles were acting out a version of their daily lives for the camera of Dick Lester, America was starting to develop its own version of England. This was the time when, Bruce Springsteen recalls, teenage boys really would try to impress the check-out girls at his local supermarket by talking in what he took to be an English accent. This artificial England they created was a fantasy island in which the stock characters of greetings-card England coexisted with this brave new world; in which beefeaters and chimney sweeps shared their half-timbered homes with fashionable young women with geometric haircuts; and in every corner there appeared a band like the Dave Clark Five that stood ready at the drop of a hat to strike up the music that would transform the room into a blur of frantic fruggery.

In their own country the Dave Clark Five remain prophets without honour to this date. For them there was to be no long-awaited reassessment. They were the first of the British Invasion bands to be more popular in the United States than they were at home. Here their core supporters were American boys like Bruce Springsteen and Tom Hanks, who was eight years old and being dragged all over California in the wake of his divorced dad. There was something about the Dave Clark Five that appealed to the buried aggression of young males. There was something bigger than life about the sound of their records that we would detect later in American heartland favourites like Kiss and Black Sabbath and Bon Jovi. There was nothing subtle about them. If the Beatles were soccer then the Dave Clark Five were American football.

When the American-based Rock & Roll Hall of Fame gave them an honour in 2008 they had still never been recognized at home. On that occasion no less a personage than Hanks came out and read a throbbing encomium in which he drew a direct line between the depression following the Kennedy assassination and the orgiastic release of listening to the Dave Clark Five on the car radio. He recalled begging his dad to turn them up when they came on the radio. When Dad said 'this ain't music', Tom thought, but didn't say, that it was music in one very important sense. It was going to 'take all the bleak days we've been through and all the heaviness of our hearts and smash it to pieces, bits and pieces'.

6

'Man, that's how life should be'

On 14 July 1964 the prints of the Beatles' first feature film, *A Hard Day's Night*, were delivered to the Beacon Theater on Broadway in New York. As a claque of back-combed first-generation Beatles fans dutifully clutched each other with excitement for the benefit of the news cameras, the canisters were gravely conducted into the theatre by three agents of Wells Fargo. Somebody had instructed these men to unholster their revolvers, presumably in order to underline the full gravity of the responsibility with which they had been entrusted. Just five months since being revealed to the nation on *The Ed Sullivan Show* via a screen so tiny, so cramped, so low in definition that the teenage audience had to pull their chairs up close to the set to have any chance of apprehending the detail of their performance, those same Beatles were suddenly being delivered into every neighbourhood movie theatre from sea to shining sea. Now, thanks to the miracle of movies, their adored faces could be projected 60 feet wide and their music reproduced at a volume which at least stood a fair chance of doing justice to its pulsating excitement.

This was the way the music really came to the masses. This is where the deal was sealed. Just as *The Blackboard Jungle* had been the vehicle that brought rock and roll to the kids who weren't old enough to hang around jukebox dives, so *A Hard Day's Night* would bring America and the Beatles close together, for more reasons than anyone suspected at the time.

A Hard Day's Night had been originated with a view to the American market. Up to that point in their career the Beatles had been playing one-nighters in venues that seated a thousand at most. The only realistic way to reach bigger numbers was to make a film. At this time film was the natural next step for any pop star who was considered big enough to graduate into show business proper. Even Cliff Richard and the Shadows had made more than one feature film by then and they weren't even popular far beyond the United Kingdom. The way forward had been set out by Elvis Presley. Presley had seen pop stardom as essentially a stepping stone to the proper, gold standard fame represented by Hollywood. Colonel Tom Parker understood that Presley's signal quality was that the camera loved him. Therefore he had his client make films as soon as he could.

A Hard Day's Night was shot in just a few weeks following the Beatles' return from their epochal visit to the United States in February and it was somehow made ready for a summer release. 1964 was a good year for British film stars in the export market. The Beatles' first film was launched in the USA just a couple of weeks after *A Shot in the Dark*, with Peter Sellers reprising his role as Inspector Clouseau, and a fortnight before Hitchcock's *Marnie*, which starred Sean Connery. United Artists launched *A Hard Day's Night* in the US with seven hundred prints, which was a lot for a pop film. Thanks to another of Brian Epstein's deals that favoured greater exposure over more revenue, United Artists, who owned the film, also owned the soundtrack; therefore it was already in profit before actually being released.

The movie was fairly well received by the traditional gatekeepers of cinematic excellence, who were not normally given to saying anything kind about a pop music film. The *New York Times* greeted it as a 'surprising pleasure', exceeding what they might have been led to expect from even 'those incredible chaps', and agreed with their peers that it was a cut above the standard cinematic attempt to ride the coat tails of pop success. They even allowed that some of it was 'a fine glomeration of mad cap clowning in the old Marx Brothers style'.

The way the film had come together provided a further example of the almost sinister portion of good fortune enjoyed by the Beatles in those early days. Because the American company financing it didn't believe it would be worth shooting in colour, the film was shot in black and white. This might have been a budgetary compromise but it gave the film a verité sheen which led people to overlook its shortcomings. It also meant film critics, who are as a breed pre-programmed to read monochrome as authenticity, were favourably disposed towards it. Creatively, the Beatles were also fortunate to work with Americans who were not based in America. The director Richard Lester, like the producer Walter Shenson, was an American who, for want of a better idea, had decided to try his hand in the UK. This meant they were both ideally placed to explain the demands of the American market to their British stars and to deal with any communication issues in the other direction. Shenson was nothing like as heavy-handed as the standard producer might have been in demanding the film make adjustments for the huge American market.

When the US distributors first saw the film there had been some talk of overdubbing the dialogue to make it more intelligible for an American audience. Paul quite reasonably countered that since British audiences were perfectly used to watching cowboy films where much of the language and all of the accents were unfamiliar then it ought not to be expecting too much of American audiences that they do the same thing when the boot was on the other foot. His argument was to be repeated endlessly down the years around other acts, with the Brits tending to argue that surely half the fun was working out what something meant, and the American marketeers, who held the view that anything which involved work was the antithesis of entertainment, usually winning in the end.

It had been agreed at the outset that they would play themselves, and the action would be confined to a couple of days in the lives of the group. It had been further agreed that there would be no love interest since this would be bound to upset the fans, most of whom had a favourite Beatle with whom they were already enjoying a torrid imaginary affair. All Elvis's films hinged on his wooing of a beautiful starlet. Since Elvis only had himself to answer for, that was acceptable for him. The Beatles had a higher loyalty. Their loyalty was to one another. The film was a celebration of that very togetherness. This was its secret sauce.

Playwright Alun Owen had been hired to write the script and he spent a couple of days on tour with them, getting an idea of how it felt to live their fugitive lives and trying to capture their mode of speech. He may have overdone the Liverpool argot, having them use the arcane 'come 'ed' instead of 'come on' and putting the word 'grotty' into the mouth of George Harrison even though neither he nor the rest of the group had ever heard it before. It was full of in-jokes that would have only meant anything to a British audience. One of its core themes, about Paul's grandfather being 'a very clean old man', was playing on the fact that the same actor, Wilfrid Brambell, was at the time playing the character of the father often described as a 'dirty old man' in the long-running TV sitcom *Steptoe and Son.*

It was an identifiably British film. Its action unfolded against a background that would have been familiar to anyone watching British light comedies of the time: city gents read *The Times* in the first-class carriage, TV producers are neurotic and faintly camp, pub sandwiches curl up beneath plastic covers, teenage fans wear duffel coats and ankle socks, gentlemen strew cloaks Walter Raleigh-style across puddles so that fine ladies may traverse building sites, anyone stuck for somewhere to go in a conversation will adopt the voice of a German officer, and constables can be relied upon to bark 'Gotcha!' when laying hands on their quarry. For the average American cinema-goer who had grown up watching films set in the pastel nowhere in which Hollywood dealt, *A Hard Day's Night* might as well have been a travelogue. Jane Smiley, growing up in St Louis, said that while she watched it for the Beatles, 'what I saw were the shots of the train, of Paddington Station, of the English countryside, of Wilfrid Brambell, who did not look like any man I had ever seen'.

Some of its inspiration came from the Maysles brothers' *Yeah! Yeah! Yeah!*. Writing about that film, no less a person than cultural critic Susan Sontag said, 'there is more vitality and art in their film on the Beatles in America than in all the American story films made this year'. The documentary, hailed at the time as an exciting new development in TV because for the first time the camera moved with the action, and Dick Lester's feature film both agree on one thing. Film directors and fans want the same simple thing from pop stars: they want to get up close. We the audience are not desperately interested in what the band have to say just so long as we can watch them say it. Ideally we want to watch them closely enough to almost smell them. The Maysles' camera did this as the Beatles confronted the delirium of their welcome into the United

States. That feeling shaped *A Hard Day's Night*, and it has shaped every rock documentary ever since.

At the same time, *A Hard Day's Night* accidentally invented the pop video. This was many years before anyone realized that there was a use for any such form, or that it needed inventing. Before *A Hard Day's Night* film-makers had shot pop performances as though constrained by the proscenium arch. Lester's film, which is at its most moving when the Beatles just sing and play, was breathtakingly different. Using as many as six cameras, some of them hand-held, Lester delivered an experience that seemed to take the enthralled young audience right inside the group. When they saw the Beatles singing 'I Should Have Known Better' in the mail van of the train or teasing Ringo during the opening of 'If I Fell' at rehearsals for the TV show, the multiple cameras captured something which had never been caught before: that traffic in secret smiles and shared delight, the traffic that can only pass between the members of a group when they're in the midst of playing a song while simultaneously basking in the fierce heat of an audience's overpowering admiration.

Something entered the heart stream of American youth as they gazed rapt at the silvery 60-foot images of these four young men at the precise instant when they were having the time of their or anyone else's lives. That something was, if anything, more powerful than the music. That something was the element that galvanized young America, the idea of being in a group. For tens of thousands of young kids, many of them either pre-teen or in junior high school, *A Hard Day's Night* offered a wide-screen advertisement for the possibility of prolonging childhood while still living large, with your closest school friends bound even closer to you by the idea of being in a group, ever the envy of those in your wider social circle who would never be able to fully penetrate your special secret society. What Dick Lester bottled in *A Hard Day's Night* in a form so powerful that only years later is it possible to appreciate fully is that beyond the songs, beyond the playing, it's the emotion flowing between the group's members which makes the idea of being in a band so appealing. A would-be pop star from Manchester, who would go on to head up the British Invasion's second wave, had already noticed this the year before when seeing them playing in a field in Urmston. 'They loved each other,' said Peter Noone. 'The way they looked at each other and shared the private jokes. That was one of the most appealing things about them.'

All young people wish to belong. All entertainment targeted at young people aims to tap into this need by encouraging them to identify with either their families or a uniformed organization of some kind. In *A Hard Day's Night* you were looking in at a new social organization so self-sufficient, so benign, so emotionally appealing that while you might never be able to break into this particular magic quartet the hope arose in your breast that you might be able to start a musical family of your own. Paul McCartney needn't have worried about America already having a surfeit of what the Beatles were providing. He didn't realize that Americans would be struck by something that he took for granted: the simple fact that they were a group. Steve Van Zandt, thirteen at the time and growing up in New Jersey, noticed it. 'With bands it was the posse, the club, the gang, the family. That meant a lot to me. It was people who separately might not mean much but together they could pursue a common goal.'

A Hard Day's Night was unwittingly a recruiting film for a new way of life; the four-man pop group had taken over the male imagination from the cowboy gang, the patrol cut off behind enemy lines and the men who had sworn a blood oath of loyalty as boys. In the action, which follows them through a couple of days travelling by train to do a TV show in London, taking unsought meetings and being exposed to the attentions of the media, what's heartening is how little use they have for the baubles of stardom, for the five-star hotel or the casino or the posh women. In truth they only need each other and their equipment. The musical numbers apart, the soul of the film is the press conference scene where the four of them return a series of asinine questions from their elders and betters with such lugubrious non-sequiturs as 'Turn left at Greenland', 'I'm a mocker' and 'Arthur' before catching each other's eyes across the melee and agreeing to sag off, as they might have said in Liverpool.

In many ways, going to see the Beatles at the movies was better than going to see them try to play live. JoAnne McCormack, who saw the film at the Bel Air Theater in Valley Stream, New York, remembered going up to the screen at the end and kissing it. Valerie Volponi of Long Island, who went to see *A Hard Day's Night* thirteen times, eventually took a notepad with her to write down the dialogue in shorthand. They were the teenagers. Their younger siblings just saw it as a way they could actually participate in a phenomenon that previously only TV had delivered to them. Ken Hanke, who was nine at the time, remembered seeing it in the State Theater in Lake Wales, Florida. He recalls the kids in the audience screaming just as hard as they would have if the group had been there. John Anderson was ten when a friend's mother took a party to see the film at the Tamalpais Theater in San Anselmo, California. Everybody rushed the screen to touch their favourite Beatle. 'They stopped the film several times,' he remembers.

For those who were kids, *A Hard Day's Night* supplied them with fantasy friends. For those who were no longer kids, it reminded them of what they missed. The film critic Roger Ebert, who was already twenty-two, later recalled, 'it moved me as few films ever have'. Then there was the effect it had on the hundreds of people who would go to make up America's next generation of rock musicians. For thousands of young American musicians wondering where to go and what to do now that the first coming of American rock and roll appeared to have run out of steam, *A Hard Day's Night* provided a tool kit.

Lester was a musician himself and therefore, knowingly or otherwise, his film betrayed a musician's true first love, which is a love for the equipment. The kit. The gear. These were the tools you could not afford. These were the tools that would transform you. Lester knew this. Throughout the film his cameras got close enough to linger on Ringo's Ludwig drum kit. The script even allowed him to touch on the depths of the drummer's relationship with said kit. This would never have happened with Elvis. Elvis seemed happy to mime with whatever the props department came up with. You couldn't do that with the Beatles. The Beatles were passionately specific. Their equipment was an extension of them. The film made particular stars of Paul's Höfner violin bass and George's twelve-string Rickenbacker guitar. Although the latter was American-made, before the film came out most American musicians had never seen one. Rickenbacker, another of those American firms which were very fast on their feet when the Beatles began happening, had laid on a demo for the group on their first visit to New York. Because George was confined to his hotel room with laryngitis at the time they actually took the instrument to his bedside. By the time they came to make *A Hard Day's Night* the Rickenbacker was a distinctive part of both their sound and their look.

American musicians Jim McGuinn, David Crosby and Gene Clark were just three of the young players of the time who had launched themselves as folk artists but had begun to suspect that the folk tide was going out. McGuinn was already performing Beatles covers alongside his usual folk songs while playing at the Troubadour in Los Angeles. This had started back on the other coast when a club in the Village advertised for 'Beatles imitators'. By the time he played the Troubadour his hair was longer but his material still wasn't going down well with the audiences who felt that pop was the work of the devil.

The Beatles, however, coming from overseas, seemed to be free of such strictures and, having at one stage been a skiffle group, they tended to afford all music the same irreverent treatment, whether it came from the Brill Building or the cotton fields. This was immediately attractive to the three American musicians, who resolved to become a group called the Jet Set. They started to comb their hair forward after the manner of the Beatles. They came out of a showing of *A Hard Day's Night* so elated that Crosby was twirling round lamp posts Gene Kelly-style. The following day they went to see it again and made a note of all the equipment the Beatles used. McGuinn immediately traded his banjo for a twelve-string guitar just like George's, their drummer Michael Clarke was equipped with a Ludwig drum kit like Ringo's, and David Crosby ordered a Gretsch like John's. Folk rock was born not from folk, not from rock, but from *A Hard Day's Night*.

By the autumn of 1964 the passion for all things British had become so intense that their first single came out under the name of the Beefeaters, which somebody had taken from a popular brand of London gin. There was even talk of them appearing in the Ruritanian uniform of the guardians of the Tower of London. American folk enthusiast Joe Boyd, who had been in Britain that same year with a caravan of touring blues artists, happened to catch the Spencer Davis Group, with their fifteen-year-old singer Stevie Winwood – who was introduced as 'Little Stevie' in honour of Stevie Wonder – doing folk tunes in a rock band style, and decided when he got back to the US that he would help put together an American folk rock group called the Lovin' Spoonful. Even West Coast purists like those who were to make up the Grateful Dead, sage, bearded men who at first thought the Beatles were strictly for teens, changed their mind after seeing the film. Jerry Garcia described it as 'a little model of good times'.

In the year-end box office numbers *A Hard Day's Night* came in ninth below those other phenomena of British entertainment, Julie Andrews in *Mary Poppins* and the Bond films *Goldfinger* and *From Russia with Love*. It overshadowed the home-grown teen movies of the year, *Bikini Beach* starring Frankie Avalon and Annette Funicello and Elvis Presley in *Viva Las Vegas*, which strongly suggested that it had tapped into something more powerful than a keenness to see the latest pop fad on the big screen.

The American kids who flocked to see *A Hard Day's Night*, and saw it repeatedly, were baby boomers and they were ready for some emotional nourishment. In most cases they had been born to couples who returned from the war, bought themselves a dream home, provided their children with material comforts and probably felt that the incalculable dividend of peace would be enough to cover any remaining emotional deficit. In this they probably underestimated the impact their changed style of life would have on their children. Turning their backs on the extended families and inner-city neighbourhoods in which they had been raised, these families had moved to the newly built suburbs. These were marketed as the perfect place to raise kids, even though, as historian David Halberstam points out, their dream family was simultaneously being pulled apart by the automobile and the TV.

Donald Fagen of Steely Dan was one such youngster who experienced a sort of emotional malnutrition as a result of his parents' blithe pursuit of the clean lines of the suburbs. He recalls they were satisfied with the 'streamlined look of the cream Olds Dynamic 88 all cozy in its car port. But for me, a subterranean in gestation with a real nasty case of otherness, it was a prison.'

In 1951 *Life* magazine dubbed these parents who had come back from the war and settled into suburbia 'The Silent Generation'. Both Bruce Springsteen and Tom Petty were growing up, albeit in different parts of the country, with fathers who belonged to that brooding cohort, and for them, as well as many others, *A Hard Day's Night* held out possibilities that went beyond the mere musical. Petty saw the film in Gainesville, Florida. 'I was into rock and roll before them, but they were the first band I saw where everything was so self-contained. They were so young and in control of what they were doing. They were the first people we could relate to who showed us that your dreams were within your reach. That's what I found so liberating about seeing the Beatles.'

In 1964, American TV schedules were still dominated by shows like *The Adventures of Ozzie and Harriet, The Patty Duke Show* and *My Three Sons*, all set in an idealized suburbia in which everybody was just like their next-door neighbour and any tensions within the family were merely misunderstandings that could be smoothed out well before the message from the sponsor. *A Hard Day's Night* was above everything an advertisement for being in a new kind of family. From its ringing opening chord to the dying echoes of its ending it promoted the virtues of private jokes, of living according to your own code, of taking the magical appeal of a gang beyond the backyard of childhood and carrying it with you into the adult world. Being in a group was like being given a magic key with which you might prolong adolescence and arrest the advent of the adult world. In Britain it signalled the end of the National Service which had hovered over the heads of the older generation of teenagers. In America it meant something deeper, which few articulated at the time but all felt in retrospect.

The Beatles don't hug in *A Hard Day's Night*. There are no secret handshakes. The Beatles might have been, as Michael Braun observed, avatars of a new kind of human but they were still Englishmen of their era, men who would have considered the idea of expressing their true feelings in anything other than song distasteful. However, Lester had observed them at close quarters. He had watched the way that when one of the four was below par for some reason the other three would cover for him without anything needing to be said, and he made sure his film communicated this. 'There was a sense of us against the world,' Lester recalled. 'As an only child I found it staggering.'

Reviewing the movie in the *Observer*, the British critic Penelope Gilliatt spotted something similar. 'They behave to one another with the kind of unbothered rudeness usually possible only between brothers and sisters. I think this feeling is at the root of the Beatles' charm. The only thing that would probably finish the Beatles with the fans, it seems to me, would be if they seemed to split up as a family.'

This couldn't have come at a better time. The apparent harmony of the First Family had been shattered in Dallas less than a year before. The suburbanization of America was isolating American teenagers from the cities they thought they had been born in, leaving them reliant on the family car to be able to see their friends. Billy Joel was one such refugee, born in the Bronx but brought up in Hicksville. Chrissie Hynde, relocated to a suburb by her father's job, made two-hour trips back to the decaying shopping centres of Akron, Ohio, but 'there was no longer anywhere in walking distance'.

Things weren't like that in the reassuringly human-scale London of *A Hard Day's Night*. Here it was possible for even a Beatle to wander off on his own and have adventures. It was a fantasy set against the background of ordinary life. And a lot of that daily life, from the glimpses of Marylebone Station and the milk-dispensing machine at the beginning to the school playing field they briefly escape into, was all clearly British. For many American viewers who had grown up on films set in Hollywood's great nowhere, this was like a black and white travelogue.

Ringo Starr, an only child, said that when he joined the Beatles 'I suddenly felt like I had three brothers'. Even for people who weren't in the band and never would be in the band, the Beatles held out the prospect of enveloping warmth. This was precisely at the time more and more of the children of the Silent Generation were starting to be affected by divorce. Warren Zanes, writer and musician, recalled, 'When it came, the British invasion was, of course, a Copernican revolution. Ed Sullivan was the mechanism through which the core message was delivered: you can do this. A generation heard it. In fucked-up homes across America, an alternative was presented.' Jann Wenner, the founder of *Rolling Stone*, who was one of that generation, came out of *A Hard Day's Night* thinking that the Beatles might be a new kind of family, only this time one that everybody could join. 'They were young, fresh and good-looking in the same sort of way that Jack Kennedy was. The kids who are your age, who are so alive and upbeat and joyous and taking the piss out of everybody – man, that's how life should be.'

7

'He can't be a man 'cause he doesn't smoke the same cigarettes as me'

All the bands who went ashore as part of the first wave of the British Invasion were naturally disposed to favour American music. They thought America was where all the best music came from. Few of them would have dreamed of arguing that a home-grown product was in any way superior. Given all that, the passions of the members of the Rolling Stones were of an entirely different order. The Stones, more than any of the other acts, were deep-end music snobs from the very beginning. Like the jazzers from whom their band had initially sprung, their preference for almost anything American was on another level entirely. When it came to any aspect of music they were, in the words of the old song, sold American to the tips of their Chelsea boots.

Their founder Brian Jones's passion for all things blues was so far off the scale that back in 1962 he had seriously attempted to present himself as a bluesman with the name Elmo Lewis. Brian Jones came from Cheltenham, where Elmos are rare. Drummer Charlie Watts was utterly obsessed with every aspect of the jazz of Birdland. Bassist Bill Wyman was in love with cowboy films. Clinchingly, the group's leading lights Mick Jagger and Keith Richards had resumed the threads of a childhood acquaintance at Dartford railway station when the former was spotted carrying an American copy of Chuck Berry's *Rockin' At The Hops* under his arm. This was in the days when British fans could only lay their hands on such items via the American Embassy in Grosvenor Square (where the US government lent out records to interested parties as a form of cultural outreach) or by ordering them directly from Chess Records at 2120 South Michigan Avenue, Chicago, and then putting their faith in the vagaries of parcel post across national frontiers.

From the start they were the most American of British groups. In the spring of 1965, when the Rolling Stones were already making their third visit to the United States, Jagger formally announced to the press that 'There isn't really anything in England today that any of us would go to see expecting to learn anything. It's all right here in America. You've got to come here to get the real thing.' It followed, then, that they had to make their records in the United States in order that they too should be the real thing. During their first American tour the previous year their manager Andrew Loog Oldham had attempted to take the band's minds off the petty humiliations of people in the street – comments on the length of their hair, the reflexive insults of TV hosts like Dean Martin – by arranging for them actually to record at Chess in Chicago, in the very studio from which much of their inspiration had come. What excited them about this wasn't merely the associations of the place – Muddy Waters, the man from whose song 'Rollin' Stone' they had taken their name, was actually in the studio when they arrived, but he was painting the ceiling rather than making music – but also the efficiency of engineer Ron Malo, who could get the sound they wanted and get it quickly.

By 1965 there was a feeling growing among British acts that American studios could impart some magical property, that they had endless supplies of a particular form of fairy dust which was for some reason not available in the studios of London. To make their case they pointed to the superior bass sound on new American hits like Wilson Pickett's 'In The Midnight Hour'. One of the reasons 1965 was shaping up to be the annus mirabilis of the seven-inch 45 was that the big hits – in the first half of the year these included 'You've Lost That Lovin' Feelin'' by the Righteous Brothers, 'All Day And All Of The Night' by the Kinks and 'Mr Tambourine Man' by the Byrds – were the products of a creative and technological arms race. The world of pop music at the time was exploding and each week's new releases were expected to include something revelatory. People were doing things that nobody had done before. The very best 45s of the year, records such as Bob Dylan's 'Like A Rolling Stone' which came out that summer, felt like hastily composed dispatches from wholly new frontiers of experience.

On 1 May 1965, when the Stones played in the posh surroundings of the Academy of Music in New York, they were just getting used to their new American reality and, although they didn't know it, on the point of producing their own 'how does it feel?' record. They and their American fans were still establishing their special relationship. The writer Lynne Tillman, who was at the Academy as an eighteen-year-old student, was drawn to the Rolling Stones not so much because they were rebellious as because their music sounded as though they ought to be rebellious. She and a friend sat with undisguised impatience through the support act, Patti LaBelle & the Bluebelles. (The tradition of the Stones' audience not being quite as keen on the black rhythm and blues acts that the Stones personally favoured was established early on.) The gap between their set and the headliners was so long and unexplained that when the Stones finally sauntered on stage the effect was almost anti-climactic. There was none of the standard show business presentation about them. They looked, she remembered later, 'as if they were going to the men's room'.

Just as America had been attracted by the fact that the Beatles were a group, the thing that drew people to the Rolling Stones in 1965, particularly in America, was the one thing they claimed to give no thought to whatsoever. This was the way they looked. Until the early 1960s the idea that entertainers must identify themselves by adopting some kind of uniform was such an accepted tenet of show business lore that even Andrew Loog Oldham had originally dressed the Stones in matching check jackets with velvet collars. By the time they got to the USA that had all been discarded. It was this subsequent refusal to bow to the first rule of show business, a homogeneity of appearance which at the time applied equally to everyone from folk-singing fishermen to troupes of tumblers, that truly marked them out.

When the Rolling Stones of 1965 appeared on stage it was in the same clothes they'd had on when they wandered in off the street. Their individual outfits were far from uniform, and because they weren't uniform they were often full of fascinating detail. There might be elephant cord hipster trousers in unexpected colours, clumpy belt buckles behind which their hips might appear even narrower, crewneck T-shirts with horizontal stripes, bleached jeans that might have been picked up in St Tropez, button-down shirts from traditional stores and neat ties in sober shades where they might be least expected, whole regions of sensual leather or suede (quietly indicative of a degree of spend), the occasional profoundly covetable T-shirt bearing the logo of an American radio station; and, as the eye inevitably travelled down, more likely than not it would eventually be met by the arresting sight of a pair of suede desert boots or scuffed white shoes with a chisel toe. The individual items of clothing were stylish but relatively conservative. The way they were worn was anything but.

What made the Rolling Stones stand out was that unlike the Beatles, the Dave Clark Five and even the Animals, they didn't appear to have dressed to go to work. Instead, they appeared to have dressed to please themselves. This was genuinely revolutionary. This was as transformational in its time as the abandonment of the music stand had been when dance band musicians turned to jazz. Henceforth it would become the norm. All bands would look the way the Stones looked because all bands wanted to make the same statement. Variations on the Stones' look would in due course be taken up first by the Byrds and then by just about every American band formed after 1965. Why? Because a similar kind of motley seemed to be eminently achievable. It also hinted that your mind was on higher things than the way you happened to look. This was of course completely untrue.

The thirteen-year-old Steve Van Zandt had looked at the Beatles and decided he would really like to start a gang of his own. 'The day before *The Ed Sullivan Show* there were literally no bands in America,' he remembered. 'Day after, everybody had a band.' But while he found the polish of a band as well practised as the Beatles slightly intimidating, he looked at the Rolling Stones and thought something different: 'We thought, maybe we could do that.' Not long after seeing them he joined a band in Middletown, New Jersey. This was one of untold thousands of groups who took their inspiration and their name from England. Van Zandt's band called themselves the Mates, which is a minor classic of the genre.

The sole sense in which the Rolling Stones appeared uniform was in the length of their hair. This was just long enough to ensure they offered a more ragged silhouette than the Beatles. Although this was certainly provocative enough to invite speculation about their sexuality in certain parts of the USA, it was never quite long enough to be described as shaggy. Instead it appeared attractively unkempt and faintly romantic. Fashion, which in the 1950s had been aspiring to sharpness in all things, was now fast moving in the opposite direction. Mick Jagger, when asked – which was often – confessed that his hair was cut by his girlfriend Chrissie Shrimpton. To most people this seemed a daringly androgynous way to live one's life.

When the Rolling Stones had made their first TV appearances in the USA the previous year, the only thing host Dean Martin could think of to say about them concerned their hair. Much of his banter, which was presumably supplied by professional writers, implied that the length of same made them wild men and as such barely human. This message seemed to be underlined when they found their next gig had them booked to play a fairground in San Antonio, Texas, on a bill that also included honky tonk singer George Jones and the Marquis Chimps, a troupe of trained chimpanzees who had come to prominence advertising tea on television. When Jagger complained that the dressing rooms were inadequate, the promoter, a veteran of D-Day and unaccustomed to dealing with rock stars, shot back with what was now a standard jibe that the band probably hadn't changed since they had been in the country. Jagger and Richards responded to this slight by stripping off and swapping clothes in front of him. The promoter, whose idea of acceptable underwear was of a piece with the rest of his value system, was amazed to see that Jagger's pants were fire-engine red. This too was revolutionary in 1964, an augury of the many other things that were going to change as the sixties picked up pace.

Much of the resentment the Stones met with was the inevitable backwash of a PR campaign ahead of their visit which was keen to

When Buddy Holly's Crickets (*above*) played the UK in 1958 a group was simply a means of performing music. Six years later, when the Beatles landed in the USA thanks to Ed Sullivan (*left and below*), a group was a way of life.

The American teen appetite for anything English, at its most intense in the months after the Kennedy assassination, needed further feeding when the Beatles went home (*right*). Ed Sullivan got the Dave Clark Five (*below*) to stay for an extra show by paying for them to have a week in the sun.

The Byrds had been coffee-house folkies until they saw the light in the shape of *A Hard Day's Night*. A year later they were taking their spin on the Beatles' music back to London and making pilgrimage to the sites where the old city was suddenly said to swing.

Like many long-haired British groups, the Rolling Stones had to get used to abuse during their early visits. For those tours they presented themselves as missionaries for the blues, sitting at the feet of Howlin' Wolf (*above*) as he guested on the teen TV show *Shindig!*. Just a year later they were in drag (*left*) to celebrate their single 'Have You Seen Your Mother, Baby, Standing In The Shadow?'

Jimmy Page (*centre*) had the idea for Led Zeppelin, a group built in Britain with the appetites of America in mind, while serving in the Yardbirds (*above*). At the height of Swinging London the style of Beatle girlfriends like Pattie Boyd (*below*) made them fashion icons in every corner of the United States.

Peter Noone (*above*) of Herman's Hermits didn't manage to hang on to the material rewards of his two years as America's favourite boyfriend but he certainly impressed Pete Townshend by appearing to entertain a mother and daughter in his room overnight. Cream, pictured below in Central Park, were signed to an American company and blazed a trail for the volume dealers of the second wave of British invaders.

San Franciscan peace and love went straight to the head of Eric Burdon, whose Caxton Hall wedding (*above*) to Angie King was a high point of the 1967 social calendar. Roger Daltrey's American wife Heather (*below*) was the one who advised him to ditch the hair products and liberate his locks, thereby releasing the Dionysian love god from the Shepherd's Bush mod.

British bands such as the Who supercharged their performance skills in small halls like Bill Graham's Fillmore theatres (*above*), where they played for American audiences who had come to listen rather than dance. Graham's team took pride in the audience's experience in the electric ballroom. This wasn't the highest priority of Peter Grant, Led Zeppelin's mountainous manager (*right*).

The unknown Elton John and Bernie Taupin (*left*) went from haunting the import shops of Soho to taking Hollywood by storm with a Troubadour run that attracted rock's glitterati and an album of songs entirely inspired by American rock and roll. The experience changed them utterly.

stress that 'a second wave of sheepdog-looking, angry-acting, guitar-playing Britons' was on the way and they were 'dirtier, streakier and more dishevelled than the Beatles and, in some places, they are more popular than the Beatles'. That was from no less a source than Associated Press. In seeking to provide an instant point of differentiation for people who couldn't be bothered with listening to the music this prefabricated schism between the acts, which was not reflective in any way of what the teenagers of the time thought, was responsible for the false opposition between the Beatles and the Stones which has pursued both down the years.

At the Academy of Music on 1 May 1965, Lynne Tillman counted just eight numbers in the Rolling Stones' set. Her personal highlight came when a lone member of the audience, who were predominantly young white girls, decided to try to gain the stage via its one means of access – the stairs from the floor of the hall. In mounting this assault the girl reckoned without the heavy-set female attendant who stood at its top. When the girl approached, Tillman recalled, this sentinel 'gave her the hip', propelling her back down the stairs. After that, nobody else tried it. Inevitably the woman was African-American. Inevitably she was the sole black face in the place during this celebration of the legacy of black American music.

In the audience that day, and whiter than most, was Tom Wolfe, who was reporting for the *New York Herald Tribune*. On this occasion he was accompanying 'Baby' Jane Holzer, the heiress and society beauty. Holzer had been a Stones fan since spending a year modelling in London in 1963. Andy Warhol had elected Holzer as his girl of the year for 1964. For posh girls like Holzer, the Stones represented the acceptable face of the working class, which meant they weren't working class at all. In his subsequent piece, Wolfe described Holzer jiggling with delight at the memory of Mick saying 'Give us a kiss!' Lines like these were part of Jagger's appeal. Hearing this kind of thing, even as acute a critic as Wolfe had bought the idea that the Stones were like the Beatles but 'more lower-class deformed'. This would have surprised the members of the Beatles as much as it would have given Mick's mother Eva the vapours. Still, if America wanted Jagger to be common he was no less happy to pretend to be so than the highly schooled British actors making their names at the time playing bits of rough.

This didn't change the fact that it was smart New York society, which traditionally looks east rather than west, that first began to grant the 1965 Rolling Stones the benedictions of chic. When they had first arrived they held a party on a boat docked on the Hudson and the guests were not the usual pop crowd. Rock writer Richard Goldstein remembered, 'there were editors from the leading fashion monthlies, their perfect figures draped in tasteful versions of the mini-wear Twiggy had made hip'. Furthermore it was Diana Vreeland, the editor of American *Vogue*, who was the first to see in Mick Jagger not a young thug so much as a face from Caravaggio, someone who could be the James Dean of the decade. That spring there was a party at Warhol's Factory for the Fifty Most Beautiful People, a party that was attended by Rudolf Nureyev, Allen Ginsberg, Tennessee Williams, Brian Jones and Judy Garland. The latter made her entrance carried shoulder-high by four men. Despite this she had trouble pulling focus away from Edie Sedgwick, who by then had replaced Jane Holzer in Warhol's star system. Jane had been the girl of 1964; 1965, which already was all about a different, altogether thinner look, called for a newer and slimmer girl of the year. Gauntness was all. All that rationing was paying off for the young princes of the British Invasion. Even Holzer enthused to Wolfe about just how deliciously thin the Rolling Stones were.

Of course this was New York, and New York is, as many have realized too late, an island off the coast of America. As the Rolling

Stones headed out of New York and began to tour the South, play-ing places like Statesboro, Georgia, and Birmingham, Alabama, they had the same sense that other visiting bands had experienced of being in a country where a small group of people already living in the twenty-first century were trying to drag many of their fellow citizens out of the nineteenth. In 1965 Lyndon Johnson was out-manoeuvring the Southern Democrats who had held civil rights legislation back for many years, but the FBI was still struggling to prosecute the lynch mob who the previous year had murdered three civil rights workers in Mississippi. At the same time the coun-try was beginning to be riven with disagreements about a foreign war that was already looking ominously unwinnable. David Hal-berstam's book about Vietnam, which was published in the spring of 1965, was called *The Making of a Quagmire*.

For the first time the folks at home could no longer be relied upon for unquestioning support of a war being waged overseas. In May 1965, a *Life* magazine reporter on board a US aircraft carrier in the South China Sea spoke to a pilot flying missions over North Vietnam. The pilot said how mad he was about the protests against the war which were growing back home. 'We're out here so these guys can grow beards and have free speech movements,' he com-plained. The journalist didn't mention that his own son, who like him was called Loudon Wainwright, had just dropped out of col-lege and was growing just such a beard and moving to the place where the free speech movement was based, San Francisco. This was going to be the American city of the near future.

Very little of this pierced the bubble in which the Rolling Stones, like every other group in that most hectic and competitive of years, were conveyed between the various obligations their manager and agent had lined up for them. They arrived at venues early in order to avoid fans and had to kill time as best they could. Security at the shows was provided often by the local law, who had no more regard for these Limey fags than for the teenagers who turned out to scream at them. The venues were either too big or too small, the technology of sound reproduction unsatisfactory, they couldn't hear themselves play, they were forever doing this and signing that, and at the end of every day somebody would poke a microphone in their faces and ask the same inane questions that they had been asked the night before and the night before that. Exquisite boredom was written on their faces in every picture.

In 1965 the groupie's trade was not sufficiently evolved to make the consolations of sex as easily available as they were to become. Thus, when the Stones arrived in Clearwater, Florida on 6 May, nearly a week after their New York date, Bill Wyman and Brian Jones, the band's most dedicated philanderers, had to content themselves with the company of two women Wyman subsequently described as models. The following morning brought two developments. The woman who had spent the night with Brian said that he had attacked her; an American member of the Stones' road crew administered a punishment beating as a result of which Brian had two badly bruised ribs. A happier piece of news was that Keith, who had remained in his room, had woken in the night with a riff going through his head. It was a riff that had come to him accompanied by the words 'I can't get no satisfaction'. Luckily he had recorded the idea on the tape machine he kept by his bed and could play it to his songwriting partner the following day.

Jagger composed some further words for it which numbered the sources of his frustration, from the false promises of advertising men to girls whose menstrual calendar made it inconvenient for him to slake his lust. A couple of days later they went to Chess in Chicago and recorded four numbers, one of which was a tilt at 'Satisfaction' – a tilt which was too bluesy, according to Andrew Oldham. Oldham wasn't a proper producer but he had the kind of ear for a hit that they needed. A week later in Hollywood they recorded the song again at RCA Studios with engineer Dave Hassinger. By then two things had been changed: Charlie had upped the tempo and introduced the distinctive drum break, and Keith Richards had a new toy. The Maestro Fuzz-Tone was a little box you connected to your amplifier. It had been introduced in 1962 with the promise to be able to make your guitar sound like anything but a guitar. Keith imagined this song being played with a horn section in the Stax style, an idiom newly popular that year through records like Otis Redding's 'Respect'. He connected the Maestro and turned the dial until it sounded to his ears like a horn section, and played the signature riff. In half an hour they had it recorded.

Great records sometimes just happen, often to the annoyance of the musicians involved, who mistakenly think that if they were to do them again they would be bound to do them better. Keith couldn't hear it. He just imagined it was going to be a track on an LP. According to everyone else in the band, and most sentient beings who heard it in the summer of 1965 – a year which was, never forget, the greatest year for hit singles ever – it was clearly a lot more than that. There was a feeling that came off the grooves of 'Satisfaction' that was without precedent, even in 1965. It was the itch you could never quite scratch.

There was nothing bluesy about 'Satisfaction', nothing attractively mournful about its cocky insistence, nothing conventionally funky about its wasp-in-the-bottle sound, nothing timeless about a bunch of lyrics that might have been ripped whole from today's supermarket tabloid, nothing sensual about the gleeful spite with which the singer delivered those lyrics, and absolutely no precedent for the evident fact that this most American-feeling, most American-sounding, most swaggering, most New World, this horniest and most restless of records had been made by five men from south London.

Prior to this the Stones' A-sides were either covers of American r&b hits or thinly disguised lifts like 'The Last Time'. It was past time for something that summed up where they were at now, and where they were at now was America. '(I Can't Get No) Satisfaction', to give it its full title, was released in the United States on 6 June 1965, which was twenty-one years after American troops had landed at Omaha Beach. It was the same week that Bob Dylan's *Bringing It All Back Home* was trumpeted in *Billboard* as turning the tide of the British Invasion, and Woody Allen's *What's New Pussycat?* opened in movie theatres. By the middle of July it had displaced the Four Tops' 'I Can't Help Myself' and the Byrds' 'Mr Tambourine Man' at the top of the *Billboard* charts. When 'Satisfaction' came out in June, Andy Warhol remembered, it seemed to be leaking out of every car radio and from every transistor pressed to every ear. To him it sounded more mechanical than musical. Warhol liked that about it.

The reason their manager wanted to put out the record so quickly was that they were booked to appear on the TV show *Shindig!* on 20 May and they needed something new to plug. *Shindig!* was one of the new youth-oriented TV shows that had sprung up in response to the British Invasion. This one was actually produced by a Brit, Jack Good, who had worked on shows like *Six-Five Special* and *Oh Boy!* and was now trying to come up with a production style that might match the energy being given off by the music. Once in the United States, Good, who was an Oxford graduate, played up his Englishness, even to the extent of appearing on camera in a three-piece suit and a bowler hat. He also knew how to ring the bells of the Rolling Stones. For 20 May he made sure that he booked alongside them Howlin' Wolf. The great blues man appeared playing 'How Many More Years' as the band literally sat at his feet like university students while the *Shindig!* dancers, who included in their number Toni Basil and Teri Garr, sat on high stools in the background and frugged.

Television was actually the Stones' medium. It suited them even more than the Beatles. Television perfectly framed the eternal drama that played out between the five of them. It also got close enough to capture the details: the simpering camp of Brian Jones; Charlie Watts' deliberate refusal to mime convincingly playing the drums; Bill Wyman's rapt concentration on the studio clock, the hips of the dancing girls and anything other than his bass guitar; Keith's slightly unsteady slashing at whichever interestingly shaped instrument he'd selected for that particular broadcast; and most of all it got close enough to capture whichever piece of business Mick Jagger had devised to suit the selling of this particular song. For 'Satisfaction' he accompanied the distinctive drum breaks with a slapping motion of his right hand aimed right into the camera. He looked like a Regency fop issuing a challenge to a duel and was imitated by teenage boys all over the world whenever the record was played.

Teenage boys were 'Satisfaction''s natural constituents. They adored the sound and strongly identified with the way the Rolling Stones seemed to be the first act to make a virtue out of slovenliness. If you had grown up in the fifties the first thing you hoped to be was slovenly. The Stones projected an imperious insolence which youth all over the world eventually bought into, every bit as much as they bought into the joy projected by the Beatles. Even within the restrictions of that appearance on *Shindig!*, the Stones were able to create their own space in which to prowl, a place from which to project their otherness. At that age, in 1965, when their fleshly appetites were still some way from sated, the thing that they projected most of all was that they appeared the randiest group ever to have drawn breath.

And with 'Satisfaction' they had done what Andrew Oldham always wanted them to do, which was reflect not the world they heard in all those old Chess sides they had pored over back in

London but the America that glinted beyond their limo, the mad clamour hammering against the windows and the roof, the crazed imprecations of the pitchmen on television claiming 'he can't be a man 'cause he doesn't smoke the same cigarettes as me', all those people providing useless information which was supposed to fire their imagination, all the promises that were bound to come up short – everything that was, in short, America.

Peter Noone remembered staying with the Stones and Tom Jones at the City Squire Hotel in New York earlier that year. 'We [Herman's Hermits] had just done "Henry VIII" on *The Ed Sullivan Show* and there were two or three thousand kids standing outside the hotel waiting for us. We all went on the roof and it must have made an impact on the Stones because they started to write pop tunes. No more of the blues stuff. They went to start and write songs cause they said, "Look what happens when you make it in America."'

Indeed it did make an impact. The Rolling Stones had come to praise America and ended up effectively being American. By the end of the year they would reach an agreement with Newark's Allen Klein for him to become their manager. From 1965 on, the Rolling Stones would put America first.

8

'Engerland swings like a
pendulum do'

On 15 April 1966, as the Rolling Stones' '19th Nervous Breakdown' jostled with Sgt Barry Sadler's 'The Ballad Of The Green Berets' for position in the *Billboard* Top 100, the weekly news magazine *Time*, which could claim fourteen million American readers every single week and liked to feel that it had a mission to make the wider world intelligible for those sitting around the dinner tables of middle America, came out with an unusual cover. It was a cover that presented a familiar city in a most unfamiliar light. The message of the cover was 'London: The Swinging City'.

This article, which turned out to be far more influential than most of the lifestyle pieces *Time* was wont to offer from time to time when the news agenda didn't throw up anything more pressing, had started life as a regular travel piece. The traces of the travel piece still remained. The cover, which was an illustration rather than a photograph, was a montage of those London sights that might have been familiar to a handful of the fewer than 9 per cent of Americans who owned a passport in the year 1966; the overwhelming majority of Americans, apart from those who had been stationed there during the war, knew London only thanks to a thousand establishing shots in a thousand movies they had seen down the years. This cover was front-loaded with the signifiers that were almost invariably in those shots. There was the red double-decker bus. There was the clock tower of the Houses of Parliament. There were crowns, there was ermine, and there were even monocled peers who could have strolled out of Gilbert and Sullivan. Sprinkled over the top of these old established symbols of Englishness were a number of newer icons. There were Union Jack spectacles, a Rolls-Royce driven by two men with long hair, and even an outright dandy who had clearly just taken the plunge into bell-bottomed trousers.

The illustration was drawn by Geoffrey Dickinson, who apologetically said he'd had much work to do here because, well, he couldn't actually claim to be a swinger. In fact this Liverpudlian didn't know a lot more about the small section of London that reputedly swung than the average *Time* reader in one of America's many towns called Springfield. Hence Geoffrey made it up. Considering how instrumental his cover was in beginning the rebranding of London from Heart of Empire to City that Swings and firing the starting gun on a period during which anyone in the world who was excited by music, film or fashion set their sights on visiting the city, this could have been the most far-reaching day's work he ever did.

At the time Dickinson finished his fantasy the actual people who were at the centre of this tiny world of Swinging London – the ones who might be able to get into stars' watering holes such as the Ad Lib in Leicester Place, who knew how to find the trailblazing fashion boutique Biba in Abingdon Road or Robert Fraser's Duke Street gallery where his friends the Stones and the Beatles might from time to time hang out – were few in number, but people from across the seas seemed to want to join them. Suddenly, everybody seemed to agree, London was happening. The Earth's axis, which during the 1950s had appeared to be permanently tilted in America's favour, was, thanks to the Beatles and a handful of other people, tilting back.

Suddenly London, previously the centre of everything musty and mysteriously venerable, was the place you went to if you were looking for things that were new and flashy. The Old Lady seemed to be enjoying the new attention. Even the Queen had awarded John Lennon, Paul McCartney, George Harrison and Richard Starkey the MBE the previous year. This was not for services to exports, which could have been patronizing, or services to music, which would have been inconceivable, but, as the citation memorably read, 'of the Beatles', which really was all that was required. The following year fashion designer Mary Quant was given the even greater honour of an OBE to recognize her pioneering work in the development of the miniskirt and the western world's consequent discovery of the pleasures of sex before marriage. It was all most unexpected for a city with so many statues. It was not what people had previously thought of when they thought of London. It was as though the world centre of Marxism had turned out to be Rome. Robert Fraser was quoted in the *Time* story saying, 'Right now, London has something that New York used to have; everybody wants to be there. There's an indefinable thing that makes people want to go there.'

There were very few normal Americans who could afford to go there. They tended to be the people who were well funded and well connected. In March 1966 the Lovin' Spoonful, whose 'Daydream' had just been a top five record on both sides of the Atlantic, were flown from the United States to rural Ireland purely to be the live entertainment at the twenty-first birthday of Guinness heir Tara Browne. If you didn't happen to be wealthy and you wanted to make the trip it helped to be endowed with exceptional beauty. One of the latter group was the young would-be actress Sharon Tate, who was in Borehamwood just outside London in 1966 making a film called *Eye of the Devil* and being hyped in a short promo film called *All Eyes on Sharon Tate* in which she was inevitably filmed dancing the Shake in a London disco with her co-star David Hemmings. The American actor Dennis Hopper, who also visited at this time, later recalled: 'That sixties time in London was the greatest. I knew I was in a place where all the creation of the world was happening. The Beatles and the Stones had just happened. It was just sensational. The art world, the fashion world, they were exploding. It was the most creative place I've ever seen.'

In 1966 even the more mass-market magazines operated in the belief that their readers were actually prepared to read. In truth, most of *Time*'s subscribers probably didn't plough through the dense columns of type that made up the actual feature. However, they would have picked up the gist from the colour shots of debutantes dancing decorously at the Scotch of St James or uniformed schoolgirls exploring Carnaby Street. These were juxtaposed with stock images of city gents swinging brollies as they crossed London bridges or louche gentlemen of a certain age playing chemin de fer at Crockfords in Mayfair. The message the feature broadcast was unmistakable. Now London was identified not with tradition and convention but with pleasure and leisure. It was as though the pea souper under which Hollywood had traditionally draped London had been lifted to reveal the erstwhile heart of empire in vibrant red, white and blue. The ancient, smoky London, which, like any ageing dowager, had preferred to be depicted in black and white, was ready for its close-up and only too happy to be seen in colour.

In *Time* there was no dwelling on the dark side, but the dark side most assuredly was still there. There was no mention in the story of the trial beginning that week at Chester Assizes, in which Ian Brady and Myra Hindley were accused of crimes of unprecedented malignity. In their police mugshots the bottle-blonde Hindley and the slicked-back Brady appeared like visitors from the least appealing regions of the decade just passed. Saddleworth Moor, where they had buried their dead, was a world almost as far removed from Swinging London as were the Midwestern lounges and rumpus rooms in which *Time*'s story was being consumed.

Everybody in Britain felt it at the time. Everybody in Britain knew that America was suddenly paying attention. It made us sit up and show our best face to the world. We were aware that for the first time in most of our lifetimes the things that were going on in the UK were being commented on, and commented on approvingly, by people in the United States. It was an unfamiliar feeling, but we liked it. Only that could possibly explain why in January the British public had gone out and bought a record called 'England Swings' by that prince among America's novelty hit-makers Roger Miller. The refrain of this epic of tweeness, which demonstrated as little regard for observable reality as it did for scansion, went 'Engerland swings like a pendulum do, bobbies on bicycles two by two'. It was like the fever dream of somebody who had been exposed to repeated screenings of *Mary Poppins*. In January 1966 it reached number 13 on the British charts.

Everybody wanted to be here. Bob Dylan had first visited London around Christmas 1962 to appear in a play for BBC Television, a play which called for somebody who looked like a beatnik. While in town he appeared in front of the greybeards of the folk circuit, who thought he was phoney. It was the younger generation who took to him. When the Beatles went to the United States, John Lennon was wearing a leather cap in emulation of the one Dylan wore on the cover of his first LP. In 1965 Dylan did his first concert tour of the UK during which his hangers-on included Donovan, members of the Animals and Marianne Faithfull. The British arts and political establishment fell at his feet, thrilled to have an American musical star singing about the seemingly black and white issues of race and nuclear dread. A year later he was back with his electric rock and roll band, an event which dramatized the schism between the apparent purity of the folk era and this new world of psychedelics and sensation. It was in Manchester that somebody shouted 'Judas!' and Dylan turned to his band and muttered, 'Play fucking loud!'

The same year, the Byrds landed in London, the city that had provided their inspiration. They hung out with the Beatles and played a few shows at which nobody could believe they actually tuned up on stage. The charitable interpretation was that this was because they were unusually serious about their craft. The truth was that they were only just getting used to their electric instruments and their drummer, who had been hired for his hair, could barely play at all. The tour, which was promoted by the splendidly named Mervin Conn, who was used to working with visiting country acts, mistakenly billed them as 'America's answer to the Beatles' when in truth anything further from the Beatles' cheery directness than Jim McGuinn singing 'Turn! Turn! Turn!' from behind spectacles which had been designed so that he couldn't look out and nobody could look in would be hard to imagine. They confused the chambermaids at their London hotels with their habit of putting wet towels around the doors to their rooms and went back home different people, even writing their next song 'Eight Miles High' under the inspiration of that 'grey, grey town, known for its sounds'.

A further measure of this changed view of the United Kingdom in the United States could be taken in the number of American musicians who, around this time, came to the UK in the hope of making a name there and then re-importing their newfound fame to their homeland. The classic case of this was Jimi Hendrix, the American guitar prodigy whose career couldn't get traction in the United States because his act was too black for the white audience and too white for the black audience. He had been kicking around Greenwich Village to no great effect for some while. It was not until the Animals' Chas Chandler sold his instruments to buy Hendrix a plane ticket to the UK in 1966 and then showcased him in front of the musical aristocracy of London, much as Mozart's father had shown off his son in front of the crowned heads of Europe, that he became an overnight sensation.

P. J. Proby tried the same thing but was held back by a tendency to overdo the outrage which seemed to belong in earlier times. Gary Leeds was the drummer during the Texan's trouser-splitting tour of Britain in 1964–65. When he returned to Los Angeles he persuaded his friends Scott Engel and John Walker that they stood more of a chance of getting attention in the UK than they did in Hollywood. Thus in February 1965, with the help of a little seed capital from a relative, they landed in Britain where they announced themselves to the record business as the Walker Brothers. Almost immediately they were successful, with vast and velvety ballads like 'Make It Easy On Yourself' and 'My Ship Is Coming In'. As an entertainment proposition they had two key qualities that were in short supply even in Swinging London. The first was the kind of voices that could handle romantic ballads. The second was the kind of preposterous good looks more usually glimpsed in Greek statuary – the kind that probably wouldn't warrant a second look if they were parking your car at a Hollywood restaurant but in the average British city they were more than capable of stopping traffic.

They weren't the only Californians who were tearing up trees in the UK. At the same time Sonny Bono, the promotion man who had welcomed the Rolling Stones to Los Angeles, was dominating the British charts in his own right with his young wife Cher. They provided a bridge between the emerging hipster lifestyle of the West Coast and old-fashioned show business with their celebrations of brotherly love, connubial bliss and the importance of not cutting your hair. The calculus of celebrity decrees that a famous couple, any famous couple, is worth many times more than the sum of its individual parts. A couple is a walking, talking story, particularly if it's a couple as unlikely as this union between a short, gnome-like man arrayed in Disney Medieval and the slender madonna on his arm who was eleven years his junior. Their being together and their clothes, the length of their hair – their whole demeanour was designed to be a provocation to respectable opinion. If for any reason respectable opinion was not provoked, the lines in Sonny's songs ideally supplied the things they should be offended by. 'They say we're young and we don't know,' sang Sonny, who was thirty, in 'I Got You Babe'. 'What do they care about the clothes I wear,' he chanted in 'Laugh At Me', indicating the suede waistcoat over the shiny shirt that he had commissioned from his hippy seamstress Bridget Milligan.

They dressed to suit their songs and they sang songs to suit the way they dressed. These were in truth pretty limited songs, but once they had the benefit of the attentions of the Wrecking Crew and arranger Harold Battiste they arrived in a cloud of sound which chimed perfectly with that jingle-jangle morning. And they behaved like old-style celebrities. They ordered six Rolls-Royces while in Britain for a TV date before deciding which two to send back to the United States. The PR said they had bought a gold watch for anybody who had helped them when they were in the country. They wore fancy dress at a time when most British bands were still wearing grey suits. The British Invasion bands had hinted that there might be a lifestyle behind the music. Sonny and Cher put the lifestyle in the foreground.

By then the papers were all over this mood of national optimism. Just two weeks following *Time*'s Swinging London story the *Sunday Times* said it was already taken for granted that 'journalists and sociologists write and talk about crazy gear and Swinging London', and Hunter Davies in the Atticus column was reporting that a man who had previously made documentaries on exotic places like Hong Kong was going to make his next one about Swinging London. All this was particularly good news to anyone who had ever dreamed of selling British goods overseas. In the issue of *Time* following the Swinging London cover edition, A. P. Spooner from the British American Chamber of Commerce wrote to say that he hoped the feature would do something 'to dispel the popular misconception that Britain continues to live in the past'. The problem with such thinking is that any country's reference points come from the past and therefore they are apt to be wheeled out when the realm needs a boost. Mr Spooner was probably one of the great minds behind the arrival of a double-decker bus at the New York department store Gimbels to launch Britain Today, a two-week promotion of the products of this fresh new Britannia, one that majored on tea, toffee, crumpets and the other products to which the British were inextricably yoked in the American imagination. On the sixth floor of Gimbels it was proudly claimed the Cross Keys would be offering a version of the authentic British pub experience for those Manhattanites desirous of rolling out the barrel or shoving the halfpenny.

By early June 1966 the *New York Times* had bought into Swinging London comprehensively enough to take a kind of moral stand about it. Under the headline 'Frivolity in Britain', a title that seemed about as likely to be reached for as 'Homosexuality in Dallas', they opined that surely this phenomenon that was going on over the water had to be primarily all about sex, as clearly advertised in the shortness of the skirts. By 1966 short skirts had taken the place of long hair in the litany of subjects comedians could make jokes about in the certainty of getting a laugh out of audiences over the age of thirty-five. Many of their alleged observations were clearly fantasy. Atticus in the *Sunday Times* even claimed that a secretary at *Vogue* had been so cold because of the shortness of her skirt that her legs froze together and she couldn't go out to lunch.

Worrying about how all this below-the-waist business might be rotting the moral fibre of the nation that had once stood alone against Hitler, and rarely missed an opportunity to remind the rest of the world of same, the *New York Times* further noted that the genuinely pressing problems of the nation's ineluctable economic decline were now dull stuff to people so suddenly 'bent on a swinging time'. The *New York Times* even dared to suggest that the UK population didn't care that their pound could now only buy $2.79 as long as they could still get their annual week in Majorca. In this, of course, the *New York Times* was entirely correct. It wasn't going to get any better either. Within two years Harold Wilson, who had been the first British Prime Minister to be persuaded to pose with the country's pop stars, would also become the first Prime Minister forced to face the unavoidable mathematics of Britain's decline, and to appear on TV to announce that his government had been forced to devalue the pound against the dollar, assuring the viewing millions with a straight face that this did not mean 'the pound in your pocket' was worth any less. The many British voters at the time who had grown up in a world order with Britain somewhere near the top took this kind of public indignity hard. Their children, however, the post-war generation, took comfort in the fact that while Britain might no longer be the workshop of the world it was clearly now the place where the world came to get its hair done.

That kind of thing goes to a nation's head. Even in those pin-striped days the British Establishment was quietly beginning its gentle pivot in the direction of pleasure. Nobody yet talked about the creative economy but what was going on seemed to offer an alternative to the traditional economic model which had always been founded on the belief that only where there was muck was there likely to be brass. Did it always have to be so? Was there now a new way of building revenue and winning prestige? This was the beginning of a stealthy shift in which the British Establishment, which had not previously been aware of the value of inclusivity, opened its arms to embrace anybody who seemed to be doing well, and it mattered not whether this was as a result of their labours with clippers and plectrum rather than slide rule and stock market. This was the beginning of Britain, historically speaking the first country to industrialize, finding a new pride in becoming the first country to turn itself over to the production of fun.

When, on 30 July 1966, England beat West Germany in the World Cup Final at Wembley, the number one record was 'Out Of Time', a Rolling Stones song sung by Chris Farlowe. There wasn't an England World Cup song at the top of the charts because there wasn't an England World Cup song. The fact of this, which appears inexplicable from the vantage point of the twenty-first century when the symbiosis between sport and entertainment is such a given, eloquently explains what a gulf there was in 1966 between football and everything else in life. I was on a school trip to France when England won that game. That the school thought it feasible to take a party of sixteen-year-old boys out of the country at the time of England's first home World Cup is testament to the breadth of this gulf.

Nevertheless the sight of Geoff Hurst galloping goal-wards in the Wembley sunshine seemed to chime with the sound of the Kinks' 'Sunny Afternoon', and seemed of a piece with the brazen sauce of Michael Caine in the trans-national hit of the year *Alfie* and the gamine prettiness of Twiggy, hailed worldwide as 'the face of 1966'. The combination raised the national mood on thermals of optimism. If ever there was a week when England seemed to be on top of the world it was that week. Five days later, only two years after they had released the soundtrack to *A Hard Day's Night* – their first entirely self-penned long-playing record, the first which a band could be said to have authored as thoroughly as the great movie directors were said to shape their films – the Beatles released a new record. They called this one *Revolver*.

9

'The dazzle and the madness
of London today!'

At the middle point of the decade England received a sharp reminder of just how foreign a country the United States remained, for all its apparent embracing of the new sounds and fashions from Swinging London. The day before England won the World Cup an American teen magazine called *Datebook* had re-published an interview with John Lennon which had been done for the *Evening Standard* by Maureen Cleave. *Datebook* was a magazine that prided itself on covering issues with a youth slant and therefore it had been keen on hearing Lennon loose off on a wide range of issues. The interview had run in the UK without causing raised eyebrows and nobody could see any reason why it would be different in the US.

Looked at from today with our outrage receptors ever tuned and quivering, the *Datebook* piece appears to bristle with provocations.

These start with the quote from Paul McCartney that sat alongside his picture on the cover and says, clearly referring to America, 'it's a lousy country where anyone black is a dirty nigger'. This line, which was in itself a crude misrepresentation of McCartney's original statement, passed wholly without comment. Everyone was too interested in the interview inside in which Lennon was quoted as saying 'we're more popular than Jesus now' and further prophesying that Christianity might not outlast rock and roll. At the time of publication nobody at the magazine thought it was anything to get hung up about. But the day before it came out a copy fell into the hands of DJ Tommy Charles, who had a show on a small radio station called WAQY in Birmingham, Alabama, colloquially known as 'Wacky 1220'. Animated by his all-American public-spiritedness and his desire to goose the ratings, Charles opened the fader and announced that if any of his listeners were offended by this attack by 'a group of foreign singers', which clearly struck at 'the very basis of our existence as God-fearing patriotic citizens', then they should demonstrate their feelings by taking all their Beatles records and souvenirs to the upcoming bonfire which somebody was thoughtfully organizing to coincide with the Beatles' appearance in Memphis in a couple of weeks' time.

What was originally framed as an argument about religion was actually a familiar complaint about America being undermined by sinister aliens. This played in to a well-established narrative about how the USA is beset by foreigners who wish it ill. The argument was less about blasphemy than about the money that had been taken out of America by these foreigners. The land of the free had been too trusting, too good-hearted, too Christian altogether in taking these English boys to their hearts, and now that they had their feet under the national table they had taken advantage of their position as honoured guests to steal their hosts away from America's defining invention which was obviously Christianity. The radio station would no longer play records by this British group who 'grew wealthy as the music idols of the younger generation'.

The story was picked up by the newspapers, swiftly went national, and soon other stations in the South, unwilling to be outstripped in their defence of the national interest, joined in, banning the playing of Beatles records and encouraging the organization of local demonstrations of disgust. In Birmingham, Alabama, a wood-chipping machine was hastily repurposed as a 'Beatle grinder' to ensure that previously loved copies of *Meet The Beatles* or *Beatles VI* could be efficiently reduced to particles of dust. The politicians piled in without delay, with a Republican Senator in Pennsylvania calling on promoters in his state to make sure that the British group never performed there again. At a hastily organized press conference in New York on 6 August, Brian Epstein was asked whether all this fuss might mean the reorganization of the Beatles' imminent American tour to avoid some of the more bonfire-happy cities on the itinerary. He said that wouldn't be necessary but he didn't sound all that sure. When the boys arrived on 11 August to begin the tour they gave another press conference to try to damp it down, which pleased nobody. What no one fully appreciated at the time is that Americans love being outraged, American politicians love to fan such outrage, and there is always a small, daytime-only radio station like WAQY that has nothing to lose by fanning it further. That same night one Bob Scoggin, the Ku Klux Klan Grand Dragon, tossed Beatles records into a fire at Chester, South Carolina. The demonstrations, like the Klan, spread far beyond the Bible Belt. In Cleveland, Ohio, the Reverend Thurmann Babbs even told his parishioners that anyone who attended that night's Beatles concert would be expelled from his congregation.

The tour, which followed on the heels of a similarly fraught trip to the Philippines, was dogged by even greater problems than picketing Klan members and disgruntled mayors. The Beatles were playing outdoors at a time when the technology couldn't begin to be equal to the job. When they played Crosley Field, a baseball stadium in Cincinnati, the rain was so heavy that the show had to be abandoned after the support acts had played because there was such a serious danger of electrocution. The Beatles had to return at lunchtime the following day, a Sunday, to perform their portion of the show, then pack up their three guitars and single set of drums and fly to St Louis to play another show that night. At every stage on the tour they were on the back foot. They had to quickly abandon any plans they had to record in Memphis at the famous Stax studios. In the same city they received a message saying that one of them would be shot on stage. When they brought the tour to a close on 29 August with a show at Candlestick Park in San Francisco their stage was set up behind second base at least 200 feet away from the nearest screaming human being and surrounded by two lines of fencing to keep those hysterical fans – and anything worse – at a safe distance. Their fee for the half-hour performance that evening was $90,000. Since the venue was undersold they were probably lucky to get it. The promoters lost money. Though nothing was said at the time, other than McCartney asking his PR to record it, it turned out to be the last time the Beatles would play in front of a paying audience.

Many of the shows on the tour had not been sold out, the audience that had come in previous years having worked out that they weren't getting much more from the experience than the performers. The Beatles had lost interest in live performance some while before. It was increasingly a chore which seemed utterly unconnected to the recordings that interested them. It belonged in a different region of their mind. This was underlined by the fact that while this was the tour immediately following the release of *Revolver* they didn't play a single song from the album in the course of it. The number one album in the USA that summer was actually their

Yesterday And Today, the last of their shoddy repackages for the American market. It wasn't until September that *Revolver*, the first of their records to be presented as an artistic statement on both sides of the Atlantic, took over at number one. They exited the stage just as the new era of extended live performances was being born. The two cities in which it was being born were San Francisco and London, both a world away from Memphis, Tennessee and Birmingham, Alabama. They were glad to have the tour over with. George Harrison sat back in his seat on the plane leaving San Francisco and said, 'Now I don't have to be a Beatle any more.'

The 'more popular than Jesus' furore had been a salutary reminder that sentiments wafted into the air of a living room in the stockbroker belt of Surrey on a cloud of cannabis smoke could incite unexpectedly violent reactions in what was still, to the Beatles, an unexpectedly violent country. It was, in its own way, an augury not just of the strength of American nativism but also of the pile-on culture of today. The Beatles only had one such controversy in their whole career. If it were now it would be happening every few months. If it were now, John Lennon would have thought what he thought but he wouldn't have said it in the first place.

Back home things were, by contrast, utterly benign. Disputes which in America might be solved by rifles were in Britain settled with a testy letter to the editor. The *Time* 'Swinging London' piece was a story that had some consequences for the people who featured in it. Britain might have loosened up but there were still certain proprieties to be observed. Jane Ormsby-Gore worked as a fashion assistant at *Vogue* at the time. The piece had said she hung out at Dolly's in Jermyn Street and quoted her as saying, 'people don't spend much time necking because they usually live fulfilled sex lives'. This looked worse in cold hard print than she'd meant it to. Since she was the daughter of Lord Harlech, formerly the British ambassador to Washington, representations were made about this quote to the editor of *Time*.

Very few people in Britain actually lived the life hinted at in the *Time* feature but, largely thanks to the efforts of the film industry, we all felt as if it was going on. If we didn't actually come to London very much, or came but didn't find the bit that swung, the cinema was very keen to take Swinging London to us. The kind of movies which in the years before the Beatles had been located in gritty industrial cities, films like *Saturday Night and Sunday Morning*, *Billy Liar* and *Room at the Top*, were now abruptly replaced by a new generation of features which proposed this demi-paradise, this new Rome, as the only place any self-respecting young person with anything about them would seek to go. Films like *The Knack*, *Darling* and *The Pleasure Girls*, which all appeared in 1965, may have been shot in black and white but they all proposed London as the city of dreams. They all seemed to begin with nice girls from the shires walking without fear along ungentrified and affordable streets in Notting Hill or Chelsea, swinging empty suitcases as they looked for the flat where they might begin a new life of adventure and glamour and men. Most of these films seemed to offer variants on the same story. Each had to have a scene where the heroine lost her virginity. Each was obliged to include a stop-motion sequence where the heroine went shopping and returned with an aspidistra. Each one seemed to find room for a mime acted out at dawn against the background of the dirty old city. There would be men in bowler hats, a scene in a casino, and one where the heroine falls in with a Bad Lot. Because music was such a key ingredient in the cultural cocktail of the time, because music carried the virus of the Swinging London idea, each film would be obliged to have at least one scene where the characters danced to some allegedly happening music.

This new young London, where youth apparently held sway, suddenly became the place in which film-makers from overseas wanted to make their films. In 1966 the Italian director Michel-angelo Antonioni, who was fascinated by the new breed of English fashion photographers and the attractive responsibility-free life they appeared to be living, pitched up in town to make his first English language film. *Blow-Up* was the film that finally made up the mind of anybody who had previously been wavering in their belief that London was the place to be. The hero of *Blow-Up* is a handsome young photographer, loosely based on David Bailey and his mates, who has had enough success to be bored with trappings such as his Rolls-Royce, who makes a fortune draping clothes on bony young women before taking their pictures, who salves his conscience about the superficial way in which he makes his preposterous living by going among the poor and the dispossessed to take their pictures. In the course of this he takes a picture in a London park which he later thinks may have unwittingly captured a murder. Cineastes have for ever since been arguing about the hidden messages of the film.

Casual cinema-goers, on the other hand, didn't bother about the message. They focused on one simple thing: the sheer amount of casual sex this photographer appeared to be getting. All the women in the film, from Veruschka to Vanessa Redgrave, show some skin. The first pubic hair glimpsed in a mainstream film belonged to Jane Birkin, playing one of two would-be models who turn up to David Hemmings' studio hoping to get their big break and end up rolling naked among the background paper. This scene was shot in full matter-of-fact daylight as if to say 'What's the fuss?' In the USA this caused more comment than in the UK. When *Blow-Up* was released in the United States it was denied the Production Code seal of approval, the mark of all major studio releases since 1930, and was compelled to be released by a subsidiary company.

Young men all over the world did not interpret David Hemmings as living a meaningless, loveless experience. They saw him as living the exact life they would have picked out for themselves if they only had been given access to the catalogue. On the basis of one viewing of *Blow-Up* they were happy to assume that photographers actually did spend their days straddling half-naked models, occasionally using the exhortatory mantra 'give it to me, give it to me'. The birds – and 'birds' seemed to capture perfectly the pert expressions and angular frames of the girls who came to his studio – were clearly queuing up to sleep with him. What more could anyone possibly want?

Thus began, in the year 1966, the Englishman's association with sex. This was clearly a very new thing indeed. English actors hadn't previously been seen as sexual creatures, certainly not in the eyes of America. English movie stars were generally good chaps, pipe-smoking, cravat-sporting, get-their-round-in officer-types like John Gregson and Leslie Howard. Boudoir bandits they had never been. This was surely something best left to the French. Similarly, English pop stars would never have been accused of having any kind of sexual allure. By 1966 this was beginning to change. Suddenly these bony, fey, self-involved boy-men with their pouts, their paisley shirts, their coy expressions and their long eyelashes – men such as Cat Stevens, Steve Marriott, Mick Jagger, Keith Moon and Peter Frampton – no longer appeared to want to look and behave like American jocks, which had previously been the way of all masculinity. They would have no use for Charles Atlas or his Dynamic Tension method. They looked as though they might actually get some sand kicked in their faces and, what's more, they would become magically more attractive as a result. A new male sexual stereotype was being born, a stereotype that Britain would give to the world, and it was *Blow-Up* that introduced it to the world.

There are no drum heroes. There are certainly no piano heroes. Nor are there saxophone heroes, harmonica heroes or even bass guitar heroes. There are, however, guitar heroes. The guitar hero is an idea we do not have the slightest difficulty selling to ourselves. The guitar hero is an idea that speaks to the depths of anybody who ever felt the heft of an electric guitar, and to many who have never got any nearer to a guitar than the back of the stalls. It turned out to be Britain's most lasting musical gift to America, and the year it was first given was 1966.

It was in 1966 that the lead guitarist began to emerge from the group and claim his own space in which to demonstrate his heroism. There already was, for some reason – possibly because the instrument looked like a weapon – something heroic about somebody with an electric guitar. In the middle of the decade, as the music began to edge away from pop songs with tidy endings to rock songs with deliberately frayed edges, rock music began to embrace the cult of the soloist. This is the individual who can only demonstrate the intensity of his feelings by ascending to the top of the guitar neck or even, in moments of particular emotional extremity, plunging that neck into the nearest stack of speakers. In 1966 Pete Townshend of the Who was doing this, and so was the new arrival in London, Jimi Hendrix. In both cases the drama of their acts was heightened by the probability that at some point they would break something. The trailer for *Blow-Up* promised the film would reflect 'the dazzle and the madness of London today' and part of that was, of course, an appearance by a band performing some of that auto-violence.

In truth, Antonioni was no more interested in pop music than most middle-aged Italian film directors but he was very taken with the Who because of the way they attacked and destroyed their equipment at the climax of their act. He wanted them for his film but since they were playing hard to get, Simon Napier-Bell, at the time managing the Yardbirds, sold him on using his group instead. The Yardbirds were famous for having been Eric Clapton's first band. Since that time the star of the group had been whoever was his replacement as lead guitarist. At the time it was Jeff Beck. The great thing about Jeff Beck is that not only could he play but also more than any other he looked and carried himself in the way that was expected of a guitar hero. In fact, if a film director could invent a guitar hero, he would look like Jeff Beck.

The guitar hero was not a British invention. The guitar hero was an English invention. To be more specific, the guitar hero was an invention of the Home Counties. The handful of players who origi-nated the style – Eric Clapton, Jeff Beck, Jimmy Page, Peter Green and Mick Taylor – were all born in or near London around the end of the Second World War. They all learned to play by copying Hank Marvin of the Shadows. They were all attracted by Chicago blues which they then adapted into a style all of their own. They weren't, as was frequently and incorrectly alleged, copying poor old Ameri-can blacks from the rural South, people with whom they had nothing in common. If they were using any music as a jumping-off point it was the brassy blues of Chicago exponents like Otis Rush and Buddy Guy and Texans like Freddie King, people who were closer to themselves in age than Robert Johnson and fully appreci-ated the value of flash. And they all, consciously or not, worked as hard on their personal appearance as they did on their scales with the inevitable result that they, rather than the usual lead singer, inevitably became the front men of whichever band they joined. Clapton in particular always gave a lot of thought to his hair, which he changed with every new group. When Bob Dylan first saw him perform in 1965 he looked at his sideburns and said, 'He looks like Wyatt Earp!'

The interesting thing about the music of the guitar heroes, and the thing that distinguished it from the style of the instrumental bands that had come before, was the way it emanated directly from the groin. Put at its most basic, this meant that one end of the instrument would be planted in the crotch while the other was pointed in the direction of the object of the musician's lust or displeasure. There may have been girls who found this display attractive but it's unlikely. The people who felt it speaking to their depths were the boys. The same would apply to every other aspect of this new Hard Rock. This was a form of music pioneered by the British but forged in the American market and particularly appealing to young males who were very attracted by music that looked difficult to play but was reassuringly easy to understand. It was played by men whom they could venerate as high priest figures while simultaneously indulging in suppressed hero worship with shades of the homoerotic about it. That's why all the guitar heroes were good-looking. Right from the beginning it was every bit as much about display as feeling, about spectacle as much as sound, about haircut as much as musical accomplishment. It was a visual as much as it was a musical idea.

If you were going to invent a guitar hero you would invent somebody with a monosyllabic comic-book name like Jeff Beck's. If you were going to draw a guitar hero you would draw somebody who looked like him. Beck had the nest of hair, he had the skinny legs, his clothes were worn with the precise panache that advertised the wearer's apparent carelessness, and his guitar was worn at the hip like the holster of the last honest man in the baddest burg in the Old West. *Blow-Up* called for him to plunge his guitar into his amplifier Pete Townshend-style as a bunch of op-art-attired students in chalk white make-up looked on with blank expressions. Then he would take up the broken fragments of the instrument and throw them into the crowd who would then fall upon them like ravening dogs. Beck enjoyed doing it, partly because he was doing it with a prop guitar. It wasn't really what he was all about. He was just playing the part.

Beck left the group not long after and the man who was playing bass in the Yardbirds when they filmed the sequence stepped up to become the leader. He would take the ritual of playing the guitar to another level entirely. He was the man who soon realized where the hunger for this kind of sensory overload was likely to be at its fiercest. When Jeff Beck got frustrated while on tour in America later that year and quit, Jimmy Page would take what he had learned and turn his next group into a band that might have been made in England but was precision-tooled for America. When he took that band there he wouldn't play for no thirty minutes.

10

'This is my bird'

Most of the British acts that became world famous during the first British Invasion of America went on to become dukes and earls in the aristocracy of rock. In the fullness of time there would be an entire industry devoted to the maintenance of their myths. There would be boxed sets detailing their every cough, their every spit. Knighthoods and honours, all the baubles a grateful nation can bestow, would in time be showered upon them, as had been the case with their scarcely better behaved predecessors, the freebooters and privateers of the original Elizabethan age. Their great recordings would be venerated as the timeless classics of the genre. The images of them, in the golden morning of their youth, would be pored over and copied by later generations who knew them only through their grandparents. It is tempting to see all these people as having come out of one single, preternaturally hip mould. That, however, would be to forget the others. Posterity may not have been so kind to these others but they played their part nonetheless in America's great love affair with English pop music in the mid-sixties.

Peter Noone came from Urmston, a suburb of Manchester. His parents were successful in business – so busy being successful that he didn't see a lot of them, but he inherited enough of their entrepreneurial zeal to make sufficient cash selling Manchester United programmes at the weekend in the early sixties to be able to afford to buy the latest pop records from the States. Noone, consequently, was the man who always had the new Bobby Rydell and Bobby Vee records. In fact he had all the Bobbies. Peter was a face-time guy from early on, whether it came to chatting up football supporters or young women. He was not a band guy. When they were tuning up he was generally on the other side of the room, admiring hairstyles and shoes. Peter could always converse easily with girls, even when most of his taciturn contemporaries found it hard. Easy charm was his ace card. He was never conventionally good-looking. However, when his older sister had her friends round they would spend time with him. They said he was cute. They said he had nice hair.

Peter's easy popularity and his lack of side were eventually noticed by the boys who formed the bands and still couldn't speak to girls. This inevitably led to him being asked to sing with a band. He had no experience of doing this but when he tried he found he had no fear. Like Mick Jagger, in a very different style, he had the front to make a success of it. Nobody felt threatened by Peter Noone because there was something boyish and guileless about him. Thus it was that he became the singer of an act labouring under the handicap of the name Peter Novak and the Heartbeats. This group did what most northern bands did in the early sixties. The back line offered limp versions of Shadows instrumentals, complete with steps, and the singer from time to time donned a pair of comedy spectacles to do impressions of Buddy Holly.

Peter Noone had obviously heard of the Beatles, who played the same circuit as the Heartbeats in the north-west of England. He had first clapped eyes on them when they were performing in a field in Urmston. This might seem an unusual place for the Beatles to be playing because it was 4 August 1963, but it had been booked before their sudden fame and thus it was being honoured. That day Noone and a member of the Heartbeats stuck around long enough to assess the competition. They watched as the Beatles took to the stage and, with all their Hamburg-hardened professionalism, took the audience with them. His fellow Heartbeat took in the polish of the slightly older and clearly more practised men and then, turning to Noone, announced his verdict. 'We're fucked,' he observed.

While no less impressed by the Beatles, Noone did not agree with his assessment of their position. Noone, though still young, had native smarts. He intuited something about how show business worked that the rest of the Heartbeats didn't. He felt their act could easily coexist with the Beatles, no matter how much better the latter were. It was all a question of positioning. Other bands, such as the Rolling Stones, might try to position themselves on the Beatles' more purist, more rhythm and blues, more mean and nasty flank. Noone felt there was more than enough room on the other, poppier, more sugar-and-spice flank. All you had to do was offer the all-round entertainment the Beatles were less likely to offer as they got bigger and more successful. This was an argument that had already been partially proven by Freddie and the Dreamers, the Barron Knights and the many other acts of the era that had learned there was no harm in being able to incorporate a little knockabout comedy into your act. As a singer Noone may have been little more than serviceable. As a quick study there were few who could touch him.

First he needed a brand. The name under which he became famous across America, at one time on such a scale that he rivalled the

Beatles and the Monkees, was Herman's Hermits. This was arrived at when a Manchester pub landlord, seeing Noone don his horn-rimmed spectacles in emulation of Buddy Holly, said, 'You don't look like him; you look more like Herman from *Rocky and Bullwinkle*.' In this the landlord had misheard something. He'd meant to liken him to Sherman Peabody, who was the bespectacled swot from the American cartoon series. It didn't matter. The band decided that henceforth Peter Noone would be Herman. If their lead singer was going to be known for his gawkiness then they would point it out before the rest of the world did.

When they were first introduced to Mickie Most, the producer said that he didn't want the band but he thought he might be able to do something with Herman. That something turned out to be to put him at the centre of what would effectively become the first boy band. The boy band and girl band tropes are now so hard-wired into the way people think about pop music in the twenty-first century that it's difficult to get people to believe that sixties acts like the Beatles, the Walker Brothers or even the Monkees were never considered boy bands, no matter what level of screams they elicited, no matter what proportion of their fans were girls. These bands set out to entertain. The screams were a by-product.

Herman's Hermits were handled differently. They were all about the girls. From their first hit, a cover of Earl-Jean's 'I'm Into Something Good' in late 1964, to their climactic 'I'm Henry VIII, I Am' (which was the fastest-selling single of all time when it came out in 1965), Herman's Hermits were aimed squarely at the maternal instincts of girls, particularly American girls. Instead of screams, the noise their puppyish act tended to elicit was the sound of a few thousand girls making the 'awwwww' sound. Herman's Hermits were the ultimate in unthreatening sex appeal. Peter Noone was fine with this. The other members of the band may have harboured ambitions of being as respected as, say, the Searchers but Noone knew what it was all about: 'Boys didn't like us because we didn't play rock and roll. We were a romantic group.'

EMI's US label Capitol, which had initially passed on the Beatles and then subsequently did the same with the scarcely less successful Dave Clark Five, took a look at Herman's Hermits, who were the next cab on the rank. They looked particularly hard at Noone's apologetic fronting of the band, decided this surely was too parochial to have any appeal outside of Kentshire or wherever it was this latest set of Limeys came from, and passed again. This time they were, if anything, even more wrong than they had been in the previous two cases. It was MGM who profited from the fact that for a short while Herman's Hermits became America's second most popular British group. Their first two albums both reached the top five in America. They were sought-after guests on all the big TV shows. They had eleven top ten singles in the United States.

They achieved all this by playing up to Americans' idea of Englishness. Noone didn't dampen down his Mancunian accent. He stressed it because it made him sound even sweeter to American ears. The pinnacle of this massively successful act of transatlantic pandering came in 1965 when they recorded a plaintive comic song called 'Mrs Brown You've Got A Lovely Daughter'. This had been originally written by an English actor named Trevor Peacock for a TV play called *The Lads* (Peacock went on to play the regular role of Jim Trott in the UK TV sitcom *The Vicar of Dibley*). It was a song about a boy meeting up with the mother of the girl who has broken his heart, assuring her that her daughter is still a pearl among girls and that, no, he doesn't want back any of the things he bought her when they were walking out. It was clearly English, not only because it used the word 'bloke' but also because America liked to think that only an English boy could possibly be as polite as the boy in the song. In Britain they didn't even put it out as a single. In America it was number one for weeks, holding off the Beatles, the Beach

Boys, the Supremes and the Four Tops. Sometimes when they performed it on TV, Noone would dress up as a schoolboy for anybody who hadn't got the point.

Noone went along with most of the visual clichés that were beloved of America's TV producers. Herman's Hermits had no problem adopting the pin-stripes and bowlers of gentlemen from the Square Mile if somebody felt it would help their latest record. The singer was still in his teens when all this was happening and slipped all too easily into the role of the fifth-former whose puppy-ish enthusiasm slightly annoyed the older boys. He knew from early on that the likes of the Stones looked down on him. What he didn't know was the Stones' manager Andrew Loog Oldham envied his success, and wished his band could be similarly commercial and could be with the same agent, Frank Barsalona, who would be instrumental in launching Jimmy Page's next band in America. Herman's Hermits released so many records during the eighteen months of their hot streak that they were increasingly being performed by session men like Page and were sometimes arranged by John Paul Jones.

Within a year of that first hit Noone's former American idols, people like Del Shannon and all the Bobbies, were yesterday's men. A lot of American jobs were lost as a consequence of America suddenly deciding it preferred to buy its music from overseas. When Herman's Hermits toured the American heartland, more often than not they would be headlining over American talent that could no longer get hired without a Brit at the top of the bill. For instance, on 6 May 1965, at the very peak of their success, they played Paducah, Kentucky, at the top of a bill that also included Bobby Vee, Little Anthony, Freddy Cannon, Brenda Holloway, the Hondells, Reparata and the Delrons, the Ikettes and Billy Stewart, most of whom would spend the rest of their career thinking how much easier life could have been if all these Brits hadn't come along and upset the applecart. The coming generation of American musicians, determined not to be caught out in the same way, responded to the same forces by presenting themselves as though they were English. Thus were the Sir Douglas Quintet, the Beau Brummels, the Left Banke, the Byrds and many more brought forth, returning the British spin on American music with something new of their own.

When Herman's Hermits arrived early in 1965 they fell directly into the open arms of America, particularly into the arms of those younger sisters of the girls who had previously been screaming for the Beatles. There was no edge to Herman's Hermits, which was an important part of their appeal. Nancy in Akron could drift off to sleep dreaming about how Peter Noone would understand all her problems. Nancy's room would be papered with posters pulled from 16 magazine, which was making hay on the back of the British Invasion. There was a similar boom in the UK at the time. *Fabulous* magazine had been launched in January 1964 and was the accidental beneficiary of Beatlemania and all that came after. Its promise was simple: twelve colour pin-ups every week for just a shilling. For the first two years they had a pin-up of the Beatles in every issue. British magazines were ahead of the United States in being able to offer colour posters, which didn't arrive in 16 until 1969. Then there was the slightly more sophisticated *Rave*, which specialized in picture spreads of photogenic stars like Steve Marriott and Cat Stevens fondling ornaments in serviced apartments in London, apartments that they clearly saw only briefly between tours.

The editor in chief of 16 was a former model called Gloria Stavers, who was a key figure in what happened on the American music scene for the next twenty years. When the Hermits first landed at JFK airport in early 1965, Gloria materialized in the car with them on the way into the city, pushing them to pose for pictures and demanding to know which one was who. 'She was pushy, and we'd never met any women like that before,' Noone remembered later. This was certainly the case. Regardless of their upbringing, their educational attainment or the shortness of their skirts, most British young women of 1965 were demure by the standards of later decades. Gloria Stavers was a type you wouldn't have come across in the UK.

Her turning up at JFK to greet them was not an unusual thing for Stavers. She often made it her mission to meet the new immigrants off the boat and, where necessary, to mould them before anyone else in America got at them. Stavers was keen that they satisfy the requirements of the detailed fantasy life being dreamed under the covers in soft toy-stuffed bedrooms from Buffalo to San Bernardino. Like Mickie Most, she took one look and decided that the group was all about the singer. Noone's gap-toothed innocence hit the same sweet spot in the girls of 1965 as Mickey Rooney had found in their mothers twenty years before. Stavers' genius was to convince the twelve-year-olds of America that even the wildest of their rock heroes were not beyond taming and were, underneath it all, just crying out for some home comfort while on the road. She wanted pictures that conveyed this idea. When they didn't happen to exist she took them herself. She would go so far as to turn up at Noone's hotel first thing in the morning just to get a picture of him waking up. She knew that such cosiness was everything her readers fantasized about. If either she or her readers had any interest in the carnal side of relationships with pop stars they never showed it. It was an essentially sentimental form of cohabitation of which they dreamed.

Her readers, like so many American teenagers of the time, were in love with this new/old way of life from across the ocean. They were the girls who would go down the local pharmacy and treat themselves to a whiff of a new fragrance from Yardley called Oh! de London. This was heavily sold on American TV with a debby voiceover cooing, 'When you're young and in love, there's no place like London.' They might try to cultivate a new way of speaking, a way that seemed to them as cool as the American accent had always seemed to English ears. They were the ones who were all over the Carnaby Street fashions that had supplanted America's traditional high school look, and consumed the newspapers and magazines that carried breathless reports of how English roses like Jane Asher and Pattie Boyd managed to maintain their poise. Girls such as Chrissie Hynde of Akron, Ohio, who bonded with her friend Nita Lee over their love of English bands, and girls who looked like Jean Shrimpton and would sew their own Empire-waist dresses, paisley-trimmed bell-bottoms and Nehru-collared shirts because you simply couldn't get things like that in the stores. Girls such as Carolyn Long from Dallas, who got her mother to copy the herringbone tunics worn by Pattie Boyd in the train scene in *A Hard Day's Night*. Boyd was the envy of every American teenage girl. *16* magazine carried a regular called 'Pattie Boyd's Beauty Box' in which George Harrison's girlfriend supposedly passed on tips on how she looked after her barnet – which, she confided to readers, was London slang for 'hair'.

At the time the average age at which America's girls married was twenty and the average age of having a baby was twenty-one. No surprise, then, that this generation embraced a lifestyle which appeared to hold out the promise of a youth endlessly extended; no surprise that they were so keen to embrace short skirts and new-fangled tights that gave them the outline of pantomime Peter Pans; no surprise that so many of them wanted to look like Twiggy, the new child beauty from Neasden.

It was all very virginal. There would not be so much as a whiff of debauchery in the pages of *16* magazine. The illusion that sustained the *16* universe, much as the illusion around Herman himself, had to be so delicately handled there was no room at all for reality to intrude. The many features about Herman that appeared in the magazine during his mid-sixties heyday might all have been couched in the first person and presented as though they were the innermost thoughts of Noone, but they were entirely invented by Stavers. She had a simple policy: she wrote what she thought her readers wanted to read. 'Somewhere in this wide, wide world there is a girl waiting just for me,' throbbed one such ghosted cri de coeur, ostensibly from the urchin of Urmston. 'I believe this with all my heart – because, you see, I too am waiting . . . waiting for her. So far, I haven't even laid eyes on her, but I know exactly what she looks like. And I know exactly what she is like – because this is the girl I love; this is my bird.' This beseeching persona which Stavers invented, modelled to an extent on the character Noone played in 'Mrs Brown You've Got A Lovely Daughter', seemed to be perpetually positioned beneath the reader's bedroom window, gripping a fistful of blooms filched from next-door's garden. This is what worked for the readers – the idea that in their own dull home life somewhere there was a secret door which they only had to open to admit their fantasy.

In real life Noone and Stavers got on well. She was a sophisticated woman, a hipster of her time. She took him to Greenwich Village where she introduced him to Phil Ochs. And she was straight with him, promising that as long as he was hot he would always have a special place in the top right-hand corner of 16's cover. These covers were designed in a self-consciously childish style with the various inhabitants of Stavers' dream world represented by tiny cut-out heads grafted on to illustrated bodies which were often driving cars or making nice with huge cuddly toys. 16 was not in any way sophisticated. It set out to ape the lovingly customized cover of a school exercise book.

A classic 16 reader was Margaret Moser, twelve at the time and badly thrown by her parents' forcing her to move from exotic New

Orleans to dull San Antonio. She went further than most in her devotion to all things English. 'Carnaby Street and anything with the faintest whiff of Limey origin was hot. I devoured every magazine with anything about England and pop music, but *16* was the best,' she later recalled. 'They knew what I wanted: photos and dreams. I wrote an elaborate essay to win a date with the Monkees' Peter Tork ... *Dear 16*, the essay began. I recently departed my beloved England where my father worked on Harley Street and we have moved to Texas. It is so uncivilised here, but I have found one thing makes life truly bearable – the Monkees. I began eighth grade speaking with a fake English accent, complete with details gleaned from magazines. I had decided I would be more interesting if I were mysterious. Mysterious meant foreign to me and England happened to be The Place.'

In the summer of 1966 DC Comics tapped into this very feeling, launching a new teenage comic called *Swing with Scooter*. This concerned the adventures of a cute English pop star of that name who decides he has to escape the excesses of his fans at home by moving to the American city of Plainsville. Here he has lots of adventures with regular American teen Cookie (who adores him and the way he talks), dodges his old girlfriend Cynthia (who has pursued him all the way from England), and foils the dastardly plans of Malibu, the Californian with the dated haircut who used to get all the girls before he came along. The cute English pop star was suddenly a stock character of American popular entertainment. At the same time the British duo Chad & Jeremy, more successful in the USA than they were in Britain, were written into the top-rating sitcom *The Dick Van Dyke Show* when they appeared as the Redcoats (Fred and Ernie) who have to stay with Rob and Laura Petrie while doing their shows and inevitably throw the whole neighbourhood into Beatlemania-style panic. Serious fiction wasn't above pulling the same trick: the 1965 novel by Thomas Pynchon, *The Crying of Lot 49*, featured a group called the Paranoids, American teenagers who sang in English accents in the hope it would help their career.

Eventually the fantasy won out over the reality. Herman's audience was lured away by the Monkees, who were launched in the early autumn of 1966. They too were fronted by a similar soft toy of a Mancunian. The Monkees were invented by a couple of movie men who had been to see *A Hard Day's Night* and decided it would be interesting to turn the sixties group phenomenon on its head by putting the focus on the fantasy life the band made when not playing music rather than the music itself and making it available to its young fans whenever they turned on the TV. At around the same time Herman's Hermits, riven by internal jealousies because of the amount of attention lavished on Noone, decided they would finally get the money they were owed by the record company by refusing to deliver a new record. This plan backfired. By then the record company didn't want another Herman's Hermits record. They felt they'd had their time.

They continued to have hits in other parts of the world and assumed that this would eventually get the attention of America. It didn't. The USA is a harsh mistress where such things are concerned. So was Gloria Stavers. Just as she counted them all in she counted them all out every bit as diligently. Noone picked up a copy of the magazine in early 1967 to find he was no longer in the top right-hand corner. He had been supplanted there by the Monkees. Gloria didn't hide the truth from him. 'I remember the day she said, quite seriously, it's over, Peter. It's gone.'

Tamra McElroy had been one of Herman's people. Born in 1954, she was of that generation of American teenagers that was just slightly too young for the Beatles and therefore her first love was Herman's Hermits. The nearest she came to seeing Noone was in August 1967 when he was due to play the Kiel Auditorium near her home in St Louis. However, school commitments and parental opposition made it impossible for them to be in the same space. She made up for it years later in the book *Idol Talk* in which she explained her dream of not just seeing him but also meeting him and not just meeting him but also eventually marrying him. There were tens of thousands of girls across the USA weaving similarly dense and richly detailed fantasies around Peter Noone in the mid-sixties. Few wrote theirs down so Tamra's account will have to stand for all of them.

In her dreams she wins a competition to meet her idol. She and Noone inevitably strike up an instant connection. However, since she is only thirteen, clearly nothing can be built upon that connection. In her dream he goes off to continue his tour while she finishes school. After school she goes to college in London. One day, far, far into the future, when she has blossomed into a confident young woman and he has tired of all the predatory mini-skirted model girls he has encountered on the road, in her dream she would be walking past Tower Bridge and there finally he would be and he would see her and he would remember her and he would marry her and they would go off to live the rest of their lives in a cottage in Shropshire because when you come from St Louis no place sounds nicer than Shropshire.

Of course that didn't happen. On that same tour when Tamra didn't manage to get to see Herman's Hermits they were supported by the Who. That's the same Who that had been tearing up the Monterey Festival a few weeks earlier that same summer. They were supporting Herman's Hermits. That's how big Peter Noone still was, even after Gloria Stavers had told him his time was up. There is often reason to believe that the cuddlier kind of pop performer tends to get more sex than the ones who put a great deal of effort into projecting themselves as Lotharios. In his own memoirs Pete Townshend recalls how when the Who were touring with Noone they could only gaze in stupefaction at the sight of the two young women emerging from Noone's hotel room. They were a pretty young woman and her scarcely less pretty young mother. It was plain to all concerned that the pair had just been obliging the gawky Mancunian with the nice hair. It's difficult to imagine that this complex coupling could have taken place without, at some stage, the chorus of 'Mrs Brown You've Got A Lovely Daughter' going through the head of at least one of the participants.

11

'Save up all your bread and fly Trans-Love Airways'

I n the Beatles' second film *Help!* there is a famous scene in which the four individual members of the group come back from a day at work to open the four individual doors of the terraced houses in which they apparently continue their modest personal lives. Two ladies in the street watch this and say how nice it is that they haven't been changed by success. The gag is that the four doors all lead directly into the same extensive play palace that has been equipped with every modern comfort. They clearly have been changed by success.

The main thing that changed the Beatles and many of those who followed in their wake was America. It broadened their horizons, lined their pockets, often provided them with partners and, because Americans appeared to be tone deaf to the differences in the way they talked and considered them all as having a generic 'British accent', allowed them to forget their origins and invent themselves all over again.

Tom Jones was a coal miner's son from the valleys of South Wales, Peter Asher the son of a Harley Street consultant, Steve Marriott's father sold jellied eels, while Mick Jagger's was the England basketball coach; Marianne Faithfull was raised in a commune, while Rod Stewart helped out at his father's newsagent on the Archway Road. All these people might have come from widely differing backgrounds in the UK, their education might have taken them to places as different as Oxford and the local engineering colleges, but when they arrived in America none of this made any difference. Nobody asked where anybody had come from. At the time it would have been as impertinent to enquire about someone's class background as it would have been impolite to ask about their ethnicity and impossible to enquire about their sexuality.

Pop sociologists tend to overestimate the effect the decade's changes had on the attitudes of the great bulk of people who grew up during that time. In fact most carried on doing what their parents had done, albeit with different hairstyles and with more money and, most importantly, with the benefits of peacetime. But what shouldn't be underestimated is the effect these circumstances had on the handful of musicians who ended up in the vanguard of those changes. This applied particularly to the generation of English musicians who had ridden the beat boom, made landfall in America during the British Invasion of 1964, discovered marijuana and LSD, and suddenly found themselves asked to step up as spokesmen for youth at a time when youth's numbers were making them the dominant force in society. Nothing in their elementary education or their often narrow upbringing in the years following the war had prepared these young men for this.

It peaked in 1967 when a good deal changed, at least on the surface, and changed very quickly. Songs no longer had to make sense, facial hair began to be interpreted as a sign of wisdom, and any-body who had mastered three chords on a guitar was suddenly expected to adopt fancy dress. In the year 1967, just three years since they had first become well known, some of the most promin-ent members of bands in the middle half of the first division of British talent would be bulleted into new lives with new expecta-tions in California, a place that was in every respect a world away from their rain-lashed, cold-water childhoods in northern Eng-land. One of these was Eric Burdon of the Animals.

I first saw the Animals on 15 May 1964. It was the first time I'd seen live rock and roll played by professionals. This being 1964, it was a package tour and I had a ticket for the first of two shows that evening at the Bradford Gaumont. The headliner was Chuck Berry. At the time Berry had only recently completed a jail sentence in Missouri for transporting an under-age girl across state lines. He had come out to find that the emergence of the Beatles and the Stones meant he was suddenly in demand in England. British DJ and collector Guy Stevens smartly decided to rebrand him as the King of Rhythm and Blues (a term that has been repurposed at regular intervals over the years to mean anything people want it to mean). This rebranding of Chuck explains why he was topping the bill over Carl Perkins. Carl was still associated with rock and roll and therefore the oldest of old hat.

Down the bill, and very glad of being caught in the glinting rays of Chuck's sun, were the Animals, a new group from Newcastle who were being managed and produced by Mickie Most and looked after on the road by a former professional wrestler called Peter Grant. The Animals finished their five-song set that night with a number which they announced they were just trying out. They warned us that it was longer than usual. They weren't kidding. Once they'd taken it from the understated intro to the full drama of its ending via an organ solo which prefigured the kind of music we would all be listening to in 1967, it had taken over four minutes. At the time four minutes was entirely unprecedented. At the time it seemed like Tolstoy.

The song was their version of 'The House Of The Rising Sun'. This was a folk favourite that had recently been brought into the spotlight via its inclusion on the first LP by Bob Dylan. (Their previous single 'Baby Let Me Take You Home' had also been borrowed from Dylan's version.) 'The House Of The Rising Sun' had been kicking around in folk repertoires for some years but nobody had thought it had hit potential. For a start it was supposed to be about a girl who was compelled to live out her days in sin and misery as a whore in a New Orleans brothel. The Animals switched the gender and didn't really make it very clear what particular variety of sin the House of the Rising Sun specialized in. That didn't much matter. The Animals' treatment had genuine power, Alan Price's organ solo had majesty and, most of all, the vocal by their pockmarked singer Eric Burdon had a conviction to it that was entirely new in British music.

Burdon sang with authority without going in for the strangled vowels and blackface mannerism favoured by so many others at the time. His version was as much Northumberland as New Orleans. You knew you'd heard something very different. So did Mickie Most, who had the best ears for a hit in the British record business. Most ordered the Animals to come down to London after one of their shows in the north, to push their equipment on a baggage cart from Euston to the studios in Kingsway. Here they performed one take to warm up and another which proved to be the keeper. It was put out on one side of a 45 in June 1964 and went on to be number one in the UK.

In the USA, where it was released soon after, it had to be divided across two sides. Nevertheless, it went to number one there as well. Few people in America knew its previous history. Teenager Ted

Polhemus of Neptune High in New Jersey remembers thinking it odd that a bunch of white kids from England would have written a song about a brothel in New Orleans. When Bob Dylan heard it he realized that this marriage of folk song and rock arrangement was exactly what he ought to have been doing in the first place. Dylan and his hipster pals in Greenwich Village may have looked down their noses at all these British pop groups who kept showing up on *Ed Sullivan* in their matching suits but they had to admit that in many ways the Brits were ahead of them. Having played the organ solo in the middle of the Animals' version, Alan Price got the 'traditional arranged' composing credit. This was part of the reason why he was the first member to leave the band the following year and was next seen drunkenly trying to be Bob Dylan's best mate backstage on his tour of Britain in 1965, as captured in the documentary film *Dont Look Back*.

The American hit required the Animals' presence in America. By the time they made their first trip to New York in the autumn of 1964 the authorities at JFK had placed a ban on Beatles-style receptions. Hence they arrived pretty much like any other business travellers. Burdon was later to claim that an edict had been handed down to ensure the media didn't mention their arrival and as a consequence they were robbed of their rightful Beatles moment. Instead they had an intimation of the many tiny humiliations that would attend being called the Animals in the United States. At JFK they were greeted by representatives of their record company who gave them the good news that each member would travel into New York in the back of a convertible. To make it even more fun each of them would be accompanied by a go-go girl wearing fishnet stockings, a furry animal suit and brandishing claws. It was humiliation rather than a triumph, no matter what spin Eric Burdon put on it. Many years later, recalling his entry into the city via the wind-whipped bridges over the East River for a BBC documentary,

Burdon remembered the cars as that archetypal American sports machine the Ford Mustang. In fact they were Sunbeam Tiger convertibles. The Sunbeam Tiger was an unsuccessful attempt by the British Rootes Group to break into the American market. Thus was the Animals' less than triumphal entry into the New World underwritten by the petty cash from a car promotion. It got worse. At an early press conference the photographers demanded that they get on their knees and growl like animals, and they duly did. Their first booking was as part of a long bill at the Paramount in New York where they had to play three shows a day on weekdays and five at the weekends. Their manager Mike Jeffrey didn't appear to have control of the situation. Looking back many years later, Burdon would say that the United States was their downfall. 'As soon as we stepped into America our assets were stripped away.'

However, they did capture the imaginations of some fans in a way few English bands did. In the course of a speech about them in 2012 – a speech in which he demonstrated how his song 'The Promised Land' was directly stolen from the Animals' arrangement of Nina Simone's 'Don't Let Me Be Misunderstood' – Bruce Springsteen remembered, 'They were the first records with full-blown class consciousness that I'd ever heard. It was the first time I heard something across the radio that mirrored my home life. The other thing that was great about the Animals was that there were no good-looking members. They weren't nice. They were aggression personified. They were cruel, which was so freeing. Eric Burdon was like your shrunken daddy with a wig on. He never had a kid's face. He always had an old man's face. Also their name was final and unforgiving.'

They kept up their standards. The records they made after visiting America were, if anything, stronger than the ones they had made before. Thanks to a meeting with Allen Klein, who treated them to the 'I can secure the million dollars that your American record company is hiding from you' line that he would later use successfully on the Stones and the Beatles, their producer Mickie Most was pointed in the direction of New York's Brill Building when he wanted new material. It was here, among the hacks writing for hire, that he found the songs 'We've Gotta Get Out Of This Place' and 'It's My Life', songs that the Animals would turn into anthems to match 'House Of The Rising Sun' – songs that would inspire Bruce Springsteen and many other young Americans.

One of the small miracles of the British Invasion was how often British groups managed to cut winning versions of songs that had been originally written expressly to be sung by American groups. Manfred Mann did it with 'Pretty Flamingo', leggiest girl on 'our block' (an expression which couldn't have meant much to an Oxford-educated lead singer); Them did it with 'Here Comes The Night', a Bert Berns song which seems set on the mean streets of Boston rather than Belfast. These were the kind of songs these young bands would probably not have had the vision to write for themselves, even if they had the skills, so the fact that they did them was a great favour to their American writers, who were usually in their cells in the Brill Building with a piano, a chair and a payphone, as well as to themselves. Nobody painted that very American picture of escape from being brought up to do just what your daddy done quite as well as the Brits.

The problem was, because they couldn't write their own songs – and, unlike lots of other acts, recognized that fact – they could never really make albums. By the end of 1966 Price had left, Chas Chandler had gone to manage Jimi Hendrix, the old group had hit the wall and Eric, whose desire to be taken seriously almost amounted to a physical ache, wanted to front a version of the band in which he could be the clear leader. He had also despaired of getting what he saw as his proper share from the hits they had already enjoyed. Mike Jeffrey had started a scheme under which they would each be paid £200 a week with the lion's share of their revenue being put into a special fund in the Bahamas. Here, he argued, it could be kept away from the British taxman. This was a major problem for the English bands who had made money in the US. This was the year when George Harrison, enraged by the Wilson government's changes which had taken the top income tax rate to 83 per cent – a move which, when combined with a 15 per cent surcharge on unearned income, made the marginal rate reach a staggering 98 per cent – wrote 'Taxman', the song that had opened their album *Revolver*. In 1966 the Animals went down to the Bahamas to visit their money. Here they were expected to live on a yacht equipped with a mobile studio. This, said Jeffrey, was where they would make their records in future, presumably on the same principle as pirate radio, beyond the reach of governments and tax jurisdictions.

Like most groups in the mid-sixties who had enjoyed a few hits, the Animals were cash-rich but bank account poor. Their earnings from records would never be huge because their royalty rates were so low – in 1965 the American record business was arguing that if the mechanical royalty rate paid to the artist were to be increased from two to three cents a side their business would no longer be viable – and you couldn't get paid a lot of money for a live show that was only half an hour long.

Then there was the question of getting your hands on whatever money you were owed. You might have a big hit in the United States, but getting paid for it was another matter. Allen Klein was a thrusting young bookmaker from Brooklyn who flew to London during this period, staying at smart hotels he could not afford and pretending to be a lot more successful than he was. From there he would lay siege to British managers like Mickie Most until they hired him to audit the American record companies and find out where the money they had earned had gone. It was Klein who explained to him that in the American record business, when royalties actually found their way to the artist it meant the system had slipped up. The standard contract was full of clauses that loaded the dice in the company's favour, such as the 10 per cent that still had to be deducted for 'breakages', despite the advent of the 45 rpm vinyl record having made it virtually impossible to break a record, and the fact that the act would only get paid half royalties on records sold overseas. The bands were too busy, too young and too impatient to bother to learn about all this. Besides, the £200 a week the Animals were given in readies was ten times what a manual worker earned in 1966. If a band was being paid something similar today they would be earning almost £4,000 a week, which would make them feel well enough off in pennies not to ask too many questions about where the pounds might be going.

Of course no grand plan could compensate for a little good housekeeping. On the final Animals tour of the States they did some dates with Chuck Berry. When Berry turned up carrying his own guitar they took it as a sign of his independent spirit. It was nothing of the kind. Instead it was the small businessman's determination to keep down costs. Chuck had learned all this the hard way. When he refused to go on stage until he had been paid in dollar bills they took this as a sign of his tough upbringing. It wasn't. It was an entirely sensible mistrust of people who promise that you will get your reward either in heaven or in the next fiscal year.

Bewilderingly the Animals' name was still making them a target for humiliation. In 1966 they were hired to feature in an American TV special called *The Dangerous Christmas of Red Riding Hood*. This starred Liza Minnelli. The Animals appeared in one sequence in which they wore wolf's ears and tails while singing a song called 'We're Gonna Howl Tonight'. As he was doing this Eric still burned to earn the same respect as the Beatles or the Byrds. Instead here he was, touring the backside of America with Herman's Hermits. On

131

the day England won the World Cup they were playing at the Civic Center in Baltimore, Maryland. The poster was hand-drawn and depicted them growling behind bars. At one show in California their road crew didn't turn up and so the band had to disguise themselves in boiler suits and baseball caps and do their own set-up. No wonder that by the end of the tour Burdon was in the market for a new beginning.

It had been all of three years since he had left his mum and dad back in Newcastle: three crowded years of mad excitement punctuating long periods of soul-sucking tedium; three years of guiltless fornication with any girl he could persuade; three years of hurtling around America brandishing Confederate flags and otherwise behaving in a provocative manner; three years of dressing up as a cowboy and playing with real guns; three years telling yourself that when you clubbed together your cash in hand so that one of you could afford a New Orleans prostitute you were doing it so that you could claim to have visited the real House of the Rising Sun; three years that were long enough for you to feel your career taking off, reaching its peak and now settling into a long, slow glide back into obscurity. Suddenly this was no longer all about the next buzz. Suddenly it was all about peace of mind, the pursuit of which had never previously been a pop priority.

In the year 1966 even rock stars kept in touch with their social circle via the post office, and it was at this time that Burdon received a letter from an old girlfriend. She was in San Francisco and she told him that there were things going on in the city by the bay which demanded his attention and would speak to his sensual appetites. These last were considerable.

Burdon had always had a limited capacity for solitude and San Francisco offered itself as a place where he could be in the thick of it once again. In 1966 it was such a small scene that it was no hardship to swiftly locate the middle of it. Within hours of his arrival he found himself in the back room of the Fillmore West with his new best mates Janis Joplin (who pressed a tab of Owsley's acid on him) and Jim Morrison (with whom he discussed not films but 'film'). Eric fell for this new world as instantly and completely as he had once fallen for the blues of John Lee Hooker. He immediately became the charter member of that most oxymoronic of minorities, the Geordie hippies. The man who had sung 'The House Of The Rising Sun' started wearing flowers in his hair without delay.

Eric Burdon set himself to praising psychedelia as energetically as he would once have campaigned for the blues. Possibly inspired by the example of Roger Miller's 'England Swings' he fronted his group the New Animals in a new single called 'San Franciscan Nights'. Just a year after the discovery of Swinging London all eyes were suddenly on San Francisco. Rarely has a place been as closely identified with a musical moment as was San Francisco in 1967. Documentary crews were scrambling on San Francisco-bound planes as feverishly as gold miners had packed for the coast back in 1848, lured by promises of sunshine, flowers and girls who had unaccountably neglected to put their clothes on. It was the kind of tip-of-the-tongue association that was made by people who didn't as a rule keep up with music. It was there in the rubbernecking news reports from Haight-Ashbury. It was there in the ubiquitous travelogue hits like 'San Francisco (Be Sure To Wear Flowers In Your Hair)', which spent a month at number one in the UK, and 'Let's Go To San Francisco' by the transparently unsound Flower Pot Men.

Everybody knew that the axis of influence had shifted from London to the city on the bay. A year after 'England Swings' had promised the world that London was where it was at, Eric Burdon, a Geordie, began his song 'San Franciscan Nights' with this spoken foreword: 'This following programme is dedicated to the city and people of San Francisco, who may not know it but they are beautiful and so is their city; this is a very personal song, so if the viewer cannot understand it, particularly those of you who are European residents, save up all your bread and fly Trans-Love Airways to San Francisco USA, then maybe you'll understand the song. It will be worth it, if not for the sake of this song but for the sake of your own peace of mind.' This was a very curious message to be fronted by a twenty-six-year-old from Wallsend whose postal address at the time was a very smart serviced flat in London's St James's.

In June 1967 the eyes of the world were on the Monterey Pop Festival. Eric and his New Animals, freshly arrayed in their motley as though recently plucked from the dressing-up box, were introduced to the crowd by the father of the San Francisco scene, Chet Helms. They played 'San Franciscan Nights'. Puffed up on its own importance, the scene was definitely in the market for anthems. This was not simply another new direction in popular music. This was the Renaissance. The Great Awakening. Just add sunshine. Burdon had tired of trying to tell people in Britain why it was all so important. 'I pointed out it was a radical movement, trying to stop a war in Vietnam, but in England it wasn't their problem.' Eric, however, was sold. He decided then and there he would leave the UK and base himself in California where henceforth he wouldn't simply talk to people. Henceforth he'd 'rap' with them, and his every human interaction would be a teaching moment for this new age. His final act in the old country would be to marry his 'old lady'.

'Her name was Angela King,' he recalled in his memoirs, which are equal parts spirituality and shagging. 'She was Anglo-Indian and that was a buzz for me as I'd made a promise at the tender age of fifteen that one of the first things I would do is have a deep, meaningful, long-lasting, memorable, erotic affair with at least one member of every ethnic racial group. This is going to save me going all the way to India, I thought, if I can cop this bird.' Musicians of Burdon's generation were highly attuned to any accusations of racism but wouldn't have begun to understand any accusation of sexism. The day that didn't end with 'some girls' was a day wasted, and if those girls were what his memoirs describe in the language of the time as 'coloured' that was even better.

It was always a stretch on Burdon's part for him to position himself as a spiritual sort because he had always prided himself on being a leading light of those Falstaffs and Flashhearts of Speakeasy society who liked to style themselves 'looners'. In this guise he even claimed that he was the egg man of 'I Am The Walrus' fame. The story dates back to the day when his girlfriend Selina (who was black, of course) snuck up behind him when he was cooking breakfast naked in his St James's flat, cracked an amyl nitrate capsule under his nose, and then as his brain proceeded to explode, slid down him and removed the egg yolk that had inevitably gathered on his penis with her mouth. He told this story to John Lennon who was so tickled he put it in his song. In the years to come, when Burdon looked back on a career that was crammed with hits but not with pay cheques, such incidents provided some compensation. It may have been this he was thinking of when he sang about 'all the good time that's been wasted having good times'.

On 6 September 1967 Eric Burdon and Angie King were married at Caxton Hall in London, the standard venue in those days for society weddings. She wore a sari. He wore an Afghan coat. The bride looked lovely. Eric had a flower behind his ear. The ceremony was covered by the newsreel cameras who were eager to be in on any rites of the flower children, because they had thoughtfully stepped into the gap vacated by the mods and rockers. 'May they be hippy ever after,' chirped the commentary. No such luck.

A small number of the people attending the ceremony were probably aware of what had actually gone on in the previous twenty-four hours. It is to be hoped that the bride wasn't one of them. In those twenty-four hours Burdon had decided to say goodbye to his bachelor days by having sexual congress with no fewer than seven of his former girlfriends. It all began at lunchtime the day before in the Hilton in Park Lane where he was due to meet Pam. After that he was lined up with Shana in Fulham, followed by early evening in Mayfair with Sylvia, Jeane from New York at nine thirty in the evening at Jimi Hendrix's place, then it was just a question of polishing off Ziggy, Sue and Eva before meeting his male friends at the bar of the Cromwellian around one in the morning. Drinks with Keith Moon and Jeff Beck followed. Later that morning, as he made his way through Green Park to the register office, with alcohol and who knows what else still coursing through his system, he doesn't recall being overcome with remorse. His mother and father, who were down from Wallsend to be with their son on this most special of days, could not possibly have guessed at what had gone down the night before.

Following the wedding ceremony the guests went to a reception in the wholesome surroundings of the Speakeasy in Margaret Street. Here the men soon gathered on one side of the room and the women on the other. This was only to be expected. Beneath their renaissance habiliments and the groovy spectacles that they couldn't see through the guests were just a bunch of averagely inhibited lower middle-class English people, much as would have been the case at many other weddings taking place in Britain that weekend. The class that rock stars could properly belong to had not yet been invented.

After the party wound up there were no cabs to take the happy couple back to Burdon's flat in St James's, where he lived like some cross between Bob Ferris and Bingo Little, so he took her home in the band's Transit, which did not greatly amuse her. In the week after the wedding they went back to his mother's in Wallsend.

While Burdon was on home ground he had his picture taken for the *Northern Echo*, reading the Bible. He wanted to stress that was what he now did every day. Read the Bible. As the photographer Ian Wright recalled, 'that didn't last long'.

Soon afterwards Burdon went off to tour with the New Animals in support of their portentous LP *Winds Of Change*. This left his new bride unable to pay the rent on their place in St James's on the money he sent her. The phone and electricity were cut off. When she complained she had no money, he suggested she should get a job, which was not very Aquarian of him. She said that the wife of a man who was supposed to be a rock superstar shouldn't have to work. She phoned to say she was coming out to see him. He said he had a new girlfriend in America so it was agreed she shouldn't bother. A few years later she turned up on his doorstep in LA, no longer looking like the radiant flower child of 1967. She had an equally desperate boyfriend with her. They needed money to get back to the UK. Could he give it to her? Showing rare foresight, Burdon decided he could but only if she signed a hastily drawn-up document relinquishing all claim on the fortune he didn't have. He never saw her again.

12

'I love Jennifer Eccles'

It is an inescapable fact of life that no matter how much feeling they put into singing songs about the purity of their hearts or the selflessness of their romantic devotion, still the overwhelming majority of rock stars end up marrying women who would probably never have looked at them twice had they not been rock stars. As a breed, much like their successful counterparts in the worlds of professional sport, high finance and even organized crime, rock stars tend to marry up. For the British rock stars of the sixties this process often began at a relatively modest, local level.

In the beginning all members of sixties groups seemed to hook up with local girls who had local names and local jobs. The Beatles' first girlfriends were Dot, Iris and Thelma, and these girls either went to college with them or they had jobs in banks. As the sixties bands grew more successful in the local area they could then graduate to taking out hairdressers or beauticians or receptionists or secretaries, the kind of girls who were marked for great things in the early sixties because they were lucky enough to have the kind of office jobs that allowed them to dress up and put a lot of effort into their appearance.

In March 1964, Allan Clarke, the twenty-one-year-old singer of Manchester group the Hollies, who had just had two top ten hits with their cover versions of American songs, married receptionist Jennifer Bowstead in Coventry. Jenni, as she was known, was only eighteen and had met him just a few months earlier when the Hollies came to Coventry to play a show. His best man, as was fast becoming traditional at beat boom nuptials, was Graham Nash, Clarke's harmony partner in the Hollies.

In 1948 Nash had met Allan (then Harold) Clarke on their first day at Ordsal Board School in Salford. They both subsequently became members of Salford Lads Club and both liked singing. The singing was the only thing that marked them out from thousands of their contemporaries growing up in terraced houses and supporting United at the time. The Hollies came together around the two's harmonies with Clarke handling lead singing duties and Nash contributing the highest of high parts. They were signed by EMI and enjoyed a string of hits beginning in 1963. Some of them were picked from the American r&b charts, a few were written by themselves, and others such as 'Bus Stop' were the product of the very English sensibility of a precocious Manchester teenager called Graham Gouldman.

Six months after Clarke's wedding Nash followed suit and married his teenage girlfriend Rose Eccles. By then the group was doing even better and so he could afford to set her up with a boutique in Manchester called Pygmalia. That attachment to the local area didn't last. While Clarke was quite happy to remain a big guy in the Manchester area, Nash was drawn towards London. He and Rose moved into a flat in Shepherd's Bush and painted the walls black, because that's what rock stars did. It couldn't have been less like the home life of Mr and Mrs Clarke, who by contrast had spent their honeymoon at the Ideal Home Exhibition.

As the decade wore on a rift opened up in the group between Clarke's homebody style of life and Nash's hipster aspirations; between Clarke's determination that they should maintain at all costs their supply of British chart singles and keep their date book full and Nash's wish to see them do something more ambitious, to make proper albums and get glowing reviews in the music papers; between Clarke's contentment with the British market and Nash's increasing interest in California. The Hollies had not broken through in America but they took every opportunity to go there, largely so that Nash could look around him. When, in the summer of 1966, they first got as far as California, Nash took one look at the Hockney swimming pools undulating in the sun and was sold before the plane had even touched down. 'I climbed to the top of a palm tree and told Clarkie I was never coming down. It was a metaphor he should have heeded.'

At a party thrown by the record company he was approached by a gnome-like figure called Rodney Bingenheimer, who, it was clear, knew more about their recording career than they did themselves, and he asked if Nash would like to come down to a recording session with the Mamas and Papas. It was there that he met Mama Cass. The following day she picked him up at his hotel and then, with the top of her Porsche let down, in unremarkably brilliant California sunshine and to the accompaniment of the Californian radio playing one hip tune after another, she drove him up, up and away from Sunset Boulevard in the direction of Laurel Canyon, where all the musicians and artists lived in magic houses on stilts. There, she took him to the home of David Crosby of the Byrds who proceeded to assemble a massive joint involving weed that was, at a conservative estimate, three times as strong as anything anyone in

Britain had ever smoked before. Since Nash had never smoked weed of any kind before, this made the whole experience even more life-altering than it might have been. For an Everly Brothers fan from rainy Salford it would have been difficult to imagine an experience that could go more profoundly to the head. When he returned from this visit there was another division between him and the rest of the Hollies. While they preferred to relax after shows with a few beers, henceforth Nash would only be interested in weed. Only with the latter, as many bands were finding at the time, was wisdom apparently guaranteed.

California had always exerted a strong pull thanks to its sunshine and its celebration of the body beautiful, but the new psychedelia, which had seemingly been discovered much as gold had been in the same place over a century earlier, promised something entirely new, and it was something with a particularly powerful pull for a Mancunian war baby like Graham Nash, for whom even the Hollies' fabulous run of hit singles would never quite suffice. Psychedelia promised credibility. Although it was every bit as dependent on catchy choruses as the pop music of the day, it set a premium on lyrical obscurity and encouraged the idea that it was the duty of pop musicians to be in the vanguard of attempts to change the world. This had never been a priority before. Nash yearned to go to this magical place where the composers of popular songs were exalted, where their artist status was secure, where you could enjoy a congenial lifestyle and write songs about that lifestyle. Much as English people had traditionally felt that in order to become an artist they had to move to Paris, Nash was drawn specifically to Laurel Canyon. He later said that to him Laurel Canyon, where the minstrels coupled, decoupled and invariably left a song about the experience on the pillow, was 'like Vienna at the turn of the century or Paris in the thirties'. He was the ultimate wide-eyed Englishman abroad.

Graham Nash craved something which didn't bother Allan Clarke. He wanted to be taken seriously. Everybody liked the Hollies. Their fellow musicians had great respect for what they did. But nothing they did seemed to matter the way that the Beatles and the Stones and the Byrds seemed to matter. As the decade passed its halfway mark there was a gathering feeling that bands ought to matter, if only because the scale of their popularity ought to put them in a position to sway the youthful masses. Nash felt this more than the rest of the Hollies did. If there was going to be a division between those acts who apparently had a higher purpose and those who were simply doing it for a lark then it mattered greatly to him that he be on the right side of that division.

In the spring of 1967 American television screened a documentary called *Inside Pop: The Rock Revolution*. This was the first proper attempt by the arts establishment to stake its claim to ownership of those pop artists who yearned to be taken seriously. Programmes like *Inside Pop* did not come bubbling up from the subculture. Instead they came from the heart of the arts establishment. In order to make sure that everybody got that message, this one was fronted by Leonard Bernstein. It was produced by the grown-ups of the pre-rock and roll era. They were energetically recruiting spokesmen for a generation and would fasten on anyone who was willing to take on the mantle.

It had two central arguments, both of which turned out to be wrong. The first was that pop music was inevitably going to get more sophisticated. The second was that the kids of today were almost genetically predisposed to have liberal attitudes. Graham Nash was filmed during a tour with Herman's Hermits arguing passionately with his unimpressed band mates that bands like theirs got through to millions of kids who would grow up to be the adults of the future and therefore they had the power to change hearts and minds. 'I think pop musicians are in a fantastic

position. They could rule the world, man,' he assured an uncon-
vinced Peter Noone. Nash, whose characteristic Mancunian chirp
is inclined to reach an even higher pitch when enthusiastic, was
particularly passionate in his commendation of Donovan. He even
went so far as to say, 'What Donovan's trying to put over will stop
wars dead. We can stop world wars before they even start.'

Much of this was Crosby's weed talking. Furthermore, many of
the English musicians of Nash's generation had been introduced to
acid at some point in the previous few months and consequently
felt they had been vouchsafed a glimpse of the infinite which had
not been revealed to earlier generations. If only everybody else
could see the world the way they had been seeing it since last Tues-
day then even the most tricky problems of humankind would be
ironed out.

Nash's burgeoning tendency to take himself seriously, his
increasing feeling that he belonged in California and the strains in
his marriage to Rose culminated in 1967 in the song that broke the
Hollies. Up until then they had had hits, first in the UK and eventually in the USA, that wore their meaning lightly. They were about
everyday situations with which the widest possible audience could
identify. The girl you fancied because you saw her every day at the
bus stop. The girl you fancied who was always two horses ahead of
you on a fairground ride. They were simple sentiments enshrined
in performances that were bracing rather than sensual. They
weren't about you. They were for the audience. When Nash was
sufficiently aroused by the sight of Marianne Faithfull in her con-
vent uniform he nonetheless disguised her name in 'Carrie Anne'.

'King Midas In Reverse', which he presented to the band in 1967,
was at the more enigmatic end of their range. He campaigned hard
to get it released as a single. It was a great record, one of their best,
but the Hollies' audience didn't hear it that way. It wasn't for them,
hence it wasn't as big a hit as the Hollies were used to. It didn't

actually go into the top ten, which for the Hollies was unknown. Why was it a relative failure? Possibly because people wouldn't accept an even slightly complicated song like 'King Midas In Reverse' from the cheerful, uncomplicated Hollies. To put over a song like that, it seemed, you had to be someone different. You had to be a group with a reputation for being deep.

Nash was bitterly disappointed and slightly embarrassed with what happened to 'King Midas In Reverse'. He had hoped it would be the record that would force the world to look at the Hollies in a new light. On that score it failed. To the rest of the group it was plain what they should do. Like a football team returning to basics after a slight wobble, it became imperative that the next Hollies single should be a safety-first choice. This time Clarke was in the driving seat, and the song 'Jennifer Eccles', named for both his and Graham's wives, was machine-tooled for radio acceptability. From its 'I love her, she loves me' sentiment to the signature playground wolf whistle which was its hook, this record was like a plea for forgiveness. Nash hated it. He hated it even more the faster it went up the charts. This was Salford not Sausalito. This was Red Barrel not Rolling Rock. This was Radio One not KSAN. In every respect it seemed like the very past Nash was trying desperately to outgrow.

The rest of the Hollies might have set their faces against the wilful obscurity of psychedelia but, like all the other British Invasion groups, they very much went for the clothes. 1967 was witness to the greatest fashion panic in the history of pop as everybody rushed to embrace this crazy new look, which seemed to have been dictated by someone with shares in a theatrical costumier seeking to offload their gaudiest habiliments before the next pantomime season. The same looks were everywhere. The moustaches that in some cases appeared to be painted on. The paisley. The scarves. The chiffon. These changes were generally led by one member of the group with the rest forced to meekly comply. It was clear who

144

was the style leader in the Hollies. Bobby Elliott, the drummer, particularly disadvantaged since he was such an early pioneer of baldness in rock, put the blame where it belonged. 'Graham was wandering around in a frock. Thanks to him we all had kaftans.'

In March 1968, as 'Jennifer Eccles' was making its remorseless, chirpy way up the charts, the Hollies, never at the centre of things, were playing in Ottawa, Canada. Here they went to a party after the show and here Nash's habitually roving eye, which had in the past been open in its appreciation of the female form, was caught instead by a soulful, Guinevere-like figure sitting with what appeared to be an antique Bible on her lap. She was clearly a world removed from the dolly birds of Manchester and Mayfair.

Joni Mitchell, the object of his admiration, was for her part struck by the way Graham Nash was dressed. He was wearing, obviously, an ankle-length velvet coat and chiffon by the yard. While they both affected surprise at meeting, they were, it turned out, each looking out for the other, in the way ambitious, networking musicians invariably do and, equally invariably, always deny doing. Nash had been warned by his friend David Crosby to look out for this twenty-four-year-old who had recently appeared out of nowhere with an improbable quantity of very good and very original songs. Crosby had produced her first LP *Song To A Seagull*, which came out that month, but in fact all he had to do with her songs was make sure the tape was running and otherwise stay out of the way.

Mitchell invited Nash back to her hotel room, which was lit by candles. She played him some of her songs. In all she played over fifteen of her songs. She played the whole of her first LP and quite a bit of what would be her second. The impact on Graham Nash was rather like that on a middling sixteenth-century wordsmith accidentally confronted by a young hopeful from the Midlands who asks if you'd like to hear some of his poems and then hits you with what would soon become world famous as Shakespeare's sonnets. In fact, in Mitchell's case it was arguably even more remarkable because she had the tunes and the tuning to go with them, and her delivery was so certain. Plus she was clearly singing about her life so what she was offering was more than entertainment. This was everything Nash wanted to do with music and had been unable to do in the Hollies. He thought what every other musician who heard Joni Mitchell in those years must have thought. Can I possibly do something like this? Can I mine my own life and experience in the way this woman has done? His mind must have been racing as she sang 'Nathan La Franeer'. How could anyone possibly get such drama from the name of a driver on a cab ride to the airport? What he probably underestimated was how highly wrought these songs were and how much sweat she had put into making them sound as though the experience had just tumbled out of her. Anyway, 'by the time she got to "Michael From Mountains" and "I Had A King" I was gone,' Nash recalled later. 'I had never heard music like that.'

It didn't turn out to be a purely professional encounter. Nash also stayed the night. But this was not the common-or-garden travelling rock star infidelity such as Nash had enjoyed on a regular basis since becoming well known. This was now research. He had now entered a new and very exclusive stratum of society. In this new world of singer-songwriters, the people who mined their personal lives for material, everybody, it seemed, slept with everybody else and it was considered almost rude not to write a song about it. Later the same year he returned to New York where he hoped to hook up with her again. This time he found she was seeing Leonard Cohen. His immediate way to salve his disappointment was by writing a song called 'Letter To A Cactus Tree' which incorporated the line 'competing with a poet for your favours'. He was clearly beginning to get the hang of it.

Meanwhile, as far as his day job was concerned, it was back to the road. Unlike the Beatles, the Hollies didn't have the luxury of being able to give up playing live and devote themselves to creating in the studio. They didn't sell enough albums to do that. Unlike the Who, they wouldn't get invited to play the big festivals or the new prestige rock venues. The Hollies had to survive by being adaptable above all things. In this they had a history. When they had been booked by Morris Levy to play the Paramount in New York in 1964 they were told they wouldn't be required to do their usual hour-long show. Instead they would be required to play just two numbers. What was really novel was they would be required to play these same two numbers ten times a day.

In the summer of 1968, not long after Graham Nash had his fateful meeting with Joni Mitchell in Ottawa, I saw the Hollies playing a residency at Batley Variety Club. This was a vast, Vegas-style lounge in a car park in the shadow of the darkest, most Satanic mills in West Yorkshire. The Hollies were good. The Hollies were always good. Of all the beat groups of the 1960s they were probably the most reliable live performers. What they didn't have was mystique, that magic ingredient which makes some groups a great deal more than the sum of their parts. Tragically, mystique was the quality Graham Nash envied most. It was the quality he saw in his new Californian friends, David Crosby and Mama Cass. He had tried. He had been with his wife Rose to Morocco where they followed the hippy trail, albeit at a safe distance. This had inspired him to write a song called 'Marrakesh Express' which his fellow Hollies felt wouldn't work for them. They were right. Nobody would buy a group from Salford singing about striped djellabas we can wear at home. The Hollies had built their career by making music for their audience. The new groups, having smoked a great deal of dope, made music for themselves.

At the Batley Variety Club, as an audience of car salesmen and hairdressers drank Double Diamond and grazed on scampi and chips, the Hollies delivered their club set. Lots of hits, faultlessly harmonized. A handful of covers. Some comic patter. They explained Bobby Elliott's wearing a cowboy hat by saying 'he has a head for figures – there's a slot in the top'. It was a show rooted in the entertainment tradition of the waning decade, designed to please everyone. This was the exact opposite of lots of the shows that were gaining ground after Monterey. These were designed to please only the newly converted.

What I couldn't know was how painful Graham Nash was finding the experience. He was like a husband who has decided to leave his wife for another woman but was meanwhile compelled to accompany her to a number of family functions. After one of these Batley shows Nash took off the white suit and floppy bow tie which was the band's outfit when they were playing for young marrieds in the West Riding of Yorkshire, went back to the Oulton Grange Hotel, which overlooked a golf course on the outskirts of Leeds, cracked open the hash he had painstakingly secreted among his luggage, took out his guitar and wrote 'Lady Of The Island' and the beginning of 'Teach Your Children'.

Graham Nash had reached a fork in the road. On one side there was the opportunity to continue as an artisan. On the other, as he and most of the music world saw it, was an opportunity to claim the prestige of an artist. What decided him was a chance meeting at the end of August 1968. Taking advantage of a short break in the Hollies' schedule he flew to Los Angeles to be with Joni Mitchell, who was now living in Laurel Canyon. When he rang her from the airport she told him that David Crosby and Stephen Stills were with her. When he got there, Crosby and Stills sang one of the songs they had been working on together and Nash chimed in with a high harmony. They were all enraptured by the effect.

It took him the rest of the year to leave the Hollies. The other four felt betrayed. His final show with them was a benefit called

Save Rave. Nash inevitably had hoped it would feature them along-side the Beatles and Jimi Hendrix. Equally inevitably it in fact featured them alongside the Easybeats and the Love Affair. It was his last gig with Clarke, his musical partner for ten years. He wore a dinner jacket and stood in the receiving line to meet Princess Margaret. David Crosby turned up in the Hollies' dressing room where he showcased his legendary diplomacy. Nobody said a word to the audience about Nash's departure, which was remarkable considering how rare such departures were in those days. The fol-lowing morning he set off for New York. He had his acoustic guitar with him. Everything else – equipment, wife, houses, contract and money – he left behind.

He spent the day after Christmas flying to Florida with his new girlfriend Joni Mitchell. The term 'girlfriend' would have seemed laughably quaint and English in the new milieu in which he would soon find his way and alter his speaking voice. As would the expres-sion 'Boxing Day'. It surely had been a long trip from Ordsal Board School. It would get even stranger in the years ahead.

13

'Squeeze my lemon till the juice runs down my leg'

On 4 January 1969 the Jimi Hendrix Experience turned up at the BBC studios at Lime Grove in Shepherd's Bush. They were booked for a live appearance on *Happening for Lulu*. The time slot was early Saturday evening. This may have been the year of Woodstock and Altamont but most TV was decidedly square. The music show was scheduled to follow an episode of *The Lucille Ball Show* whose hilarious premise was that the star wore a trouser suit and danced like a youngster. It was followed by an episode of *The Morecambe and Wise Show* where their musical guests were Kenny Ball & His Jazzmen. It was two years after the Summer of Love but this was still the predominant flavour of popular entertainment.

Things on the show didn't go according to plan. The story that bassist Noel Redding subsequently told was that Hendrix was informed that he would have to duet with Lulu on the play-out tune 'Hey Joe', that he was too polite to object and so he got round it by interrupting their version of 'Hey Joe' and announcing that he was going to play a tribute to Cream, who had just announced they were splitting. This unscheduled detour into 'Sunshine Of Your Love' forced the show to overrun slightly and kept the news waiting. As was becoming traditional on these occasions, the band were told they would never work again. It was unheard of for the smooth running of a network TV show to be interrupted by anyone, let alone a beat group.

The idea of doing a duet with the performer who had his or her name above the title was not in any way unusual at the time. Later in 1969 Tom Jones duetted with Crosby, Stills, Nash & Young on the Welsh singer's big-rating TV show in the States. At the same time Scott Walker was starring in his own variety show on BBC. It had been accepted ever since the Beatles had made their breakthrough thanks to *The Ed Sullivan Show* that if you wanted to be on TV you had to play by TV's rules. 1969 was the year when that began to change. The Hendrix/Lulu incident was an early straw in the wind. The new breed of rock bands who were making the running would no longer have much truck with TV because TV could no longer deal with how big they were, how wilful they were and increasingly how loud they were. By the end of 1969 Led Zeppelin, who were all three of those things, had proved it was possible to become almost as big as the Beatles without needing television at all.

The Yardbirds had broken up at the end of 1967 at the close of an American tour. To mark the occasion they took a picture of their manager Peter Grant posing with the dollar bills they had earned in its course. Jimmy Page was determined to carry on with a new group. The first person he asked to be the lead singer of his new band was Terry Reid. Terry had been tipped for success by lots of people. He could play guitar and he could sing. However, his true X factor was that he was handsome; certainly as handsome as you could ever wish a rock star to be. Rock star handsome is not the same as film star handsome or pop star handsome. Rock star handsomeness requires the pretence that your appearance is the furthest thing from your mind. You need to act as though you're far too busy pursuing your trade to give a thought to whether you look handsome or not. This is how you come to look rock star handsome.

Terry had just signed a contract as a solo artist so he passed on the offer, thereby condemning himself to a lifetime of assuring interviewers that he really, genuinely had no regrets. Being a nice guy, he suggested that Page ought to try a guy called Robert Plant whom he'd seen playing with a band in the Midlands.

'Is he good-looking?' asked Page.

'What's that got to do with it?' said Reid.

In that simple exchange, which goes some way to explaining how come fifty years later Jimmy Page resides in a listed building in the most expensive part of London while the last time I saw Terry Reid he was lodging temporarily at the home of his accountant, is the nub of what made Led Zeppelin arguably the most successful English band in the USA. By the time they were through there was no single photograph that could ever have encompassed the amount of cash they took from the country. They took more money out of the US economy than the Beatles did and they did it in a very different way. Whereas the Beatles had charmed America, Led Zeppelin ravished it.

Led Zeppelin were hand-tooled for America. From the beginning they had a following in the UK but America was always where they seemed to belong. Even in their early days in the late sixties when they were still playing pubs in the UK and hippy dancehalls in the USA, intimacy was never their speed; from the very beginning there was something about them and their music that seemed to be reaching out to new dimensions, to a form of entertainment of unprecedented loudness, to a species of presentation that would be a stranger to all forms of modesty, to a sort of music that seemed to have little to do with the lives lived by the audience and everything to do with the Viking grandeur represented by the men stalking the stage. They needed America, not merely because it was the biggest market, not merely because it was where you could make more money in a night than you could make in a week in the UK; they needed America because it gave them a focus. It gave them something to consume, to conquer, to subdue. They sacked the cities of the American plain. They plundered the nation's treasure houses, leaving nothing on the table. Their attitude was, from the very beginning, forged in Peter Grant's tours with the Animals and tempered by Jimmy Page's time with the fracturing Yardbirds. We bend the knee to nobody. Not to record companies, not to radio, not to promoters. They carried themselves like an invading army and did many of the things traditionally done by invading armies, albeit in a different sphere. They had their leader delivered on a room service trolley to a bunch of groupies, as though he were a rare delicacy. They worked their way through the most expensive delicacies on the menus of the toniest hotels and then demanded egg and chips with brown sauce. Such are the not always attractive appetites of the wealthy English abroad. This sort of thing was Led Zeppelin all over.

All bands have mixed motivations. Only in the case of Led Zeppelin was the motivation to accumulate cash quite so high in the mix. Their manager Peter Grant had seen enough bands out-earned by their promoters to be determined to do business in a very different way. Led Zeppelin would no longer work for the promoters. The promoters would in future work for Led Zeppelin. Page, for his part, had seen enough with the Yardbirds to know that if you wished to make money you went where there were the most people with the most money, and that meant the United States. As soon as he could, after trying things out in laughably small London pubs like the Fishmongers Arms in Wood Green and Cooks Ferry Inn in Edmonton, where John Bonham's drum kit was too big to get on the stage, Grant pointed them at the place where their scale would count for something. Led Zeppelin knew what the Who had come to realize and the Beatles never wished to know: the way to really make money in America was to tour and tour and tour again.

Led Zeppelin is where the sixties come to an end. Led Zeppelin is where the rock business gets big. The Beatles had never really bothered about scale. Even when they played Shea Stadium it was essentially with the same equipment that they would use to play a theatre. They knew they were breaking the mould in attendances but in performance terms they didn't do anything different. They played for thirty-five minutes because why would anybody want more? They had an enhanced PA system of sorts but it was estimated that the crowd at Shea were producing 135 decibels. This was exactly twice as many dB as the sound equipment used by the band was capable of generating. It wasn't until 1965, when they were playing Ithaca in New York State where there were no screams, that the Rolling Stones actually got to hear themselves. 'Bloody awful we were,' remembered Bill Wyman.

By the beginning of 1970 that had all changed. It had changed so dramatically that the balance of power between audience and performer had fundamentally altered. There was now no noise an audience could possibly make which could be heard above the band. There was no longer any point in people screaming. The job of the audience was now to sit quietly during the music and then to applaud wildly at the end.

The person who more than anyone else changed this state of affairs was a gentleman from the East End of London called Charlie Watkins. Charlie, whose preferred instrument was the accordion, ran a firm called Watkins Electric Music whose initial letters were to become world famous as a synonym for loudness. He was already in his forties at the time and ran a business manufacturing and selling musical and electronic equipment. He was called upon to invent the first rock PA system for the Byrds when they came to Britain in 1965. After a lot of trial and error he managed to assemble something that worked. Charlie's was later the technology that made it possible for the Windsor Jazz Festival to have audiences of more than a few hundred. He it was who put together the PA system that the Rolling Stones used when they played Hyde Park in 1969. He came up with the first monitor to enable Roger Chapman of Family for the first time to hear himself above the band as he performed. He provided the sound system for Janis Joplin when she played in the UK and she was so impressed she paid for the same equipment to be delivered to her in the USA. In 1974, having accomplished a revolution, Charlie Watkins sold his factory, got out of the rock and roll business and devoted himself to his beloved accordion. Despite being a key figure in the conquest of America by loud British groups around the turn of the decade he'd never particularly liked rock and roll anyway.

By the time the Stones did a proper tour of America in 1969, when they first embraced this new culture of bigger/louder/greater by having their own butler announce them as 'the greatest rock and roll band in the world', Led Zeppelin were already in many ways the category leaders. On the 1969 tour Charlie Watts was complaining that for the first time he had to play for ninety minutes. Live performance was turning into an arms race. The Stones had to do that because Led Zeppelin were already inching towards the two-hour mark. This was said to be the minimum time Zeppelin required in order to do their stuff. In fact they often complained when the running orders of festivals meant that they had to keep it snappy. If everybody in the group couldn't do their solo spot, they groused, then it wasn't a proper Led Zeppelin show. This was when the new adjective of approval was 'incredible'. Only 'incredible', it seemed, could sum up the enormity of the new rock experience that you had just been exposed to. When your breath had been taken away by unimaginable volume, when you had been dazzled by extended displays of instrumental prowess, when you had been dazed by being exposed to sounds you had never previously heard, when the experience had been far beyond what you might have previously referred to as entertainment, then you could only fall back on the word 'incredible'.

The new rock, which was being spearheaded by the Who, was louder for a start. Much, much louder. When the Who played on *The Smothers Brothers Comedy Hour* in 1967, Keith Moon secreted explosives in his bass drum which were then triggered at the climax of 'My Generation'. Not even he knew how much explosive he had used but when it was detonated it shut down transmission of the show and left Pete Townshend with hearing damage which continues to this day. However, at the time the hunger for greater sensation came before anyone's concerns about public health. In Townshend's memoirs he notes that the drive for greater volume is driven first within bands – the bass player wants more amplification to be heard over the guitarist, who then retaliates in kind – and then between groups because volume is largely a matter of expenditure. At the same time Black Sabbath were coming out of Birmingham with a strapline on their ads that read 'makes Led Zeppelin sound like a kindergarten house band'.

Some of this was just a measured response to the fact that in America bands were starting to play larger venues which demanded to be filled with sound. Noddy Holder of Slade, one British success that never made a dent in the hide of middle America, remembered going to America for the first time in 1973, gazing upon the cavernous emptiness of one such venue in San Diego and wondering how it would be possible to fill it with sound. It was only when he saw the headliner Humble Pie setting up their gear with microphones positioned to convey the sound of individual amplifiers into the PA mix that he realized they did things differently in this country. Holder took to watching Steve Marriott from the side of the stage to see how he managed to communicate with an audience who were increasingly likely to be stoned. There was no intimacy. This was a big show for a big space.

Led Zeppelin began with a plan hatched with their agent Frank Barsalona. They would start off playing dancehalls and hippy venues like the Fillmore theatres and the Boston Tea Party. Because their outgoings would cancel out the revenue they would lose money doing this but they would be gathering a following. It was a following that didn't rely on their records being played on the radio. What Led Zeppelin were about was the live experience. Because people tend to over-enthuse about live experiences on the grounds that they were there and the person they're enthusing to wasn't, this means that word of mouth is more powerful than press or radio can ever be. Therefore the idea was that when you came back to the same area you would play a bigger venue for more people and then you would start to make money. By the time of their fifth tour of America, which began in the spring of 1970, they were playing large indoor venues and they had decided that they no longer needed to have a support act.

Between them, Led Zeppelin and their agent invented the idea that the rock concert business was not only here to stay but it was also as profitable as any other branch of the legit business. Through his agency Premier Talent, Barsalona pioneered the idea of the rock concert as the main event, and he used British bands like Led Zeppelin and the Who, who were known for putting on the kind of show that left their audiences open-mouthed, as the spearhead of his efforts. If anybody could be said to have foreseen the concert business of today, where people pay huge sums to be able to say they've seen their favourites, it was Barsalona, though even he couldn't imagine that the top price of $5 in 1971 would be dwarfed by the hundreds of dollars people are prepared to pay today. In 1969 Led Zeppelin were playing America's many civic auditoriums, the kind of places the people had once attended to hear symphony orchestras or political speeches. Two years later they were playing arenas, the kind of facilities that sprung up all over the States whenever a ball team's owner threatened to relocate to another city. As the buildings got bigger, Led Zeppelin graduated from offering a performance to putting on a spectacle.

All the reviews of the shows on that tour touch on the same elements. The first was just how loud it was. The second was how so much of the two-and-a-half-hour show was devoted to extended displays of virtuosity, something that few had bothered to provide in the previous decade. The third was the age of the audience, who were universally agreed to be still in high school, which meant they were tapping into a younger generation than the people who'd flocked to the Beatles and the Stones. The fourth was that the reviewers, part of that generation who had flocked to the Beatles and the Stones, thought it was all a bit empty. What gets forgotten in the great Classic Rock Love-in of the twenty-first century is that musicians like Keith Richards and George Harrison really didn't care for Led Zeppelin at all. But what mattered most was the size of the venues and the numbers in them – 18,000 in Vancouver, 14,000 in Salt Lake City, 18,000 in Inglewood, 12,000 in Pittsburgh, 16,000 in Philadelphia. This meant that by the time they had all paid the ruinous ticket price of $5, somebody was making a lot of money. This was already ahead of Frank Barsalona's plan.

What none of the reviewers referred to was the thing that really recommended Led Zeppelin to America and the thing that Page had clearly already been thinking about when he asked Terry Reid about whether Robert Plant was good-looking: sex. Right from the beginning Led Zeppelin were more closely identified with the notion of sex than any other band, and this applied particularly when they were out there somewhere in America plying their profitable trade and getting away with things that nobody else in the world would be able to get away with.

'On tour' had previously referred to the tiresome necessity of getting between cities in order to play shows. With the late sixties tours of the big English rock groups, the Who, the Rolling Stones and most of all Led Zeppelin, 'on tour' began to be seen in the public mind as an end in itself. It was a reference to a fabulous new means of permanent escape from tiresome duty, a roller coaster of sensation, a subsidized caravanserai of drink, drugs and debauchery from which no sane twenty-year-old man would ever wish to be delivered. And while the young male fans could afford their own drink and obtain their own drugs, it was the debauchery they really wished to know more about.

There had always been sex on rock and roll tours but it was rarely brought into the light. The Los Angeles scene-maker Kim Fowley claimed that the first time he saw a groupie in action was at Manfred Mann's hotel in Los Angeles in 1965. 'Her name was Liz. She was about eighteen years old. She was the first girl I ever saw walk into a hotel room for the express purpose of fucking a rock star. She said, "Do you know Paul Jones in Manfred Mann?" I said, "Yeah." And she said, "Well, I want to fuck him."'

The year before Liz's entrance this had not been the way nice girls behaved. The first time the Beatles came to New York in 1964 they stayed at the Plaza Hotel. Following that the management decided they didn't need any further disruption and so on later visits they stayed at the Warwick. In her memoir *Be My Baby*, Ronnie Spector remembers being invited to visit the Beatles at the Warwick with her fellow Ronettes. The Beatles had taken over an entire floor which was transformed into one huge bachelor apartment. Food and drink of all kinds was permanently available. TVs were left on in every room. In every room there was a record player. The latest 45s were strewn across the floor. It looked like the living quarters of four teenagers whose parents had left them alone for the weekend and before they left had provided them with sufficient spending cash to slake absolutely any of their appetites.

Despite having huge hits on both sides of the Atlantic and having toured with the Rolling Stones, the twenty-year-old Ronnie Spector was still a virgin. Later in the evening, when the Beatles' people began to clear the room and the other Ronettes began to slip away, Ronnie remained. She was still there when people began drifting in the direction of one of the bedrooms. When John Lennon took her hand and they followed the crowd she found they were all watching one member of the Beatles' entourage having adventurous intercourse with a woman of around twenty while another member of their entourage took pictures. Lennon helped himself to the only real chair in the room and pulled Ronnie on to his lap. She was soon aware of his arousal. 'I may have been dumb back then but I knew when it was time to get up off a guy's lap. So I did.'

As she points out in her book, this was 1964, and back then you couldn't watch people having sex in a film, let alone watch them being filmed. The fastest and most consequential sexual revolution ever to take place anywhere was the one that raged through America in the years between the Beatles' arrival at JFK in 1964 and the Woodstock Festival of 1969. It was just five short years, roughly the duration of a parliament. Some people say that pop music caused it. What's beyond doubt is that pop music was at the centre of it.

In November 1968 a piece by Ellen Sander ran in a New York underground paper called *The Realist*. Sander was one of the first women rock journalists and had watched with interest the emergence of a new tribe who were happy to be referred to as groupies. She understood that they were fans of the musicians but what they really craved was the status that came with being seen with – and sometimes being seen to have sex with – their heroes. She noted that they were pickier than their detractors might think. In their estimation lead singers clearly had more prestige than bass players, and singers who wrote their own songs were the most sexually desirable of all. In that respect groupies have more in common with rock critics than the latter would care to admit.

The groupies had egos too. They were similarly keen on being recognized for their work. There were the Hollywood girls who called themselves Miss Christine and Miss Pamela as though they were characters in a nineteenth-century novel. Frank Zappa, who considered groupies a wonderful manifestation of the sexual revolution and even hired them to babysit his children, had encouraged them to form a group called the GTOs (which stood for Girls Together Outrageously). They were quite happy to be known for sleeping with rock stars.

Pete Townshend had noticed this phenomenon when touring the American continent with the Who in 1967. In his autobiography he recalls the 'extremely good-looking, effervescently crazy' girl whom someone had invited on to the tour bus between Toronto and Edmonton. When Keith Moon tied her to a seat with loose ribbons and pretended to rape her he tried to intervene only to be told to fuck off. By the girl. Moon and the band's bass player John Entwistle then paid the girl a thousand dollars to sleep with Townshend, after which he contracted gonorrhoea and did what an increasing number of travelling English rockers did in those days: had the injection. This and the whole groupie experience was a rite of passage for most of the touring musicians of his generation. For some, like Entwistle, who eventually expired in the bed of a stripper in Paradise, Nevada, in 2002, old habits clearly died hard.

In 1969 groupies hunted in packs. For her piece, Sander met Cynthia and Dianne, who were so keen to be known as the Plastercasters of Chicago that they actually handed out business cards announcing themselves as such. These two, she noted, were slightly more rounded and Midwestern than their bony Hollywood sisters. It could be that they came up with the idea of getting rock stars to pose while they made a mould from which they could create a plaster statue of their penis because pulchritude alone might not be enough to see them admitted backstage or into a band's hotel. What was most surprising about the Plastercasters was their clear preference for English penises.

In the course of their work they had learned a somewhat imperfect lexicon of English slang terms relating to body parts and bodily functions. This is why they had written to a wide range of English musical talent, from the Beatles down to Mandala, and asked if they would be interested in having their Hampton Wicks preserved for posterity. They happily explained the process to Sander. One of them mixed the dental alginates which ensured that every bump and vein would be faithfully translated. As this was going on, the other dispassionately fellated the celebrated musician into the tumescence required to put his manhood into the material. From then on it was a race against time to make sure that the penis didn't soften before the plaster hardened. A list of their clients read like Saturday night at the Isle of Wight Festival: Jimi Hendrix, Procol Harum, Traffic, the Who and Jeff Beck. They laughed about how they had become famous even though some straight people – most older people – couldn't believe what they actually used the plaster for. In fact the straight media was so off the pace when it came to the things that actually went on that when the Yardbirds had come to town in 1967 the *Chicago Tribune* said they'd come along to make a plastercast of Jeff's leg! People knew that the girls of 1969 were a good deal more forward than the girls of 1964 but they wouldn't have believed exactly what that for-wardness might entail.

In 1968, *Rolling Stone* published its own report on the groupie phenomenon and it was such a successful part of the paper that they put it out as a paperback. The first groupie interviewed, Kyle, was also said to 'prefer Britishers'. 'I think a lot of my interest in English musicians is that they are completely different,' she said. 'Their personalities are different; the way they've been brought up is different. I like English musicians not only because of the sex trip but they're very uninhibited. They're not hung up on masculinity. English musicians can joke around and have fun. Put their arms around each other and pinch each other on the ass. They wrestle a lot. American males just stick with their dope.'

John Woolf, tour manager for the Who at this time, recalled, 'America is unreal to an Englishman. The biggest thing about America was the sex drive. It was always, "quick, we've got to get to LA". New York was OK. Chicago had the Plaster Casters, but the tours were always looking forward to LA. It was like looking for-ward to Christmas.' He also says that Keith Moon loved America because 'the women were so much looser. Every time you turned round one of them wanted to give you head.'

Marianne Faithfull noted that the attentions of Los Angeles groupies would inevitably result in a change in sexual expectations among rock star boyfriends. According to her memoirs, after one visit to the city where his every whim was attended to Mick Jagger tried to interest her in the idea of ice-cream-flavoured douches. She reflected that it would be middle class to complain about her rock star boyfriend getting his sexual appetites slaked by Hollywood women, and besides, she knew that she couldn't compete with what they were happy to do.

The gods of the British Invasion celebrated fellatio, the kind of sexual privilege that was freely available to them but could only be got by mere mortals when there was a ring and a mortgage involved. It was celebrated in the title of the Emerson, Lake & Palmer album *Brain Salad Surgery*, the working zip incorporated in the cover of the Rolling Stones' *Sticky Fingers*, Mick Ronson's 'going down' on David Bowie on stage during the Ziggy Stardust tour, the giant inflatable phallus with which the Stones climaxed their show on the 1975 tour, the Led Zeppelin song that exhorted the beloved to squeeze his lemon until the juice ran down his leg, and the old roadies' challenge which went 'no head, no backstage pass'. Sexual subjection was the price of admission to the royal court.

The term 'cock rock' was first used by feminists in 1970 but in truth it wasn't properly invented until 1978 when Deep Purple had broken up and their singer David Coverdale, who aped Plant's leonine mane and focus on the crotch, formed a group whose second album had a cover which featured a naked woman sitting astride an enormous serpent. The group were called Whitesnake, which clearly meant 'penis' even for those who were a bit slow when it came to metaphors.

There was a golden period of about three years, roughly between the Rolling Stones' *Sticky Fingers* and Led Zeppelin's *Physical Graffiti*, when – thanks to a magical conjunction of their hairless chests, their chiselled chins and their rent boy trousers, with music that was an unapologetically lubricious, tail-dragging reinvention of rock and roll, all stamped with the charm of their native unwillingness to take anything wholly seriously – it was widely agreed that the sexiest thing on earth you could be was an English rock star. Between the two aforementioned groups, plus the Who and Bad Company, it seemed for a while that the impossible had been achieved. The nation of back-to-backs and cobbled streets which had brought forth George Formby and Gracie Fields, the homeland to which Basil Radford and Naunton Wayne had fought their way in order to catch a Test match, the battered old island which had been kept safe for democracy by Kenneth More and John Mills, the diamond set in a silver sea which for years had considered the most excitement its small children could take was Muffin the Mule, the country which even at this late date still had a grand total of three television channels all of which closed down before midnight, was suddenly, unaccountably, thrillingly seen as sexy. As these hollow-cheeked heroes, whose ages were still under the thirty-year mark, who had no need of the personal trainer or special diet to stay in trim, were pictured tripping on and off monogrammed planes – wreathed in chiffon scarves, their coltish old ladies on their elbows, being wafted from one American city to the next, being delivered by limousine down the goods ramp of one sports arena or another while knots of high school kids looked on enthralled – they seemed like members of some new, impossibly glamorous tribe. There is a picture of Keith Richards snapped in 1972, at the precise moment that he achieved peak Keef. He is leaning on a wall at the American border, no doubt as a pack of dogs go through his luggage. He is festooned with scarves. He is wearing mirror shades. He is exquisitely bored. The photographer has asked him to stand next to a sign which says, 'Patience, please. A drug-free America comes first.' It seems to represent the moment at which the classic image of the rock star was perfected and, what's more, it was perfected in the shape of an Englishman.

In 1969 it seemed as though a new sexual stereotype was being born. This derived from England but somehow looked its best when in the sunshine and plenty of the United States. It was such a powerful stereotype and so popular with the young women of America that in retrospect it seems amazing that a company like Mattel didn't take the opportunity to launch a toy called 'English Rock Star' to do battle with GI Joe in the action figure market. With their glistening chests, cascading ringlets and tiny waists, with microphone stands appearing to grow from their crotches, English singers like Robert Plant and Roger Daltrey offered a potent new twist on the traditional male sex symbol. They looked like swordsmen and carried themselves like scaffolders. They looked like Romantic poets but even the tiniest scratch betrayed the bit of rough beneath.

Because there weren't a great deal of prominent female stars at the time – the only women at the Woodstock Festival, which happened that August, were Janis Joplin and Joan Baez – if you wanted sex appeal it was the men you looked to. This may be difficult to imagine from the standpoint of the present era, where most of the biggest stars in popular music are female, but such was the case.

Miss Pamela of the GTOs was there in August 1969 when Led Zeppelin came into town. In her memoirs she describes the preparatory preening that took place in the hen house prior to the arrival of the cocks. 'When Led Zeppelin was due to hit town, the groupie section went into the highest gear possible; you could hear garter belts sliding up young thighs all over Hollywood. Led Zeppelin was a formidable bunch, disguised in velvets and satins, epitomizing the Glorious English Pop Star to perfection; underneath the flowing curls and ruffles lurked slippery, threatening thrill bumps.'

She was in a club called Thee Experience trying to pretend she was not waiting for them to arrive:

Robert Plant was the first to walk in, tossing his gorgeous lion's mane into the faces of enslaved sycophants. He walked like royalty, his shoulders thrown back, declaring his mighty status in this lowly little club. He was followed by the king of rowdy glaring roadies, Richard Cole, who seemed to be scanning the room for likely-looking jailbait. They were surrounded in seconds by seductive ready-willing-and-able girls, who piled up at their table like clusters of grapes going bad. I was noticing that the whole group was there except for Mr Page, when Richard Cole stumbled over and handed me a scrap of paper with Jimmy's number at the Continental Hyatt House scribbled on it. He leaned into me and mumbled thickly in my ear, 'He's waiting for you.'

Word soon got back home. That wasn't the kind of thing that happened to bands in Doncaster. But it was soon the very kind of thing the bands at home were discussing excitedly over pints in the Ship in Wardour Street or across the tomato-shaped sauce dispensers at the Blue Boar on the M1 in the middle of the night. This was more like it. This sounded like the life. Not surprising, then, that in the following year it seemed that every English band that could consider themselves in any way volume dealers – Savoy Brown, Ten Years After, John Mayall & the Bluesbreakers, Jethro Tull, Mott the Hoople, Joe Cocker and his Grease Band, Pink Floyd, Blodwyn Pig, Humble Pie, Black Sabbath, the Faces, yea, even Toe Fat – inserted their still-flat stomachs into their most preposterous loon pants and headed for America. Thanks to the example of Led Zeppelin they travelled with hope in their hearts and a dream in their trousers.

14

'Blue jean baby, LA lady'

Since the very first Englishman presumed to think of launching himself as a rock and roll singer it had been assumed that the very first thing he would have to do, if this transformation were to have the remotest chance of taking place, was change his name. In the 1950s manager Larry Parnes had demanded that every member of his stable of would-be rock talent from England abandon the greengrocers' names with which they had been issued at the register office and adopt instead some surname that had the thrusting qualities associated with the New World. In this manner Reg Smith became Marty Wilde and Ronald Wycherley would henceforth be known as Billy Fury.

Such changes weren't always decreed by managers. Every bit as often it was a case of the individual concerned looking at his birth certificate and concluding that what he read there was simply inconsistent with his chosen profession. Much as would-be conjurors or wrestlers concluded that they couldn't possibly pursue their chosen trade unless they were known as the Great Marvo or the Beast, the young Harry Webb simply had to become Cliff Richard before he could put his name on the label of a record, and his guitarist Brian Rankin would be obliged to re-enter the room one fateful day and announce himself as Hank Marvin. It was the least they could do to recognize the essentially American nature of the trade they were entering.

This need to pass themselves off as American continued well into the sixties. When the unknown Beatles backed Johnny Gentle on a tour of Scotland in 1960, Paul McCartney briefly styled himself as Paul Ramon, obviously feeling that if he hoped to cut a figure as a rock star he had to begin with a name that smacked less of Liverpool. When the Rolling Stones signed to Decca in 1963 their manager Andrew Loog Oldham unilaterally removed the terminal consonant from their guitarist's second name, reasoning that Keith Richard was rock star-edgy whereas Keith Richards was merely butcher's boy-cosy. The Stones' bassist Bill had already, without having to be told, swapped his given name of Perks for Wyman, a name that had something of the whiff of the frontier about it. At around the same time, for similar reasons, Liverpool drummer Richard Starkey became Ringo Starr, and the drummer of the Searchers, with even greater urgency, changed his name from Christopher Crummey to Chris Curtis. If you were a lead singer the need to change your name to something with a little swagger to it became somehow even more pressing. Thus the singer of Manfred Mann had decided early on that he could no longer be known as Paul Pond, opting instead for Paul Jones, a name redolent of piracy and the American War of Independence. Jones was also the choice of a new surname for belter of the valleys Tom. It might not be entirely impossible to imagine the words 'Thomas Woodward' on a Vegas marquee but it seems foolish to saddle yourself with it when it could be changed at the stroke of an agent's pen.

Those beat boom bands emerging from the north-west of England at the time, those who billed the singer separately, were the first to ditch their given names for fear they'd cramp their styles. By presenting themselves as Gerry and the Pacemakers or Freddie and the Dreamers they could avoid the cobbled-street connotations of names like Marsden and Garrity; in this way William Ashton could be reborn as the chromium-plated Billy J. Kramer in front of his backing band the Dakotas, David Grundy could translate himself into Dave Berry, Fred Heath might re-emerge as Johnny Kidd, and Glyn Ellis could open his arms and advance towards the spotlight as Wayne Fontana, which was a surname he borrowed from Elvis Presley's drummer, a surname for which you will search in vain in the parish records of Levenshulme.

Some groups had names that referred to places they could only have known from atlases. The Nashville Teens came from Woking in Surrey, the Stormsville Shakers from Guildford. One Scottish group looking for the name of a suitably American city to come before 'Rollers' threw a dart at a map of the USA which landed near Bay City, Michigan, while a north London group searching for some transatlantic fairy dust took the name of the house in which they rehearsed, added the American term for a political conference and became Fairport Convention.

When David Jones of Brixton had to change his name because fellow Englishman Davy Jones of the Monkees had beaten him to fame, he adopted 'Bowie'. Jones was a member of that generation of English boys who had grown up with a toy holster and a cap gun at their hips and had somehow absorbed as much American history as British. Reasoning that nobody with the surname Baldwin would ever become a rock star, the session player and arranger John swapped his name for John Paul Jones, a name with Revolutionary

War associations. These people intuited that America conferred status in a way that Britain did not, which is why the names of so many best-sellers begin with the word 'American' and so few of them begin with the word 'British'. 'American' didn't simply denote nationality. Where music was concerned it also denoted authenticity. Authenticity is the one quality that everyone in rock and roll most urgently needs to fake.

It was in the winter of 1967, during a particularly dispiriting run at the Club Latino in South Shields – a name that pulses with all the yearning the English grow up feeling for warmer climes – that Reg Dwight of Pinner decided he'd had enough of playing keyboards in the backing band of Long John Baldry. Not only was he determined to go out on his own but he was going to go out on his own under a new name he had just invented, comprised of the first name of the band's saxophonist and the first name of its six-foot-seven, extravagantly camp singer. Dwight truly picked his time to unveil the plan he had been hatching for some while. Like a balding man determined not to postpone the reckoning of his first public outing with his new toupee, Reg announced the results of his personal rebranding exercise to the other members of Bluesology while on a bus taking them from Heathrow airport after a very cold tour of Scotland. They responded as any bunch of English musicians would to news that one of their number would no longer be known as Reg Dwight, which was a perfectly good name for a jobbing joiner, but instead as Elton John, a name that glinted with Western Promise, a name that would surely never be associated with any form of manual labour, a name that was as good as an announcement that he would henceforth be getting above his station: they laughed openly.

It took a while for his new name to settle in with his contacts in the music business, among whom he was known for being a good session piano player and also the kind of record nerd who could be easily compensated by being allowed to help himself to promos from the cupboard. For such a ferreter after vinyl, Reg seemed the perfect name. He soon linked up with a seventeen-year-old from Lincolnshire called Bernie Taupin, who had written to the same record company offering his poems as lyrics. The pair were so poor they moved back into Elton's mother's home in Pinner where, between trips into the West End to rifle the import bins in Musicland in Soho and take advantage of any opportunity to sit with successful musicians and pick up tips, they began to write songs.

Their modus operandi was unique because it all started with Taupin's lyrics. Once he had finished the words, which were effectively poems, he handed them to Elton, who composed a tune and devised a way of singing them. This meant that the direction of their music was dictated by whatever happened to be capturing the imagination of Bernie at the time. A lot of that inspiration came from hanging around in record shops. A lot of that inspiration came from a place they had never been to and never really expected to go to. America.

As the sixties came to a close America was waking from its near decade-long infatuation with first England and then psychedelia and rediscovering the ancient consolations of a new kind of patriotism. At this time the taste-makers, who were without exception based on the coasts, began to look back to the places from which they had come and hanker for the Real America, which they contrasted with the meretricious values of the fleshpots in which they had fetched up. Acts that had previously wanted to record in San Francisco or New York now boasted of how they'd made their new one in Nashville, Tennessee, or Muscle Shoals, Alabama. Only there, they argued, did they feel in touch with the Real America. The covers of these records began to show the signs of this new orientation. They featured the artists leaning against ancient barns that seemed about to fall down or posing alongside elderly relatives who had no teeth and had clearly worked with their hands.

These were the gold rush years following *Sgt Pepper*, when LP sales were rising dramatically year on year, when the music business was starting to learn from the packaged goods business, when records began to appear in jackets that projected the ambitions of the musicians far ahead of the actual music. These covers were catnip to young record collectors like Elton John and Bernie Taupin back in London, who became besotted by this ageless-seeming music that was hidden away in these inscrutable packages. They pored over *Déjà Vu* by Crosby, Stills, Nash & Young in which the band arrayed themselves like Civil War soldiery, and the first solo album of Leon Russell from which he stared out like an unforgiving preacher man. They spent hours looking at the Flying Burrito Brothers posing in their Nudie finery in a junk yard for *The Gilded Palace Of Sin*, at the old man on the cover of *Uncle Charlie And His Dog Teddy* by the Nitty Gritty Dirt Band, at the erstwhile psychedelic adventurers the Grateful Dead apparently waiting for a bus on *Workingman's Dead*, at the patched denim on the back cover of Neil Young's *After The Gold Rush* and, most of all, at the first two albums by the Band. All this seemed to speak to these two boys in Pinner.

In the years 1969 and 1970 those first two albums by the Band reset the compasses of many prominent musicians. Eric Clapton said that hearing them was what made him want to step away from Cream and do something more modest. George Harrison was so struck by them that he went to Woodstock to discover more of this strange land that had given birth to their new/old sound. It wasn't just the superstars who were taken by songs like 'The Weight' and 'The Night They Drove Old Dixie Down'. They also suddenly pointed the way forward for the blamelessly obscure Reg and his friend Bernie in Pinner. They had previously been unsuccessfully trying to write hits for balladeers like Engelbert Humperdinck or self-consciously searching for a voice they could call their own. This gave them a way of doing neither. In his autobiography *Me*, Elton John credits the first two Band albums with being 'like somebody switching a torch on and showing us a new path to follow, a way we could do what we wanted to do'.

In this time they wrote the songs that dominated *Elton John*, which was his real debut album, *Tumbleweed Connection* and *Madman Across The Water*. These records became respectively their attempt to woo America, their attempt to imagine America and their attempt to reflect the actual experience of having at last gone to America. This was the period that brought forth 'Border Song', 'Country Comfort', 'Tiny Dancer' and scores of other songs about the American experience that the Americans had somehow never got round to writing. It was the greatest repudiation of the injunction to 'write what you know' anywhere in the performing arts. It was the most successful example of cultural appropriation in the history of popular music.

The two boys worked their bizarre magic in separate rooms. Bernie would be in one, his typewriter presumably set to American Gothic, hammering away at lyrics about hot-blooded young men who were a century, thousands of miles and many degrees of latitude removed from Pinner, men who were resolved to take up their father's gun, don the grey of 'the cause' and head to New Orleans where they had it on good authority the old South would make its last stand. Taupin would rip them off the roller of his typewriter and hand them to Elton at the piano in the next room where they would be instantly put through the mill of his new style, which involved sieving everything he had ever learned, from his piano lessons at the Royal Academy of Music to his many sessions recording covers of novelty songs for budget labels, through the fine mesh of the first two albums by Leon Russell. All over the world at the time musicians who had been to the edge of psychedelia, peered over and seen naught but empty self-indulgence, were seizing on the perceived authenticity of the Band as a bold new direction. It nonetheless beggars belief that the most feverish traffic in the rolling cadences of gospel-influenced rock music and near-seditious ideas about the Civil War and Reconstruction should at the time have been emanating from a three-bedroom semi in north-west London.

These were the dog days of the British record business, the age of Mungo Jerry and Edison Lighthouse. At the time it appeared there were only two ways for a new act to break through in the UK. You could be a pop group that might get a chart hit or you could become an underground hit by being big on the college circuit. If you belonged in neither basket, and particularly if you happened to be playing what sounded like American music without happening to be American, then there was only one way to do it: launch yourself in America where, it was held, there was a market for this kind of thing and then hope that the spectacle of you doing so would help you take off in your native land. It was like trying to do in the USA what the Walker Brothers and Jimi Hendrix had done in the UK.

Not everyone was successful. In April 1970 a group of hopeful country-rockers who called themselves Brinsley Schwarz and were backed by some investors hoping to be able to break into the music business had tried to do this by getting themselves a down-the-bill support slot on a show at the Fillmore in New York. This was a venue which at that time was possessed of a unique cachet thanks to the number of live albums recorded there. The idea was to get this group on the bill at the Fillmore, fly over a load of English media to cover the event and have the venue deposit some of its famous charisma on these five very uncharismatic Englishmen.

In the event the jaunt was a logistical catastrophe, made immeasurably worse by the fact that both band and media were so intoxicated with the thrill of being in New York that they smoked and drank themselves into a state where they were no longer in a position to take advantage of the opportunity. The journalists couldn't think of anything particularly glowing to say about the band that had been the reason for the entire exercise but they did notice that when it came to live performance there seemed to be a competence gap opening up between America and Europe. The abiding memory of Nick Lowe, the bassist with the group, was listening to Van Morrison and his band who were headlining over them and realizing that when it came to the demands of performing live they were in another league altogether. Lowe was taking on board one of the great truths about the difference between British and American musicians. Whereas most of the former learn to play in order to do their own songs, most of the latter are more likely to have served some kind of apprenticeship as members of a bar band. Bar band was a term unknown in the UK at the time. Bar bands were expected to be able to play the songs that the people in the bar wished to dance to. To flourish in the world of bar bands demanded musicians who had a good ear, were quick studies and could stay in tune. You could hear all that hard-won expertise in the sound of the band backing Van Morrison.

Nick Lowe wasn't the only English musician waking up to this. The pub rock movement, which arose in London in 1971 when a bunch of London players were impressed by the American bar band Eggs Over Easy, who had visited the city on a tour supported by the American Embassy, was the English response. Brinsley Schwarz the group spent the next few years getting themselves into the order they should have been in when they undertook the trip. In 1974 the Band came to London to play and borrowed Brinsley Schwarz's headquarters to rehearse in. In Will Birch's book about Nick Lowe he recounts how as the Band played, the members of Brinsley Schwarz listened from outside like schoolboys granted a peek at first-team training. They had spent years trying to perfect the

Band's sound and had assumed they just didn't have the right equipment. They were amazed to hear that as soon as the Band picked up their equipment and played, they sounded like the Band.

Just as the dust was beginning to settle over the Brinsley Schwarz debacle, Dick James, who was first Elton John's publisher and then the head of his record label, proposed doing a similar thing. Elton had got some attention in England but not enough to launch him. He needed to happen in America first. Therefore it was proposed that Elton and his band should go all the way to Los Angeles and play a number of shows at the Troubadour. This was the fabled club where the likes of Joni Mitchell, Neil Young, Gordon Lightfoot and James Taylor had first been unveiled. You didn't play the Troubadour in order to reach the American public. You played the Troubadour to reach the people in the business. You played the Troubadour to create the illusion that you were happening and in order that you might happen. The idea was that if you wanted the chance to make an impact with three hundred million Americans you had to begin by making an impact with about twenty-five of them.

In 1970 it was clear that the Beatles were in the process of breaking up and so America was particularly susceptible to the promise of a replacement phenomenon from the same source. It so happened that Dick James had been the Beatles' publisher. In the light of that fact the PR plan couldn't have been simpler. *Le Tout Hollywood* must come out to the Troubadour and welcome the new signing from the man who brought us the Beatles.

In the USA, Elton's record company was owned by a film company, and movie companies believe in opening big or not at all. In the run-up to Elton's opening the company's PR man, Norman Winter, called Robert Hilburn, the music editor of the *Los Angeles Times*, every day for a week, to make sure he was going to be there to see this entirely unknown singer. Furthermore, Winter and his staff were at the airport to greet Elton's arrival with a London bus bearing the mortifying legend 'Elton John has arrived'. This vehicle then drove them to their hotel. If there is a slower way of negotiating the rush hour traffic in the city of Los Angeles than a double-decker London bus it has yet to be found. Elton and his party simmered with the embarrassment of being looked at by the locals and felt that they were being set up for humiliation on a grand scale.

The more they heard about the level of expectation that Norm Winter and his team had cranked up the sicker they felt. Norm's plan was that the artist, who was widely unknown on two continents, would be introduced on the first night by no less a figure than Neil Diamond. Diamond had already been responsible for 'I'm A Believer', 'Cracklin' Rosie', 'Sweet Caroline' and quite enough globe-girdling hits not to need to be pimping himself out as John the Baptist for some Limey messiah who had not yet graduated from bubbling under to the chart proper. For his own nerdish, Musicland-browsing, *ZigZag*-reading part, Bernie Taupin was deeply embarrassed at the fact that they were being supported at the Troubadour by David Ackles, the very American singer-songwriter whose Elektra LPs they had reverentially played on the home hi-fi with the two headphone sockets back in Pinner. This whole trip was shaping up like a giant practical joke. It appeared inevitable that they would be caught in the act of carrying coals to Newcastle, found guilty in the highest court of Impersonating Rock Stars, laughed out of Hollywood, put on the next double-decker bus to the airport and banished back to Blighty, there to resume their previous obscurity and for Elton to take up once again the abandoned mantle of Reg because, as all Englishmen know in their secret hearts, once a Reg, always a Reg.

Fifty years after it took place, the story of Elton John's subsequent opening at the Troubadour on 25 August 1970 was given a central place in *Rocketman*, the film inspired by the life and career of Elton John. The film played with the facts, because films are always slightly disappointed with the facts. The facts in this case are that it was the first of eight shows he played over six nights. Neil Diamond did indeed introduce him. Diamond was only the first of the stars that Norman had decreed the audience would be studded with. In the Troubadour that first night – to see an act who but a few weeks earlier had been entertaining underwhelmed audiences at St Mary's College in Twickenham and the Country Club on Haverstock Hill in London, and whose next big day in his British gig diary would be an actual support slot with the folk rock group Fotheringay – were Brian Wilson, Mike Love, Don Henley, Randy Newman, Quincy Jones, Linda Ronstadt, and Crosby, Stills and Nash. There were plenty of less famous people there who were nonetheless seasoned observers of how these things usually turn out. One such was the British pop songwriter Roger Greenaway, who later remembered, 'If Elton had died at the Troubadour, that would have been the end of it.'

For a while it looked like it might go that way. For the first few numbers Robert Hilburn, who had turned up in response to Norm Winter's incessant badgering, was convinced he was going to suffer just such a death. For a start Elton had taken the stage wearing some new clothes he had bought from the London boutique Mr Freedom. The bright yellow dungarees and matching workmen's boots with blue wings sprouting from them understandably threw people a little. This was not the costume of a singer-songwriter. Then they began. Elton and his well-rehearsed two-piece band were playing the songs efficiently enough but they weren't selling them in any way. The cover of the *Elton John* album had depicted a shadowy, introspective figure and that was what they appeared to be getting. The songs were OK but they were hardly prime enough steak to get by without sizzle.

And then something happened. Reaching into that deep well of

profound fear which animates all great live performances, the artist formerly known as Reg stood up, kicked the piano stool away in
that time-honoured tantrum of abandon pioneered by Little Richard and Jerry Lee Lewis, and accessed levels of energy he had not
previously believed he had. In his autobiography he claims that it
was the sight of Leon Russell, the man whose act he had shame-
lessly appropriated, surveying him from the second row that made
him do it. It may have been purely on the spur of the moment. It
may have been something he'd been thinking about. Fifty years
later the writer Richard Williams remembered meeting him that
August and being surprised to hear him say that he'd decided that
the quality he most needed was showmanship. This was as surprising to hear from Elton as it would have been to hear from Nick
Drake at the time. In later years Elton said, 'I really became Elton
John at the Troubadour that night. After that, there was no holding
me back, in a lot of senses.' He had learned an important lesson
about America. If you didn't want to die on stage you had to follow
the advice a Hamburg club owner had given the young Beatles a
decade earlier: *Mach Schau*!

It worked. Linda Ronstadt recalled, 'When he got to "Take Me
To The Pilot" the place levitated.' Bernie Taupin was looking at the
audience. 'It was almost movie-esque,' he remembered. 'People
were tentative to begin with, then came smiles, and then tumultuous applause. Robert Hilburn got it.'

Furthermore, he passed it on, because in those days that's what
newspapers could do. Under the headline 'New Rock Talent' Hilburn's review in the *Los Angeles Times* described Elton John's music
as 'staggeringly original', which was taking generosity a little far. In
terms of having an effect on his career it was certainly the most
powerful review he ever got. After that he didn't need much more.
Within days clubs and theatres around the country were wanting
to book him and his album was all over the FM radio. Hilburn's

was also probably the best review he ever had in his career. Dick James's plan had been to unveil him to the taste-makers and have them hand down their verdict to the great unwashed. He couldn't possibly have dared dream that it would work out as well as it did. Roger Greenaway remembers driving to LAX later that week and hearing a DJ say, 'We have a new messiah in town. His name is Elton John.' 'I don't think any one ever became that big, literally overnight, in America.'

In the wake of the tour 'Your Song' was released as a single and became a hit on both sides of the Atlantic. The reverse sell plan had worked, triumphantly so. Elton John returned to the UK as a conquering hero. His next album *Tumbleweed Connection* was full of songs about the Old West, about taking up your father's gun, about burning down the Mission, about how sad it is that Deep America had been ploughed under in the name of progress. All this Americana was written at a piano in Pinner. It sounded as though it had been recorded in Woodstock; it was actually recorded just off Wardour Street. The cover was a sepia picture of an old railway station, out in the badlands, the kind of spooky terminus where desperados might wait for a train. It was actually photographed on the Bluebell Railway in Sussex.

The lives of the two main characters in the story were changed not just professionally but also personally by that first visit to America. By the time the next Elton John album, *Madman Across The Water*, came out in 1971 their imagined experiences of America had been supplanted by real ones. There was the inevitable song called 'Holiday Inn', hymning America's budget hotel chain with premature world-weariness in a way that only made it seem even more exotic to people in England who still dreamed of staying in any kind of hotel. There was another song called 'Levon', a name applied only to the drummer with the Band. But now that two members of the Band had felt moved to fly down to catch one of their Troubadour shows it appeared that their idols were suddenly their peers.

When Elton and Bernie returned they were changed in another important respect. Elton, who was twenty-three, had left the UK still a virgin. While in California, understandably bucked by his great success at the Troubadour, he'd made contact with John Reid, the record executive he had befriended back in London, and had his first sexual experience. At the time the idea that any entertainer should be openly gay was so foreign to people's experience that nobody in the band or the entourage suspected. When he got back to London he and Reid began looking for a flat together. Still people didn't cotton on.

Bernie Taupin, who had turned twenty just a few months before the triumphant tour, had, by his own admission, 'hardly been kissed'. Within days of arriving in Los Angeles he had hooked up with an eighteen-year-old American girl called Maxine Feibelman and was discovering that if you were hot in LA romance is not something you have to find. Instead it simply comes to you. When he came home, Bernie did the simple romantic thing any love-lorn twenty-year-old would do to stay in touch with a holiday romance and sent her air mail letters talking excitedly about how busy he was and how he couldn't wait to see her again. In addition he performed the grand romantic gesture most twenty-year-olds didn't have in their armoury: he made sure that the opening track of Elton's new album was dedicated to her. It began 'Blue jean baby, LA lady . . .'

When they married in 1971 he was clear that the song was inspired by her. Following their divorce in 1976 he tended to say it had been inspired by lots of different girls. However, in recent years he has said, 'I was trying to capture the spirit of the time, encapsulated by the women we met – especially at the clothes stores up and down the Strip. They were free spirits, sexy in hip-huggers and lacy blouses, and very ethereal, the way they moved. So different from what I'd been used to in England. They'd mother you and sleep with you – it was the perfect Oedipal complex.'

Years later, that song 'Tiny Dancer' inspired a memorable sequence in the film *Almost Famous* in which all the occupants of a tour bus – the moustachioed rock gods, their amazing ladies, the wide-eyed rock journalist, even the hard-bitten tour manager – join in to swell the chorus of a song that became an emblem of the rock life in the seventies and the state of luxurious adolescence it provided for those, like Reg and Bernie from Pinner, who had enjoyed the very special good fortune of entering it at the very top level, much as the Beatles had done a mere six years earlier.

15

'This mellow-thighed chick just put my spine out of place'

traveller making a first trip from the United Kingdom to the United States in the third decade of the twenty-first century need never worry about how to pass the yawning distances involved. Today's travellers would carry with them on to the plane the latest in mile-melting technology, fully charged with specially chosen music, electronic pastimes and sword and sorcery epics of the small screen without apparent end. In our digital era boredom may not have been banished entirely but it has been ameliorated by the availability of endless distraction. Furthermore, the flying machines themselves are kitted out with options to ensure that at no point during the journey between the old world and the new should anyone have to resort to the means transatlantic travellers would have used to entertain themselves when taking the same flight in 1971. These activities inevitably involved a lot of smoking (which was permitted), drinking (which was encouraged) and bantering with flirtatious cabin staff (something that the entire 1971 flying experience, apparently modelled on a branch of the Playboy club miraculously achieving an altitude of 30,000 feet, openly promoted). Once you had exhausted all these pathways to sin you would be thrown back into your solitude and left to gaze wonderingly out of the window and think about where your life might be going.

David Bowie made his journey in the winter of 1971, just as the United Kingdom was preparing to change from pounds, shillings and pence to the new decimal coinage. His new manager Tony Defries, who had talked his American record company Mercury into paying for the trip even though he wasn't going to commit his future to them, didn't accompany him. Nor did his wife Angie, who was left behind in Beckenham waiting for their first child to be born. He didn't have the appropriate work permits that would enable him to play any shows and therefore there was no point Mick Ronson going with him. In fact he probably preferred it that way. If you're about to undergo a life-changing experience it's best to do so without witnesses. Because Bowie was travelling solo, these precious four weeks of supercharged me-time, this flight into his own personal dreamworld, this record company-subsidized cross between a promotional jaunt and a fact-finding tour would prove to be the most formative of his entire life. What made it formative was the fact that he travelled alone. This meant that whatever he experienced he experienced alone, internalized alone, wove into myth alone, artfully exaggerated, carefully edited and transformed into material alone, without anyone witnessing the fact that he was doing so. Everywhere he went in those four weeks he was in the company of an entirely fresh group of people. If they wished to know what had happened at his last stop they would have to take it from him.

Because he was alone he was thrown into the company of more Americans than he would have encountered had he made his first landfall in the same way that the Beatles or the Rolling Stones or Led Zeppelin had. Unlike them he was not in a travelling party. Unlike them his impressions of the place were not sieved through the fine mesh of English snobbery or kept at arm's length by British defensiveness. Because he was on his own he spent much of his time simply looking and listening with the result that America entered more deeply into David Bowie's soul than it did any of his peers'.

He had been primed for it all his life. Bowie was one of those who had grown up smitten not simply with American music but with everything American. It was Bowie who as a child had suddenly announced that he was obsessed with American football and had written so persuasively on the subject to the American Embassy in London that they invited him up there and presented him with a ball and some shoulder pads. When he decided that there wasn't room for him and the other David Jones in the music business he borrowed the surname of a dead American frontiersman.

Most Britons enjoy their first trip to the United States but there is a particular sub-group for whom the experience is life-changing, a group who can spend hours gawping at American traffic signs or noting the minutely different spellings of common words or staying up with the TV long after it ceases to provide either entertainment or information and wondering how one country could possibly have so much call for intimate ointments; these English people are ministering to a deep internal need for sensation which only America can answer, a need which is almost guaranteed to burst forth in song.

Preparing for the winter cold of the eastern seaboard with an electric blue fake fur coat bought from Universal Witness in the Fulham Road, his long hair curtaining one eye after the manner of

Veronica Lake and, buried in his luggage, two of the male gowns he'd recently bought from the London designer Mr Fish, Bowie flew into Dulles airport in Washington on 21 January. Thanks to his appearance he took longer than expected coming through immigration and customs. There he was met by a cross-generational deputation of the Oberman family of Silver Spring, Maryland. Ron Oberman was the head of publicity at Bowie's American label Mercury and had organized his visit. Because it was a low-budget project he had arranged for Bowie to spend the first nights with his family. In Silver Spring his appearance caused even more of a stir than it would have done at home in Kent. The younger Oberman brother remembers that when the family dined at a local steak house that evening the staff had to draw the curtains around their booth to protect them from the startled eyes of the other diners.

Before Bowie flew out, Oberman had sought to manage his expectations. Because there was no Musicians Union exchange agreement allowing him to perform he was warned that he would spend most of his time talking to press and radio people. The word he used was 'rapping'. This was the language of hipsters in 1971. Bowie responded in kind, telling the British underground paper *Friends* before his departure that despite having no work permit to perform live he was nonetheless taking his 'box'.

Ron Oberman conducted him to interviews at radio stations and with the underground press in Washington, Baltimore and Philadelphia before taking him to New York by train. There he was handed over to Ed Kelleher and Paul Nelson, which was his good fortune. Throughout his trip the people who had the job of showing Bowie around operated in that shadowy, liminal world between talent spotting and rock journalism, a world that had grown up in response to the record companies' pressing need to be able to identify the next big thing but one. These taste-makers owed their standing to the fact that they could always be relied upon to recommend a new artist who wasn't known to everyone else. If that artist happened to come from a few thousand miles away, a distance from which their credentials could not be examined, then so much the better.

Because these people hadn't seen David Bowie in his native habitat – playing under-attended gigs, taking the bus, tainted with the tag of the one-hit wonder because of 'Space Oddity', subject to a whispering campaign that he might be too much of a dilettante ever to make it big, and if only he would drop the mime – they were more inclined to take him at his own estimation than they would have been had he been one of their own. This was so often the case with the transatlantic transformation. When it's one of your own you can see how hard they're trying, their every failure is engraved on your memory, their minor triumphs all too often ascribed to outrageous good fortune, and, because you know where they came from, they can never quite trail the clouds of mystique that accompany somebody from across the pond. People from overseas cannot be mapped. They are impossible to read, which is why they are so often given more, far more, than the benefit of the doubt.

Paul Nelson, who died in 2006, could fairly claim to be one of rock's true lightning conductors. Nelson had credentials. Nelson knew Bob Dylan when he was still using his family name, and it was a folkie friend of Nelson's at the University of Minnesota from whom Dylan borrowed a bunch of records and then never returned them, records which were in many ways the foundation of his entire act. Nelson saw it as his role to spread good ideas. It was Nelson who played the unreleased Bob Dylan songs 'Only A Hobo' and 'Mama, You Been On My Mind' to Rod Stewart. Stewart was smart enough to record them, thus providing the soulful base of his early records *Gasoline Alley* and *Never A Dull Moment*.

Similarly, Nelson took Bowie to see Tim Hardin play in Greenwich Village on the day that the jury in the Charles Manson trial brought in guilty verdicts for the 1969 Sharon Tate murders. Keen to establish common ground between him and the singer-songwriter Bowie tried to get backstage to see him. It struck Nelson that Bowie seemed to be trying to shed any last vestiges of the pop star image he felt he had in the UK. 'All the while he was in New York he made it a point to look as unkempt as possible, wearing sloppy sweaters and jeans, rarely shaving and telling everyone he met he just wanted to sing his songs and play guitar in small clubs.' Having been played *Loaded*, the new album by the Velvet Underground which was not yet released in the UK, he went along to see them at the Electric Circus and forced his way backstage after the show, gushing to the singer about how much he had enjoyed the show, not realizing that he was talking to Doug Yule and not Lou Reed, who had quit the group in disgust only weeks earlier.

In just a few weeks Bowie was exposed to a wider range of the American experience than he would have been had he gone there as an established act. He was taken up to New England by Nelson who introduced him to the record producer and music critic Jon Landau, then he was shipped out to the Midwest, which was where Mercury was headquartered, and interviewed by Dave Marsh for *Creem*, at the time the leading title in trying to establish a hard rock/punk rock aesthetic for American acts. Years later Bowie would recall, 'The country was still alien and the music that was coming out of the cities was far more urban than it was in Britain. I couldn't believe the country could be so free, so intoxicating and so dangerous. It suddenly made Beckenham seem very small, very timid and very English. I needed to get out of that whole British sensibility, and that's what I did with Ziggy Stardust.'

He then flew to Texas on his own. It was here, he would later claim, that somebody somewhere, taking exception to his mode of dress, called him a fag and pulled a gun on him. It's not inconceivable that something of the sort happened. He clearly decided that this was the kind of story he wished to be able to tell about himself. His next destination was San Francisco, the one city in the United States where neither sartorial flamboyance nor pan-sexuality would cause much of a stir. Here he would be interviewed by John Mendelssohn, America's most nakedly ambitious rock journalist, for a piece in *Rolling Stone*. In San Francisco he bought himself an engineer's cap at a women's department store called House of Paris and told a DJ at KSAN that his last LP was 'very simply, a collection of reminiscences about my experiences as a shaven-headed transvestite'. They went on to an interview at a station in San Jose where Mendelssohn encouraged him to play *Fun House*, the new record from the Stooges. Their singer was called Iggy Pop.

With each stop he seemed to be adding to his lacquer of confidence. The trip was about to reach its climax. Taking the Saturday morning flight down to Los Angeles with Mendelssohn, he was met at the airport by a diminutive label rep and scenester called Rodney Bingenheimer, the same man who had offered himself as the best friend of Graham Nash five years earlier. They had barely got out of the airport when Bowie started talking about the idea he had had for a character called Ziggy Stardust.

In his book *The Tipping Point*, Malcolm Gladwell argues that, to begin a cultural epidemic of any kind, you need three groups of people. You need mavens, who know a lot of things; you need salesmen, who are skilled in framing a message; and you need connectors, who know a lot of people. During his 1971 visit David Bowie enjoyed the benediction of all three. Paul Nelson was a maven; John Mendelssohn, who combined writing about rock with putting himself out there as the leader of a group called Christopher Milk, was a communicator; Rodney Bingenheimer, who had begun his Hollywood career as a stand-in for the Monkees' Davy Jones, served an apprenticeship with Sonny and Cher, steadily oiled his way into the good graces of the beautiful people and presently worked for Mercury in the promotions department, was the connector extraordinaire.

In Hollywood, Bingenheimer introduced Bowie to his patron Tom Ayres, an old record business hand who was working at the time with the Sir Douglas Quintet, the Andy Warhol starlet Ultra Violet and former rockabilly god Gene Vincent. Bowie even lodged with Ayres at a house in Hollywood that had been occupied by the Gish sisters back in the Golden Age of the movies. Under that roof it must have seemed the perfect place to ponder the decadence of show business, the lustre of success and the dreams that always meet a tragic end. There was even a recording studio plus an engineer in the house, and when Gene Vincent wasn't using it Bowie would go in there and work on a new song of his own called 'Hang On To Yourself', which he also tried to pitch to Vincent. When he had radio station appointments he was ferried to them in Ayres' Cadillac convertible. Such treatment was bound to go even to a harder head than his.

On Valentine's Day 1971, the same day that Carole King's *Tapestry* was released, Mercury Records hired the home of lawyer Paul Fegen, high above the Strip, to introduce Bowie to Hollywood. He must have been tired by that point. Earlier that day he had made the elementary Anglo mistake of underestimating the length of American streets by walking miles down Hollywood Boulevard to attend a Christopher Milk rehearsal at A&M Studios. At the party he wore his gown, sat on a waterbed, produced his box and serenaded the leggy girls in hot pants. He turned up to an interview at a radio station in Long Beach with one such girl called Kaji who sat next to him in the studio while he was interviewed.

When reports of his activity got back to the East Coast the people who had taken him around New York were amazed. Back there he had been, according to Nelson, 'this deliberately drab, troubled but serious moth' and now he had transformed 'into a certifiable flaming creature – all glitter and glam, lipstick and gowns – butterflying his way through some notoriously bright Hollywood nights'.

When he returned to a newly decimalized England on 18 February it was with a suitcase full of albums that were unavailable in the UK, the beginnings of an idea for songs about a character called Ziggy and a determination to make music in the tradition of the Stooges and Velvet Underground albums he had heard in the States. There was no reason he couldn't try. He had a management company who were prepared to pick up the cost of making albums on spec and so he followed *Hunky Dory*, which was made that spring, with the record that became known as *The Rise And Fall Of Ziggy Stardust And The Spiders From Mars*, almost finishing the latter before the former was out.

At the time the Stooges' music wasn't happening in the USA and Bowie's music wasn't happening in the UK. There was abrasive, determinedly edgy rock and roll being made on both sides of the Atlantic. The problem was that the people making it in Britain, the likes of T. Rex and Slade, were not hip and the people making it in the US, the likes of the Stooges and the MC5, were not popular.

What Bowie came up with in the months following his return in songs like 'Suffragette City' crossed the abrasiveness of the latter with the *Top of the Pops* appeal of the former. The songs that he wrote and recorded under the direct inspiration of his American visit included 'Andy Warhol' (one of the people he'd failed to meet on his visit to New York) and a classic wide-eyed New York song 'Queen Bitch', which starts with him up on the eleventh floor watching the cruisers below. All the songs on *Ziggy Stardust* came studded with Americanisms like 'jamming good', 'cats from Japan', 'loaded', 'the nazz', 'God-given ass' and the mellow-thighed chick who put his spine out of place; on stage he started talking about sidewalks and elevators. He was like one of those characters in an

Ealing comedy who has spent so long at the Troxy or with his nose in a comic that he falls into using a hard-boiled language which could only have been learned from America.

On 1 April, *Rolling Stone* appeared with a feature about Bowie by John Mendelssohn headlined 'Pantomime Rock?' The picture accompanying it showed Bowie in one of Michael Fish's gowns. At the time, when the smoke of Woodstock was yet to clear, such images could still shock. As ever, the image travelled to places the word couldn't. Some of the first people to be impressed by it were the members of Andy Warhol's court who were appearing in his production of *Pork* in New York. Warhol's art dealer decided he could bring the production to London and so when it opened there in the middle of August 1971, the members of the American cast decided to catch up with this new exotic by going to one of his shows at the Country Club on Haverstock Hill. Here they were surprised and slightly disappointed to find Bowie and Ronson sitting on stools and playing their boxes. But when they bonded in person they brought him out of himself. Just as his American wife had encouraged him to wear the gowns and was going to do anything it took to bring him to public attention, so these noisy New Yorkers Cherry Vanilla, Tony Zanetta and Leee Black Childers appointed themselves his personal claque. Thus when *Ziggy Stardust* was finally recorded later that year it was effectively an Anglo-American production.

It was the American attention that reintroduced David Bowie to his home country. In Britain he was still regarded as an interesting joker who could always be relied upon to give good copy. Now that he had taken to turning up in what appeared to be drag he had introduced a new dimension to the usual game of 'doing press'. Whether he was aware of it or not he was foreshadowing the pop world of today where a new look is often all the story anyone needs.

In America, crucially, where they are always inclined to attribute a seriousness of purpose to anything they happen to like, the words mattered more. American critics were the first people to give Bowie more than the benefit of the doubt. This came in July 1971 when Nancy Erlich gave over her pop music column in no less an organ than the *New York Times* to three albums from Britain which proved, she said, that music could be more than mere entertainment. One was by Mike Heron of the Incredible String Band, another was by Marc Bolan and T. Rex, and the third, a two-year-old album which could only be bought in the United States if you went to a shop that sold imports, was by David Bowie. Pulling herself to her full critical height, Erlich pronounced him 'the most intellectually brilliant man yet to choose the long-playing album as his means of expression'.

It would be difficult to imagine an accolade more guaranteed to give a rock star an erection than this. She didn't just say that the record was good for the usual reasons that records are good, because they had good songs with interesting lyrics or good tunes. Her line asserted instead that artists were suddenly of a wholly different order from craftsmen. Artists were possessed of unique insight and they could choose to apply this insight across everything from sculpture to film direction. In this case, one had just decided to alight upon pop music. Every inch of critical slack David Bowie was cut in his subsequent long career, the omniscience that people were happy to attribute to him even when he couldn't get a hit to save his life, can be traced back to that review in the *New York Times*. Ironically, at the time the review appeared Bowie was back in England working on a bunch of songs that had much of the dumb simplicity he'd learned from the Stooges.

The transatlantic traffic wasn't all one-way. Following Bowie back to London later in 1971, Rodney Bingenheimer ended up living in Ealing Broadway. Here he attended a club called the Cellar where he watched young Britons in tank tops and clumpy shoes dance to Slade and the Sweet. On his return he took the idea back to Hollywood where he persuaded Tom Ayres to back him in starting what eventually became Rodney's English Disco. This was an institution along the lines of the English muffin in bearing little resemblance to any original in the old country but providing a lot of pleasure nonetheless.

For a while in the early seventies it thrived. It had no liquor licence, which meant it was easier for the girls who were the club's primary attraction to get in without showing ID. These rake-thin, under-parented girls from beyond the Hills would doll themselves up like *fin de siècle* strumpets, in which state they were irresistible to the visiting English rock royalty attracted by the Watney's Red Barrel in the VIP room. Even Elvis Presley, who valued a seedy night out as much as the next man, came on one occasion.

Hollywood, the eventual terminus of most American tours, became Sin City as far as the visiting Brits were concerned. Armies of road-horny Anglo rockers arrived there and felt that having an ocean and a continent between them and their wives, who were living in some manor house back in the rolling English countryside, was sufficient to allow them to get away with anything. It wasn't until they checked in at the Continental Hyatt House that Black Sabbath realized the women who had apparently sprouted at their elbows were members of a sisterhood who had refined the traditional fascination for musicians into something like a professional calling. 'They were a lot more forward than we were used to in Britain,' reflected Black Sabbath's Tony Iommi.

The girls who had snagged themselves a pop star back in Britain in the previous decade began to realize that they were now dealing with a level of competition which was entirely new. Sometimes desperate measures were called for. In the spring of 1971 the girlfriends of the Faces were flown out to spend time with them in Los Angeles during a break in the tour. It was at this juncture that Jan Osborne, the girlfriend of drummer Kenney Jones, openly refused to return to the UK until the two of them were safely married. In those pre-digital days it wasn't difficult for the things that happened on tour to remain on tour. Only at the end of the tour might some photographer get into Rodney's English Disco and snap a shot of members of Led Zeppelin surrounded by strumpets. There were few markets for such a picture but one of them was the English music weeklies. Among the keenest subscribers to those weeklies were the families of the rock stars who used them as a way to find out how they were being received over there. The story is recounted in the memoirs of the American music journalist Lisa Robinson that when returning from one US tour Robert Plant was met at the gate by his wife, brandishing a copy of the *Melody Maker* featuring one of these very incriminating pictures. 'Maureen,' sighed Plant in the seigneurial voice of a son of Empire returning laden with pineapples from visiting his distant plantations, 'you *know* we don't take that paper.'

16

'We were dignified people – we were artists'

On 10 December 1971, during a Who show at the Long Beach Municipal Auditorium, Pete Townshend famously berated the audience to 'either sit down or lay down but shut up. This is a rock and roll concert – not a fucking tea party!'

Townshend's choice of words betrays a great deal about what had changed about the live experience around the turn of the decade. He had no difficulty describing their performance as a concert. In their whole career the Beatles never played anything that could warrant such a formal description. The reference to the audience sitting throughout – even though what he and the band were purveying at the time could with some justification be described as the most incendiary live rock and roll ever placed before the public – indicates that the audience were expected to appreciate what was going on rather than simply, as had been the case a few years earlier, twist and shout. The concert they put on that night had a shape to it which would increasingly be adopted by many major English bands. It began with a couple of old hits calculated to get the blood pumping and to remind the audience of their shared history, a rock classic from the fifties to stress the lineage they shared with the great originators, and then it was four from their new album *Who's Next*, a couple of reliable warhorses, five from their rock opera *Tommy*, and then their closing anthem 'My Generation'.

No other British band played as many rock and roll concerts in the United States as the Who did at the end of the sixties and into the seventies. No other British band took the same risks in doing things during those concerts that had not been done before. No other rock and roll musician thought as much about what it all meant as Townshend did, and how it meant something different in the United States from what it meant in the United Kingdom. The rock and roll concert as we have come to know it was invented by the Who and it was invented in America.

The first year of their great learning was 1967. They were still out on the road going toe to toe with live audiences when the Beatles and Stones were inclined to think that all the answers could be found in the studio. This gave them a unique perspective on how the world was changing. Their 1967 datebook demonstrates the range. The Who began that year playing the Marine Ballroom in Morecambe where they were supported by the Doodlebugs and local organist Harold Graham, and finished it playing the 4,000-seat Long Island Arena with Vanilla Fudge. Between those dates a new world of live performance had been born. It didn't merely change the way the music was performed. It changed the music itself.

The Who had arrived late in America. In Britain they were, like the Beatles, the Kinks and the Rolling Stones, a singles band for the simple reason that in the middle of the decade that was the only kind of band there was. In those days eighteen months was still the average life expectancy of the career of a singles band. Nobody with any sense would plan or invest in the expectation that the career was going to be any longer than that.

On that basis, by the time the Who began to happen in the United States their career in the UK should by rights have been coming to an end. They didn't enjoy the same luxury as the Beatles of entering in triumph and being received by the nation at one sitting on *The Ed Sullivan Show*. They didn't have a huge, era-defining hit like 'Satisfaction'. By the time they got there in 1967 something of the novelty of Englishness had worn off. It was clear to Townshend that they would have to do everything the slow way. This meant confronting the overpowering, non-negotiable fact that the USA, unlike the UK, was a big country. In fact it wasn't a country at all. It was more helpful to think of it as a continent made up of smaller nation states that had precious little to do with one another. In such a continent there was no more reason to believe that the good news would spread from Detroit to Austin than to believe that a hit record in Italy guaranteed you a warm welcome in Norway.

By the end of the 1960s there were reckoned to be seven thousand radio stations in the United States. In Britain there was, effectively, one. A tour of Britain would take a couple of weeks and would be organized by just one promoter. No rock act had done a proper tour of the United States because it could only be organized by dealing with many local promoters, and besides, the country was so big the chances were that by the time you arrived in the last city you would no longer be popular in the first.

When the Who first arrived in April 1967, the Beatles were getting ready to release *Sgt Pepper*, the Kinks were unable to play in the United States because they were on an AFM blacklist, and the Rolling Stones had their own problems with court cases and the erratic behaviour of Brian Jones. Therefore, purely by accident the Who were uniquely well positioned to take part in the revolution in live music that was beginning to happen in the United States at that time.

In that year alone they saw how things had been, how they were and how they would be in the future. At first their American agent Frank Barsalona was so keen to get them booked anywhere that he wangled them on to a Murray the K show at the RKO theatre in New York. Here they were billed to appear with Mitch Ryder, Wilson Pickett, the Blues Magoos, Mandala, Chicago Loop, Jim and Jean, the Blues Project, Cream and some comedians. The idea of this show, which was built on the assumption that pop music was a perishable product, was that it ran five times a day for ten days.

The initial running order called for the Who to do four numbers. When they argued that this was insufficient time to put over what they were about, the four were reduced to two. In the face of this limitation Pete Townshend reasoned that the only thing that mattered about the show was the climax. Wearing a jacket he had jerry-rigged with twinkling fairy lights, he threw his guitar up in the air during 'My Generation'. The audience, not unreasonably, waited for him to catch it and were amazed to see it fall to the stage. America had never seen this kind of disregard for private property. Furthermore they had never heard such noise.

Al Kooper, who was on the same bill as a member of the Blues Project, was watching from the wings. He noted that Keith Moon's drum kit had far more drums than the standard American arrangement. For a start he had two bass drums. On the first it said 'the'. On the second was the word 'Who'. As the band's allotted ten minutes came to an end, Moon would kick his drum kit over and the band would exit wreathed in theatrical smoke. Then, as soon as the curtains were drawn and the next band had come on, they would put it all back together, ready to repeat the whole performance in an hour's time.

The Murray the K show had been put together on the same basis as a programme at the movies would have been at the time. People would come in when they felt like it and leave when they had had enough, no matter what stage had been reached in the performance. What the promoters found with the Who was that some members of the audience were just staying in their seats and waiting for the Who to come back. Within the next year the concept that this new rock they were playing was as perishable as the old pop would come under challenge, as would the very idea of an audience ever having had enough. The place it would come under challenge was America. The band that would challenge it was the Who.

In June 1967 they flew back to America. This time they stayed for three months and played almost every major city. They wowed the hippies with their appearance at the Monterey Festival, making sure that they destroyed their equipment before the headliner Jimi Hendrix could do the same with his. When introducing them, Eric Burdon said, 'I promise this group will destroy you in more ways than one.' On the same visit they also amazed the teenagers when they supported Herman's Hermits by starting to play before the curtain went up and not stopping between songs in case of boos. By then Keith had changed the design on his bass drums. The legend now read 'Keith Moon. Patent British Exploding Drummer.' They grossed just over $1,000 a night. Most of that was spent on breakages. At the end of the tour John Entwistle had to borrow $100 to avoid flying home coach.

In Britain at the time they would often do gigs for as little as £60. In Britain there was no plan, no sense of a world to conquer, no sense that you toured when you had an album to promote. You simply played in order to put food on the table, booking anywhere close enough to London not to require you to have to pay for hotel rooms. In Britain, the bridge between the old world of the package tour and the modern world of the arena tour was provided by the universities. In the years between 1967 and 1975 they put on big acts at affordable prices. The album that made the Who, 1970's *Live At Leeds*, was recorded in the refectory of Leeds University in front of a bunch of students who sat on the parquet floor and clapped respectfully at the end of each number. In the USA, the bridge between the old world and the new was provided by Bill Graham.

Bill Graham had come up through the alternative theatre scene and the hangover was evident in the way he would refer to his promotions as 'my shows'. Graham's is the dark brown voice you hear introducing the artists on all the famous live albums recorded at his Fillmore theatres, either in San Francisco or New York. The reputation of the Fillmores as being the hippest gig you could play was spread by the hundreds of live albums that were recorded in them, first by the San Francisco bands like the Grateful Dead who had come up through them and then by the visiting English bands like Cream and the Nice who wanted to say they'd recorded there. For them, playing the Fillmore was like visiting jazzers being invited to play Birdland. It was a mark of quality. The ambience of the Fillmore was more like the old jazz clubs than the out-of-town sports arenas the bands were being increasingly directed towards. The Fillmore in San Francisco had an official capacity of 900 but there were often 1,500 in there. The audience would very often be the same local heads who had been there the night before. They weren't over-enthralled simply to be in the presence of legends, not even on the night of 10 May 1968 when the bill at the Fillmore East was made up of Sly and the Family Stone and the Jimi Hendrix Experience. They sat in battered old cinema seats, they listened and they clapped. The whoop was not yet obligatory.

Bill Graham had an ego and he did very well financially out of the early days when the big bands would play for a flat fee and he would maximize his profits by making sure he accommodated as many people as the buildings would hold. That said, he had a show-man's love for the show and was always concerned that the public should enjoy the evening. There was no liquor licence and the only food available was the pile of apples in the lobby with a sign that said, 'Please take one.' More to the point, Graham wanted the artists to feel that they had had a good time, that they appreciated the PA system and the professionalism of his staff enough to want to return. But he only dispensed one variety of love and that was the tough kind. Hippies who attempted to explain how the place ought to be run would often find themselves in a very dark place at the sharp end of Graham's jabbing finger. Much the same could apply with the musicians. The first time Eric Clapton met Graham was when the guitarist was intent on stepping out to take the air between Cream sets and the promoter asked where the hell he thought he was going. At the end of the evening, whether that evening had involved Jethro Tull, Led Zeppelin or the Hampton Grease Band, the audience would be wafted towards the exits with a recording of England's oldest popular song 'Greensleeves'.

In April 1969 the Fillmore East offered Ten Years After, the Nice and Family. On 30 May, Led Zeppelin were supported by Woody Herman and his Thundering Herd and Delaney & Bonnie. In November it was Joe Cocker, Fleetwood Mac, King Crimson and the Voices of East Harlem. In June 1970 it was Fairport Convention, Traffic and Mott the Hoople. Bill Graham would not have described what he did as 'curation' but he was consciously trying to create a unique experience, and when he made unexpected pairings such as that night when he put on Led Zeppelin with the Woody Herman jazz orchestra, he was knowingly trying to create something that hadn't been there before.

Pete Townshend credits Graham with pioneering what he christened 'the electric ballroom syndrome', where the acts looked out and saw for the first time an audience who gave the appearance of listening to their music harder than they had listened to it themselves. A lot of this was down to drugs. Eric Clapton had noticed towards the end of Cream that things in the USA were different. Whereas when Cream played in the UK there would be a knot of mainly male fans of their playing gathered near the stage while the rest of the place would be occupied by mainly female dancers, in San Francisco there was evidence of an altogether more introspective attitude to his music which he had never noticed before. Townshend was the first person to sense the effect this had on the kind of music they made. 'In the electric ballroom we grew extraordinarily. We were able to experiment. We were able to take chances. Before that there was blues jamming. We hadn't done that because we were more of a pop group. We found we were able to experiment not just on the length of songs but on song cycles. The effect was of a cameo of music which might not actually elicit a response until it was clearly over and then everybody would go "YEAAHHHH! Rock and roll!" Not for what you'd just done but kind of for the idea of it.'

What they learned in the electric ballroom was reflected in the shift between the six hits they played at Monterey in 1967 and the twenty-two they did just two years later at Woodstock, the bulk of which came from their rock opera *Tommy*. What the Who learned about dynamics and the sustaining of intensity in the electric ballroom would come to fruition in 1970 on *Live At Leeds*. Townshend recalled, 'Somehow, Bill had hit on it. He gave us dignity. We felt we weren't the pop plebs we had been when we went out with Herman's Hermits and we were told to shut up and get in the back of the bus. We were dignified people – we were artists.'

The Who did something that few British bands before or since have done. They really worked at America, long after the novelty had worn off for so many other bands. Between 1967 and 1980 there was only one year when the Who didn't tour the United States. This new focus eventually changed everything about the group.

Roger Daltrey, a genuinely unreconstructed working-class bloke from west London, met his second wife, the model Heather Taylor, in New York. She was the one who, on waking up with him to find that his hair had reverted to its natural curls in the night as the effects of the Dippity Do styling gel wore off, told him he had to keep it that way, at a stroke doing as much to extend his career as anything short of 'Won't Get Fooled Again'. 'We couldn't believe our luck,' Daltrey recalled of that period. 'All these beautiful, exotic American girls and they were all into us. Heather told me that British boys took American girls by storm. We were sharper dressers. We strutted around like peacocks. And we were better in bed.'

Keith Moon was able to burnish his legend as a yob for a bunch of American rock writers who would have been horrified to meet a yob with whom they happened to share a nationality. In a Holiday Inn room in a town called Rolling Meadows in the year 1967, Pete Townshend says he first heard the word of God. America provided John Entwistle with the income stream he needed to be able to afford the life of a landed rock star without the advantage of having written a lot of hits.

By 1971 Bill Graham was closing his two Fillmores because the acts were getting too big to be subsumed into one of his shows and the managers and agents were getting too wise to how much more money they could make by doing their own deals in bigger venues. However, for those few years Graham had a profound effect on the music as well as the expectations of both musicians and fans. He retired for a while but then came back. He couldn't keep away from either the excitement or the money. Even he couldn't have predicted how much money would eventually flow from what *Life* magazine in June 1968 had dubbed 'the New Rock – the music that's hooked the whole vibrating world', the originators of which were Brits but the biggest customers for which were Americans. Graham died in a helicopter in 1991 on his way to one of his gigs.

Nobody in a position to explain the murky finances of modern touring can be relied on to tell you the truth about them but Bill Graham got close to spelling it out in his autobiography, describing what happened in the first few years of the 1970s as the demand grew to outstrip the supply:

> More and more people wanted to see the acts. Unless the band was willing to give us three dates, we could not satisfy the demand. Bands began to realize that if they could make as much in one date as they could in three, they wouldn't have to stay out on the road as long. Rock and roll had started in the clubs and the streets and the parks. Then it became a game of supply and demand. It wasn't just who had the better amps or piano or stage crew. It got to the point where bands were earning money far beyond their wildest dreams. Musicians realized, 'God, I can have a second car. I can have a home in the country. I can have a sailboat. I can have everything I want.' What else did they need? The time to enjoy these things. Because the road was always the same, the conclusion they reached was 'I want to make more money in less time'. Result? Stadiums.

In the years following Woodstock every long-haired British band with a Marshall stack visited the United States. There was never any question in their minds about doing this. It was, after all, why they had joined. Everything about it thrilled them down to the depths of their English souls. Furthermore, they had the excuse of knowing that America wanted them to visit. The music they brought was the music America was buying. They were pushing on an open door. The audience for this new bare-chested, eardrum-threatening, doggedly excessive rock was growing as it was swelled by the ranks of the younger brothers and sisters of the people who had flocked to Max Yasgur's farm in Bethel, New York for the 1969 Woodstock festival. In the face of this increased demand and the inability of the bands to say no to bigger and bigger offers the gigs had to get bigger and bigger until it seemed that the whole point of them was their scale.

The sixth of April 1974 saw the biggest of them all take place at the Ontario Motor Speedway in California. On this occasion ABC television had hired some promoters to lay on an event they called the California Jam. The TV producers probably had something mellow in mind, which was why the opening acts were Americans like Seals and Crofts and the Eagles. The promoters, however, knew what sold tickets to the teens and twenties, to the kind who would be prepared to make the hour's drive out of Los Angeles to broil in the heat and dust of a California plain. This was why they made sure the headliners were the British acts who were increasingly popular with the younger audience, the kind of acts whose calling card was loudness and bombast. The plan worked because it certainly sold tickets. Tens of thousands turned up and paid their $15 at the gate, and it was estimated that by the time the audience were pitched on the plain waiting for Black Sabbath, who had flown over from the UK purely to play the show, this was the largest ticketed gig of all time with almost 200,000 in the audience. Nobody was counting properly, which enabled the participants to claim in later years that there were as many as 350,000.

The California Jam would be a harbinger of a future where the only things that would really matter were the depth of the sponsor's pockets and the number of things bands were prepared to overlook in pursuit of a cheque bigger than any they had previously received. The dramatic change in scale that had happened between the 1960s and the 1970s meant there was suddenly a dislocation between the kind of shows the members of bands had grown up attending and the kind of shows they were now being paid to play. The American music commentator Anthony De Curtis, recalling his feelings about it many years later, noticed a change around this time. 'Suddenly these British bands didn't seem to have any sense of larger social purpose and they were just regarded as marauders. They just wanted to make as much money as possible, get high as much as possible and go back home.' The California Jam was the kind of grotesquely inflated experience that could have happened only because the members of the bands involved had never themselves endured the unmitigated misery of being in the audience at such a gig. If they had, they wouldn't have played one.

On this occasion Black Sabbath did their diabolical business incongruously in the heat of the afternoon. Following this there was a mere two-hour hiatus before Deep Purple. This was caused by the fact that Ritchie Blackmore locked himself in his trailer and refused to take the stage until it was dusk. At the end of Deep Purple's act Blackmore further bolstered his reputation as rock's foremost crosspatch by launching his guitar into the TV camera at the side of the stage and then proceeding to make very heavy weather indeed of noisily destroying a number of instruments. This had the virtue of further spinning out Deep Purple's stage time to ensure that by the time the headliners Emerson, Lake & Palmer were approaching 'The Great Gates Of Kiev' and Keith Emerson had been strapped into his stunt Steinway in which he would be elevated 15 feet above the stage prior to being rotated through 360° in what was intended to be their crowning *coup de théâtre*, the California Jam audience were just a bit too fatigued to enthuse as he might justifiably have hoped.

The California Jam marked the moment when peace and love were swapped for bread and circuses, when the promise of Monterey and Woodstock – where the crowd had thrilled to hearing things they had never heard before – turned into the exaltation of rock as empty spectacle for their younger brothers and sisters, when the story of wide-eyed Britishers coming to the USA with hope in their heart and a tumult in their trousers culminated in the image of Deep Purple's newly acquired lead singer David Coverdale, who a few months earlier had been working in a clothes shop in North Yorkshire, feeling nervously in his back pocket throughout their set. He did this because that's where he had put the cheque he had just got from their American record company, Warner Brothers. It was the safest place to keep something that none of his forerunners from the 1960s had ever had their hands on: a cheque for a million dollars.

17

'They travelled 3,000 miles to die here'

Only people from smaller countries speak of 'breaking America' as though this vast, various nation were a single nut that only required to be hit at the correct angle in order to yield. American performers have never looked at it in the same way. They have always looked at the country with the eyes of Presidential hopefuls, knowing that it is more helpful to think of it as a number of distinct regions or markets separated by different histories, different ethnicities, different climates and different time zones, and that nothing worth achieving in America can ever be achieved quickly. This is what the English acts had to learn. It was never easy.

Nobody worked harder at 'breaking America' than the Who, and nobody knew better that you never do. However, they had the first thing required, which is a work ethic. For all their excesses, for all the regularity with which in the early days they spent their performance fees on room service, for all the many occasions when Keith Moon's authentically insane experiments with improvised explosives would force them to vacate an expensive hotel midway through a booking, for all the fact that whenever presented with a choice between the sensible option and the crazy one they unfailingly plumped for the latter, still nobody knew better than the Who that putting your mark on America was a job of work and not a subsidized holiday.

When they travelled by scheduled airline in the early days they had to endure the standard slings and arrows from their fellow passengers, from jibes about the length of their hair to asides about the British government's devaluation of the pound in 1967. When they travelled by bus they had to live with each other and the tension would regularly turn physical. After a few years had gone by no British rock star knew better what it cost to make it there than Pete Townshend. By 1971 he had seen an entire ragged army of graduates of the Blue Boar school of British rockers go to America, overspend on room service, contract social diseases and then quietly slink back to Britain, never to return. That year he wrote in *Melody Maker*, 'The first trip to the States of any major English act is always treated as a group's big next step. They wave happily from the top steps of a VC 10 and set off to make their fortune. A couple of months later, after the most gruelling and exhausting work they have probably ever done in their lives, they return triumphantly home and start to tell lies. "It was great!" "We made thousands!" It went terribly, and they lost thousands.'

The British public couldn't be expected to understand this. If a British band came back from America having played the odd prestigious venue, having drawn the odd well-known face to their backstage party, having made some token entry on some airplay chart, the British public were only too happy to accept that they had made it over there. In fact it was not so simple. Most of these bands sank without trace. In the same year that Townshend delivered his truth about his compatriots, American musician Al Kooper rented a limousine to take his new friends Elton John and Bernie Taupin out to see the historic sites around Lexington and Concord associated with the American War of Independence. This was where, he liked to explain, his ancestors had seen off their ancestors. On this visit Elton's eye was caught by a plaque which announced this as 'the tomb of the British soldiers' and went on, 'they travelled 3,000 miles to die here'. Elton thought for a moment and said, 'The thing is – this has happened to so many British bands lately.'

Elton could afford the gallows humour. Although it was still early days he'd certainly made it off the beach when it came to establishing himself in America and from that position he'd been able to watch subsequent waves being mowed down in the shallows. An assiduous student of airplay reports, sales charts and concert returns, Elton knew the difference between getting your record released in America, playing a few gigs in America, having a party thrown for you by the American record company, and making any kind of real impression on the place. At that time an endless stream of hairy men and weighty materiel was being shipped from Heathrow to JFK every day and in many cases the actual demand for the imported services was minimal. The bands who made these trips were obeying greater imperatives. English record companies, who had signed these acts relatively cheaply, ushered them in the direction of passport control in the hope they might make more money for them in the bigger market. If they didn't, they didn't lose anything. The musicians themselves looked upon going there as the next step on a ladder they had first mounted upon signing a record deal. It was the destination they did not look beyond. Their first trip to America, where the streets were paved with gold and Led Zeppelin-style fame awaited them. For many of them the first trip to America would be their last.

This was a process which was closely observed from the UK. In every quarter, from the Speakeasy in Margaret Street to the branches of Smith's where almost a million copies of music papers were sold every week, there were three little words indicating a new category of success, three little words that people whispered in wonder: Big In America. Those same papers breathlessly tracked the progress of this new category of Briton abroad via the correspondents they retained over there, often on both coasts. So much space had to be filled every week in their letters from America that British readers who had never been inside the portals of London's Marquee felt as if they could find their way to the bathrooms of New York's CBGB or Rodney's English Disco in Hollywood, so often did they vicariously visit there in the overseas column of their favourite weekly. The correspondents who held these coveted jobs saw themselves as having a duty to be supportive and could generally be depended upon to put an optimistic gloss on how well the British acts were going over in the United States, fully realizing how vital it was to be able to go back to Britain with your head held high, even though inside you might be dying.

Sometimes the bands went to America and then simply broke up. That first foot on American soil, long dreamed of but rarely thought about, would often have the effect of bringing to a head problems that had already been there. For instance, on the day in April 1969 when Family, the living example of the 'hard-gigging five piece' who had never been more than a middling draw in the UK, were due to open at the Fillmore East on a full English bill which also included the Nice and Ten Years After, their bass player Ric Grech announced he was leaving to join Eric Clapton's Blind Faith. 'We died,' recalled singer Roger Chapman of the subsequent gig. For many bands the experience of going to the States was the last one they ever shared. Half of the British bands who played New York's Fillmore East in 1970 – jazz-rock outfit Manfred Mann

Chapter III, Scotland's Clouds, the blues band Chicken Shack, the former Cliff Bennett and the Rebel Rousers (musicians now known as Toe Fat) and power trio Quatermass among them – flew home to Heathrow and quietly de-merged.

Then there were the proverbial musical and personal differences brought to a head by too many days and nights on a bus covering unfeasibly long distances. It was during an American tour in the same year that Keith Emerson decided he was going to wind up the Nice. He did this because he didn't think their vocalist Lee Jackson was good enough for them to make it in the USA, and while supporting King Crimson at the Fillmore East he had heard Greg Lake, who he thought was just the man to replace him. As if Lake's departure wasn't enough of a problem for King Crimson leader Robert Fripp, in the course of a car journey up the Pacific Coast Highway fellow members Ian McDonald and Michael Giles announced that they too were leaving King Crimson. They were surprised and overwhelmed by what the American touring experience had taken out of them and became just a few of the many who fell by the wayside in those days after the thrill of the first visit had worn off. Often it was a combination of homesickness and struggle that brought things to a head. As soon as the work side of life is becoming a struggle the personal side of life becomes difficult to manage. The Bonzo Dog Band cut short their American tour in November 1969 partly because it had taken four days for a message to reach them from the UK that Roger Ruskin Spear's wife was ill. Viv Stanshall, who had somehow become their manager when the last sane professional walked out, blamed the agency for booking them into unsuitable venues and the record company for not getting their albums in the stores. The band never returned to the United States. The news item in *Rolling Stone* reporting the facts was bluntly headlined 'Bonzo Dog runs, fucks itself'.

Townshend wasn't joking about how hard these tourists had to work. The progressive band Yes did two tours of the United States in 1972. In November of that year they played a different American city every night. They had just one night off in the whole month. Interviewed during an American tour in 1971, Ray Thomas of the Moody Blues said, 'You really have no conception of touring and the strain until you have toured America the hard way, driving yourself from New York to Washington and working until you are so tired and ill you are on the verge of collapse. On our first tour in 1969 it was nothing to find somebody in the band in tears from sheer exhaustion.' Before the days of 'tour support', when artists would have the tours underwritten by their record company in the hope that their appearances would boost sales, touring bands were compelled to live off the land. Thomas remembered one occasion when Justin Hayward, who was ill with the flu, was told off by their manager for ordering a room service meal because they simply couldn't afford it.

Most British acts that went to the USA avoided the highs and the lows but came home instead with a reminder of their professional mortality. Ian Hunter, the leader of Mott the Hoople, did posterity a considerable service when he recorded his personal impressions of touring America in 1972. His memoir, called with tongue in cheek *Diary of a Rock'n'roll Star*, because he was never quite that, more than makes up for the thousands of British musicians who went to the United States in the seventies, underwent comparable experiences, never quite broke into the American market, never quite recovered from the experience of not breaking into the American market, and sadly never got round to putting their impressions down on paper.

There's nothing blasé about Hunter's account. He makes no effort in his book to conceal the thrill of his band's great adventure in the land of plenty. It's almost as if he understands that all these visiting rock musicians who went to America in the seventies were travelling on behalf of the fans and readers back in the UK who never dared think they would ever get there themselves. There's nothing even faux blasé about Hunter's account. He lists the facilities that are available to passengers on the plane for the benefit of readers who haven't flown before, which would have been most of them. He's too enthralled by the place to put any energy into making himself look cool. Once arrived on the West Coast he remarks upon everything from the quality of the pornography he can take back to his hotel room to the toothpicks the Americans use to prevent their overstuffed sandwiches from bursting open; from the ready availability of every form of vice and indulgence delivered to your door to the sign outside the Continental Hyatt House welcoming Mott the Hoople; from the array of services that can theoretically be summoned by the rows of buttons on a hotel room phone to the mere $3 it cost to fill the band's rented Mercury with gasoline.

The British reader in the year 1974, when the book came out, didn't need to have spelled out the contrast between all this bounty and the cramped lifestyle back in strike-bound Blighty. Hunter had left his own car, a Ford Anglia, outside his flat in Wembley, which is some measure of how the term 'rock'n'roll star' denoted something very different back in London in those days. He sunbathes on the roof of his California hotel wearing trunks he has bought from Woolworths, regrets the passing of an earlier generation of groupies who were into the music, and decides against a trip to Disneyland on the grounds that the theme park has apparently banned anyone with long hair from visiting. (In fact this ban, which had been in operation throughout the sixties, had been rescinded by the time of Hunter's visit. But only just. There were some Holiday Inns where the management would still insist on long-haired guests wearing bathing caps before they could use the pool.)

The gigs Mott the Hoople played on this visit were the usual mixed bag of prestige slots, special favours for the agent and unsuccessful efforts to get them in front of a mass audience – the same unsatisfactory assortment most visiting British bands were faced with at the time. Thus Mott the Hoople found themselves supporting transcendental jazzer John McLaughlin one night and caveman metal band Bloodrock the next. In Los Angeles they were thrust on stage in front of 35,000 who'd been drawn there by the promise of Stevie Wonder, the Four Seasons, Chuck Berry and the Bee Gees. When they played in front of their actual fans, who were inevitably concentrated in Los Angeles and New York and sparse anywhere in the middle of the country, they went down well and enjoyed the experience. When things went wrong, on the other hand, they felt they might be the victims of a case of mistaken identity on a massive scale, involving hundreds of puzzled-looking guys in Afghan coats who had been chosen for this indiscriminate export drive on the basis of somebody having put a pin in one of those rock family trees Pete Frame would lovingly design in the pages of *ZigZag*. Driving down Sunset Boulevard, Hunter cast a mordant eye over a giant billboard for the British jazz-rock band If and, while envying them the exposure, noted that since they had already broken up this might possibly be a bit of a waste.

Hunter was honest with himself about the size of the task facing Mott the Hoople if they were to make any impression in this giant country. In America, thousands of people hadn't heard of his band but thousands had. The problem was, those thousands were distributed over such a wide area that it was impractical to make contact with them. What they couldn't generate in the United States was the spark required to start a fire. All it had taken to make Mott the Hoople well known in England was a couple of appearances on *Top of the Pops*. America had no comparable promotional G-spot. Hunter was thirty-three years old by this time and he knew that the band had to keep getting bigger in order to survive. 'Come on, America,' he pleads at one point. 'Take us in out of the cold. We're trying hard to catch you but you're so fucking big.'

Here he was not just referring to the size of the country. He was also talking about the size of the impact you needed to make once people saw you. In New York, he and the band were given tickets to go and see an English band playing at Madison Square Garden. This large indoor facility with a capacity of 20,000 in the middle of Manhattan had only recently begun hosting rock shows. When Chris Dreja of the Yardbirds was first told that Jimmy Page's band was playing in Madison Square Garden in 1971 he had assumed they had the name of the venue wrong because he couldn't imagine a musical act filling so large a space. The headliner on the occasion Mott the Hoople went was Jethro Tull.

A one-legged, flute-playing, codpiece-to-the-fore repudiation of the conventional wisdom that English bands hoping to make it in the USA had first to jettison the very idiosyncrasies the English hold so dear, Jethro Tull were, if anything, more popular in the USA than they were in the UK. This was despite their specializing in complex musical tales that appeared to have been cooked up in some student dramatic society, indulging themselves in on-stage business redolent of the BBC's 1940s radio comedy show *Much Binding in the Marsh*, and taking their name from a pioneer of English agriculture. Their Madison Square Garden shows in December 1972 came at the end of a US tour that had begun in the spring. It was their eleventh tour of the United States and their experience was evident in everything they did. They had gone there first in 1969, out of curiosity as much as anything, and lost money on their first two tours. When the third tour went into profit they realized that while in the UK they had probably reached a plateau, in the USA they could keep on reaching new people. In an interview in 1971, front man Ian Anderson described America as the place to play and England the place to live. Anderson was already starting to prepare for the big American tours as seriously as an actor. 'You give up smoking and do deep breathing exercises. We rehearse before a tour and gradually work up to it, with a final dress rehearsal. When we're on tour it's total involvement. The first week home after a tour of the States is written off completely to adjust to the time changes.'

How exactly Jethro Tull's support act that night at Madison Square Garden came to be Roxy Music is not exactly clear. Roxy Music at the time were England's new darlings. Roxy Music had happened in the kind of way that a band can only happen in England. With staggering speed. Approximately five people – managers, record executives, journalists, style-mongers and Pete Townshend – had decided that they were going to be the next big thing and, behold, they duly were the next big thing. Their first album had come out in England that spring and captivated the taste-makers on the basis of its cover alone. They then followed it with a single, 'Virginia Plain', which even proved popular with the great unwashed who followed the uppers and downers and hanging-arounders in the weekly singles chart. Everybody in Britain wished to touch the hem of Roxy Music's garment. It seemed they could do no wrong.

It seemed obvious to all concerned that Roxy Music's next step should be America. In the interviews before they went they talked of how excited they were and how America was their second home and it was where all their favourites – which included Fred Astaire as well as Elvis Presley – came from and how New York was going to welcome them with open arms. It was not to be. Their second gig in the United States was a twenty-five-minute set in a cavernous exhibition centre of the kind they had not the slightest experience of filling, playing without benefit of a sound check, with the bass not making itself felt in the mix until fifteen minutes had gone by in front of a bunch of American Jethro Tull fans who were frankly puzzled as to what they were supposed to be seeing and hearing.

Roxy Music at the Garden was the first example of what would be one of the recurring features of the Special Relationship from 1972 on. Over the years there would be many such blind dates between Main Street America and Smart Aleck Englishness and they all seemed fated to misfire. It would be replayed with a different cast many times in the future. This was what was bound to happen when a country which has a hundred different ways to denote sophistication comes face to face with a country that meets all such excursions with the same disapproving adjective.

Roxy Music marks the point at which America fell out with Britain for the first time since the Beatles arrived in 1964. Some American observers found this disappointing. Journalist Lenny Kaye, covering the Madison Square Garden show for *Rock Scene* magazine, described the two young Tull fans sitting in the seventh row passing their hash pipe between them, watching what was unfolding on stage without comment until one turned to the other and said, 'Boy, are they weird!' Kaye was confident that all these Jethro Tull fans would need was greater familiarity, more radio play, to change their views. He was wrong. America would never take to the same thrusting, arty Roxy Music that the British had taken to their hearts. It would be another decade before Roxy Music had a big hit in the USA and then it was with a very different sound, a much changed and far less confrontational vibe.

America would not be hurried along at the urging of change as had happened in the UK. America was not going to respond to the challenge of getting on the bus. America would never be susceptible to fashion's key driver, which as ever is the fear of being out of fashion. The *New York Times*, while noting that Roxy Music were, much like the headliners Jethro Tull, another British band attempting to fuse disparate genres into a new whole, described their efforts to perform in the face of the crowd's 'benign indifference' as slightly embarrassing. America's less benign reaction was better expressed

Within a year of Elton John's American debut Bernie Taupin was marrying Maxine Feibelman, the 'Tiny Dancer' of the song, in a ceremony that raised eyebrows in Market Rasen (*left*). Also in 1971 the unknown David Bowie (*below*) travelled to the United States for the first time, playing for the smart set from a waterbed at a Hollywood party. He too returned to Britain utterly changed by the experience.

Led Zeppelin's sex appeal worked on boys, girls and groupies, for whom their end-of-tour visits to Los Angeles were carnal jamborees. In the days before social media, wives and girlfriends of British band members only got to know about this via the odd stray picture turning up in the British music papers.

Rodney Bingenheimer's English Disco in Hollywood was the place where the girls came to bag themselves an English rock star, and visiting performers like Dave Hill of Slade (*above*) came to live out their side of the fantasy. By 1974 bands like Black Sabbath, Deep Purple and ELP were jetting in for massive paydays such as the California Jam (*right*) where David Coverdale (*below*) performed with a cheque for a million dollars in his back pocket.

The prospect of American success transformed the economics and the aesthetics of British music. Elton John adapted to the demands of massive shows at venues like the Los Angeles Dodgers Stadium in 1975 (*top*) . Rod Stewart's high-profile affair with movie star Britt Ekland (*above and left*) promoted him in the show business pecking order. His 1975 album *Atlantic Crossing* was made in America for the American market and was so successful it seemed to render him stateless.

The Sex Pistols pretended not to be interested in breaking America but couldn't resist its lure. Their manager tried to make things different by entering via the southern states but they were already so far beyond their moment that it was inevitable they would finish their tour by breaking up in San Francisco in January 1978.

The bands that came out of the English New Wave were ambivalent about America. Artists like Elvis Costello craved the acclaim of the country and the billboards above Sunset Strip while simultaneously acting as though they were above it all. This tension is what led to Costello's brawl with Bonnie Bramlett in 1979, which set his career back years.

The 1982 arrival in America of acts like Culture Club (*above*), Eurythmics and Duran Duran, which owed a lot to the video revolution, a resurgent British fashion industry and America's fascination with sexual identity, was hailed as a second British invasion. By the time of the Live Aid concert in 1985 (*below*) the two countries seemed further apart than ever.

By the middle of the 1980s the USA was back in the driving seat of world music for the first time since the age of Elvis, thanks to massive solo superstars like Bruce Springsteen (*above*) and Madonna (*below*). When they sang, they sang of America, and the British lapped it up.

in the review of their first album in the Detroit rock and roll magazine *Creem* where Robot A. Hull said that the worst thing about it was that the cover was so godawful synthetic you might want to display it on your coffee table and that the singer's name was pronounced 'fairy – and that's exactly what he is'.

It was years before the members of Roxy Music could talk about their feelings following that show. In the twenty-first century, guitarist Phil Manzanera remembers taking the stage with his tiny little amp. 'We just came off in a complete daze and then watched Jethro Tull play incredibly and with all the lights and the PA and everything; we thought "Ah, oh dear, how do we do this?" So we had a lot to learn, and then we were put on supporting the strangest people, you know, Edgar Winter and Humble Pie, and it was all totally wrong and difficult and we had to try and learn how to play with the big boys – which we never did, really.'

After the gig Mott the Hoople found themselves in Roxy Music's dressing room making musicians' small talk, which must have added significantly to Roxy Music's discomfiture. Bryan Ferry avoided Ian Hunter's eye. This wasn't surprising. When an Englishman has just performed such an emphatically underwhelming debut in New York and come face to face with the fact that the currency which buys him so much at home is not legal tender on his travels, the very last thing he wishes to see is a friendly face from home.

Many of the artists who rolled off the UK production line in the early 1970s fell under the umbrella of glam and few of them had an easy time of it in the United States. Marc Bolan, for one, was somewhat premature in marking his conquest of America in 1972 by sprinkling dollar bills from his seventh-floor balcony at the City Squire Hotel. Even though he had enjoyed a genuine US hit with 'Get It On', retitled 'Bang A Gong' to protect delicate American sensibilities, he never managed to deliver in concert the knee-trembler that his records could deliver. He did his best to fill the gap when he played Carnegie Hall in early 1972 by turning up the volume past the point of good sense. The *New York Times* got their revenge by reviewing the publicity rather than the concert, pointing out that the spotlights sweeping the sky on 57th Street, the blanket radio coverage and the thousands of dollars spent on advertising had 'all the elements of hyped superstardom', and said what a pity it was that this tiny man at the centre of it all couldn't live up to it. For all his bravado, Bolan was terrified of exactly this kind of reaction and had dealt with his nerves by drinking two bottles of champagne and doing some substandard cocaine before taking the stage. Worse than that, he appeared in a T-shirt bearing a picture of himself. This is the kind of thing the English are prepared to take as a joke but the Americans read as evidence of the kind of vanity they will not readily forgive. Interviewing Bolan in New York in May 1972, Ritchie Yorke of the *NME* concluded, 'It would seem the days have gone when every English musical discovery, no matter how minor, automatically broke through in the States', but was content to reproduce Bolan's account of how swimmingly it had all been going, how John Lennon wanted to come to their gig at Carnegie Hall but couldn't get a ticket and how he had seen Paul Simon dancing in the aisle. Simon wasn't dancing in the aisles for long. According to Bolan's manager Tony Secunda, who broke with him after that show, Bolan was sitting on the steps outside when a disgusted Paul Simon exited the venue and went stalking off into the night saying, 'This is fucking bullshit, man.'

Slade's failure to make any impression in the US was made worse by the manner in which they were launched there. Their manager Chas Chandler, formerly a member of the Animals, felt they had to arrive as a proven success and was even happy to have them billed as the heirs to the Beatles' crown. Before their 1973 visit he called a press conference at Gatwick airport in the hope of getting a 'not since the Beatles' story going. It didn't work. Dave Hill's announcement that he had a new stage costume with padded shoulders in honour of American football and would be playing a new raygun-shaped guitar bearing the legend 'Superyob' didn't help. They never had a prayer. Taking the stage in their mirrored hats and platform boots only underlined the contrast between their 'anything for a laugh' approach and the stern artisanal values and instrumental heavy-lifting of headliners like Johnny Winter and Humble Pie. They were written off as pretenders before they had even begun. Watching Humble Pie night after night, Noddy Holder realized that while he and his friends had a bunch of concise, catchy songs, that was no substitute for Humble Pie's ability to fill up two hours with rock noise. Noise was the quality British bands like Ten Years After, Savoy Brown and Black Sabbath all had. They could deliver yards of the stuff. If all else failed they could, if necessary, batter audiences into submission. The message was starting to come back to the UK. To make it in America you had to be obvious.

Sometimes it was just a question of luck. It's possible that Queen would have made more of an impact on their 1974 tour, when they supported Mott the Hoople, if they hadn't had to abandon it in New York in May when Brian May went down with hepatitis. By then Ian Hunter was leading a new line-up of Mott the Hoople with a new guitarist replacing Mick Ralphs, who had gone off to join Bad Company, a band put together and managed by Led Zeppelin's Peter Grant with a view to making it in the USA. Their first album went to number one. By 1975 they had made so much money that they were forced to leave the UK and live in Malibu. By then Ian Hunter was starting again as a solo act.

The artists that magazines choose to feature on their covers reflect the prejudices of the editors. The choices are also made in the hope of attracting new readers. In the light of this it's interesting to note how few British acts were featured on the cover of *Rolling*

Stone in the first half of the 1970s. The Beatles, the Rolling Stones and the Who were regularly represented, both individually and collectively, as they continue to be to the present day, but there were precious few new members of that exclusive club beyond Elton John and Rod Stewart. David Bowie appeared alongside the line 'Are you man enough for David Bowie?' in November 1972 when he was touring the USA behind *Ziggy Stardust*, but then he wasn't seen again for another four years until he'd reached the safe harbour of a number one single with 'Fame', which was his first genuine American hit. By then he'd shrugged off his drag, parted company with his English musicians, embraced disco and, for the avoidance of doubt, put out an album called *Young Americans*. He knew as well as anyone: if you were going to make it in the United States you had to go native.

18

'See you, suckers!'

O n 15 August 1975, in the same week that the Birmingham Six were jailed – a bad decision that would not be reversed until 1991 – and the motor manufacturer British Leyland came into government ownership – a bad decision that would not succeed in its objective of rescuing the British car industry from extinction – a new Rod Stewart album called *Atlantic Crossing* was released. This was an album that many people in Britain, most prominent among them the members of his band the Faces, also thought would turn out to be an admittedly less momentous but no less bad decision.

In terms of his standing in the United States they were entirely incorrect, but when it came to the effect that record would have on his image in the United Kingdom they could have been on to something. *Atlantic Crossing* would triumphantly reset his career as a solo act but it would also bring about the end of the band with whom he had ridden to fame, a band who to many represented something profoundly English, a bunch of musicians drawn together more by the bonds of friendship and the conviviality of the public bar than the stroke of an agent's pen. On a broader front and in the fullness of time, *Atlantic Crossing* would ultimately provide a template for those rock purists and Little Englanders who held that America in general and Hollywood in particular was the root of most of the corruption in the world, the place that lay in wait for Englishmen and stole their souls. It's at this point in the familiar story of British acts making it in the United States that national pride quietly curdled into national resentment, and 'doing well over there' all too easily shaded into 'selling out over there'.

The cover of *Atlantic Crossing* for a start was quite the statement. It was given over to an airbrush illustration by the English émigré artist Peter Lloyd. This depicted the singer with one foot back in the old country (with a flag of St Andrew flying from the top of the Palace of Westminster) and his front foot stepping over the towers of Manhattan to be planted in the United States. Seen from the vantage point of Britain this could all too easily be read as 'See you, suckers!' Ever since 1969 Rod Stewart had pursued parallel careers as the singer in the Faces, one of the most popular live acts either side of the Atlantic, and as a solo artist, in which capacity it just so happened that he made records that far outsold those of the band. Up until 1975 the solo records had been made for a different, European company. With *Atlantic Crossing*, that changed. He was now signed to the same American label as the band. This did not afford the latter any comfort whatsoever. It was taken as read that if Warner Bros had a choice they would rather get behind Rod the solo artist, even if only on the grounds that it is always easier to deal with one person rather than the five people in a group. The other members of the Faces were acutely aware that if *Atlantic Crossing* did well then it would probably be curtains for them.

Former leading light Ronnie Lane had already left and drummer Kenney Jones had gone public about the fact that Rod's unavailability to play certain shows during the summer of 1975 had cost him $500,000 'and put the rest of us in a predicament'. The other thing that had put them in a predicament was that Ron Wood was simultaneously moonlighting with the Rolling Stones and doing his own solo records. These last, Ron speculated in an interview, did not sell very well because Warner Bros promoted Rod's at the expense of his. (There has yet to be a proven case of a company actively seeking to stop members of the public buying one of its products in order to aid its own negotiations with talent. Talent, however, continues to believe this is the case. It's the music business equivalent of the Deep State. Always suspected but never proven.) Most tellingly of all, when Ronnie Lane had left the band in 1973 they had replaced him with the Japanese bass guitarist Tetsu Yamauchi and were now talking of further bolstering their line-up with the Texan Jesse Ed Davis, thereby breaking the link with the bunch of London boys they had been when they formed the band.

Much as the previous decade had appeared to be the era of the group, the seventies, thanks to Elton John, James Taylor, Cat Stevens and Carole King, appeared to be shaping up as the time for single men or women. In 1975 Rod Stewart had acquired the best asset any single male solo singer could have, which was a celebrity girlfriend. Comprising one half of a power couple quadrupled an artist's media coverage in those pre-digital days because it gave the papers and magazines a reason to be interested in you which was above and beyond the merely musical. If the other party happened to be a photogenic movie actress this coverage was multiplied further. With his new relationship, Rod Stewart advanced emphatically from the pop section to the front page.

He was introduced to Britt Ekland in Hollywood by Joan Collins and her husband Ron Kass, which was a clear indication of what he was getting into. Ekland's two previous paramours had been Peter Sellers, from whom she had learned much about the fathomless insecurity of the male star, and impresario Lou Adler, from whom she had learned that the big beasts of the music business often behave with a sense of entitlement to which they never give a second thought. Britt was a couple of years older than Rod and certainly knew more about show business than he did but she was excited by the idea of being with somebody her own age because at last she could have the young life she felt she had missed out on. For Britt, going out with Rod was a slight step down into a funkier ambience. For him, it was a step up to the Presidential Suite, from the rock shows to the chat shows, from the public bar to the private room. Rod's PR man Tony Toon, who had always seen it as his job to get Rod in the papers rather than keep him out of them, triumphantly hailed their romance as making them a Burton and Taylor for the seventies.

Whether or not Rod Stewart had ever consciously considered projecting himself as such, the label 'ladies man' was one that, thanks to the combination of songs like 'Maggie May', his hectic social life and his genuinely inimitable appearance, tended to have little trouble attaching itself to him. This was still the era when the gatekeepers of the media wielded the power not only to give but also to withhold the pages of newsprint or hours of airplay that might make the difference between success and failure. In Britain they had a further string to their bow. They could bestow or withhold the favour of the nation; and this being Britain, that favour rarely came without a dash of sanctimony. It's forgotten now, but in 1975 Rod Stewart had, in living memory, been the great hope of British rock. In 1975 it still wasn't many years since he had been the lad of choice for both the *NME* and John Peel. Now that he was swanning about the world so clearly enjoying the fruits of his success, and with a Hollywood star on his arm, he had clearly traded up from the union bar to the penthouse suite and was suddenly persona non grata. Whereas the Americans will generally accept that one of the inevitable consequences of doing well is that you will make a lot of money and one of the consequences of making a lot of money is that you will change, the British pretend not to be able to see why these clearly transformed creatures cannot continue to act the way they had previously acted back in their scuffling days. In Rod's case this wasn't helped by his tendency to flaunt his wealth and an occasional insensitivity to how things looked. He would be the one who would say that a woman's place was in the home. In April 1975 he was interviewed for *Rolling Stone* by Cameron Crowe in the back of a limo on the way to a gig in San Bernardino. Also in the limo was the child film star Tatum O'Neal drinking from a bottle of Blue Nun. She was eleven years old and her father had asked Rod to look after her for the day. The fact that this went unremarked at the time is an indication of just what an anything-goes world it was in 1975.

It wouldn't remain that way for long. Things were starting to tighten up as a handful of English rock stars returned from the new world clearly having made more money than they knew what to do with. In the nineteenth century the wealthy sons of the British Empire invested the booty from their overseas estates in country houses close to London. When it came to decor they favoured a heavy style as though to suggest that their wealth had been passed down rather than acquired with indecent haste. By 1975 Rod Stewart, like an increasing number of rock stars, had just such a place. This was in Windsor, which was handy for both Heathrow airport and the Queen. It had been bought from a peer of the realm who could no longer afford its upkeep. There were ten bedrooms. There were horses in the paddock. There were trophies of big game on the walls. Almost immediately it was further transformed into a perfect example of rock star baronial of the kind that was being pioneered by the new generation of rock stars flush with dollar income. A Wurlitzer jukebox was installed in the old servants' hall. Holes were knocked in walls to facilitate the installation of a miniature railway. Into this splendour were inserted the living habits of the English working class on the budget of the upper middle. His pre-Ekland girlfriend Dee Harrington was instructed to start serving up the traditional English Sunday roast as soon as the sound of his traditional Italian Lamborghini coming up the drive indicated that the young master was returned from the footy.

Rod and Dee Harrington's Swedish replacement spent some time in Windsor but from 1975 on the focus was on the United States. At this point in the 1970s, Harold Wilson's Labour government's determination to raise the higher rate of tax had resulted in a few successful acts deciding that since they did most of their work overseas, and made most of their money overseas, it might be sensible to go and live overseas, at least for a full tax year. Most of the records by British acts that made number one in the *Billboard* charts in 1975 – from the second album by the Average White Band through Elton John's *Rock Of The Westies* to Wings' *Venus And Mars* – were recorded far away from Britain for reasons that were more fiscal than musical. Asked why his new album *Numbers* had been recorded in Canada, the not yet completely ethereal Cat Stevens claimed it was because the studio had a nice view of a lake.

The tax exile question was just beginning to be added to the quiver of questions with which English reporters sought to prosecute their time-honoured mission of putting the high and mighty in their place. When Rod Stewart was interviewed by Steve Clarke for the *NME* at a press junket in Dublin that July he was compelled to deny that he had just been turned back at Heathrow because entering the country would have forced him to pay a tax bill of £750,000. Reporters have always had a sketchy grasp of tax affairs, as some of their own returns would probably attest. However, in the course of a stormy press conference in Dublin one reporter was sufficiently seized with self-righteousness to shout, 'Why don't you make your contribution to the British economy? They need the money.'

Atlantic Crossing was his first record for an American record company after a stint with a European one, and in every single respect it had clearly been made with American success in mind. It had an American producer, Tom Dowd, with American musicians like the Muscle Shoals rhythm section. It was the first one not to feature any of the contributions of his mates from the Faces. It even opened with 'Three Time Loser', a self-penned number in which the singer bemoans the fact that he caught the disease up in Monterey, shook it off in East Virginia and now finds his consolation 'jacking off' to *Playboy*, suggesting that he now even performed self-abuse with the American market in mind. It could scarcely have been any more American had it been made by Bob Seger.

It was Rod's first experience of recording in America and he was to find that they did things very differently there. Dowd set aside three weeks for its making and mixing and then delivered it in less time, telling Rod that in his experience it was the records that took longer that went wrong. Rod was dazzled by how quickly the American musicians could arrive at a way of playing a song and how little they would vary from take to take. He soon discovered that there was no point asking the Muscle Shoals musicians to play knock-down, drag-out rock and roll because it simply wasn't in their blood. The other thing that wasn't in their blood was alcohol, partly because Muscle Shoals, Alabama, was in a dry county, and partly because it wasn't their custom. Dowd actually called him in to do the vocal for 'Sailing' in the forenoon, which was shock enough, and furthermore without lubrication, which made it a doubly novel experience. It was all a far cry from those long-drawn-out, boozy sessions with his old mates in the London studio where his earlier albums had been made. Maybe it was this that his old fans missed when the record came out. With *Atlantic Crossing* it seemed that some essence of Willesden had passed out of Rod Stewart's music; it was a quality that not all the Muscle Shoals in the world could ever quite make up for.

In August he was playing Anaheim, California, with the Faces, who still conducted themselves like a band of mates. The openers were a group called Fleetwood Mac, another bunch of Brits who had decided to devote themselves to the American market. On this occasion the *Rolling Stone* reporter witnessed Rod Stewart's arrival in the backstage area 'in full make-up, blinking his blue eyelids and swigging from a bottle of Courvoisier'. He was accompanied everywhere by his highly publicized new partner. He was defensive about Ekland's presence, pointing out how important she was to him professionally, that she did his make-up, took photographs and had been the person to advise him that the new record should have one fast side and one slow side. On this occasion she was accompanied by Victoria, her ten-year-old daughter by Peter Sellers, and was recorded putting pressure on Rod to make sure she could travel with them the following day on the Learjet 'because her father only lets her fly TWA'.

Britt and Rod had just moved in together at Rod's new American home. This was in the upmarket Holmby Hills section of LA. He had paid $750,000 for this twenty-room mansion and had given Britt a spare $100,000 to spend on decorating it. As a result there were candelabra, silver artichoke tables, a pair of pelicans made of ostrich eggs, and a couple of sofas backed with elephant tusks and upholstered in cowhide. Ekland's memoirs further confide that they called on Sotheby's in Los Angeles for '£6,000 of Old Masters'. One of the strangest features of the way this tribe of peripatetic young men came back from the sheds of America laden with cash and determined to put down roots is how many of them chose to invest that cash in places that seemed built more for show than comfort; how much of the money they had made playing for hot, sweaty crowds was lavished on cold marble floors and fragile ornaments; how these people who had been essentially rootless since first they got in the back of the Transit at the age of eighteen should, when finally given unlimited choice and unlimited budget, decide on places to settle that seemed to have so few of the properties that most of us would associate with home.

Having spent so much on the place, Rod was unable to resist the opportunity to show it off. The couple were photographed on the diving board of his pool, she in a bikini, he in budgie smugglers with a football parked between his legs. This was exactly the kind of flash behaviour that in time we came to expect of the new generation of rock stars. Nowadays only Premier League footballers would make these kind of gestures. Back in 1975, successful footballers lived in houses as modest as their bank managers and the nearest they would have come to the lifestyle of a Rod Stewart would have been via an eight-track in the glove compartment of their Cortina. Rod, on the other hand, had an AC Cobra, an Excalibur and a Lamborghini in his garage in Holmby Hills. The latter he had had air-freighted from Rome to Los Angeles for £2,000. This was in the days when £2,000 was a decent annual salary.

Rod Stewart interviews were already starting to become difficult. He prevaricated in his interview for *Rolling Stone*, saying that he hadn't decided whether he was going to stay with the Faces or not and even suggesting they might make another album together, possibly in Australia, where they were set to go in the course of a tour in the winter. He told the interviewer that he missed playing in the UK because there were some songs where the audience sang every word and he hardly needed to sing himself. He would like to hear them sing 'Sailing', which had been number one in the UK for four weeks but, he thought, wouldn't be in the States. 'I don't think it's an American single.'

By the time the piece appeared at the beginning of November the prevarication was all over. The rest of the Faces were presented with a magazine which had on its cover, instead of the usual picture of the members of the Faces wreathed in alcoholic amity, their lead singer in a practised clinch with Britt Ekland. The cover announced 'Rod Stewart and his new pal Britt Ekland'. The feature inside, in which the interview with the pal was longer than any of the interviews with the other band members, was headlined 'Rod Stewart faces the American dream', and went on: 'A solo spotlight, a Hollywood mansion, a glamorous girlfriend and lower taxes. Every picture tells a story, don't it?' This clearly confirmed everything his detractors back home had been saying. He had gone native. He was lost in showbiz.

On 18 December at a press conference in London he announced that the Faces were breaking up. The planned tour of Asia and Australia had been cancelled. The reason provided was the fact that Ron Wood was joining the Rolling Stones, but no less significant was the fact that Rod was in the process of forming his own band. Which he subsequently did. And he prospered. Of all the people who left big bands in the mid-seventies hoping to carve a solo career Rod Stewart was the most successful. And has remained so. The man who in 1975, at the age of thirty, said that he wouldn't want to be doing what he was doing when he was forty would turn out still to be doing it in 2020 at the age of seventy-five. These days his property dealings are still big news in papers all over the world and his Beverly Hills mansion still merits a spread in *Architectural Digest*. And still it seems the remaining members of the Faces, Ron Wood and Kenney Jones, stand ready to get the band back together at the smallest excuse.

The Faces' keyboard player Ian McLagan, who died in 2014, said of *Atlantic Crossing*, 'It's very sterile, unemotional . . . he wasn't stretching himself . . . Down deep he hasn't changed at all, but he's all into that Hollywood thing.' True to that same 'Hollywood thing' he let Britt Ekland go in 1977, trading her in for the first in a number of younger, equally blonde models. She sued him for what was just starting to be called 'palimony' and reached a settlement out of court. In her score-settling memoir *True Britt* she makes no bones about her role in changing him. She says that Rod Stewart was always self-conscious about his humble beginnings and that she was the one who gave him an appreciation of culture and the arts. 'I was a walking encyclopaedia on where to dress, where to dine and where to find antiquity. I had shown Rod, my proletarian bard, a new style of living but he was never to shake himself free from the tawdrier facets of his environment.'

Somebody had to become the poster boy for the new tax exile class of rock star. For a variety of reasons – the way he was seen to ditch his old band mates, the speed with which he seemed to move from blonde to blonde like an ageing roué worried about his virility, his unapologetic embracing of the kind of nice things that such millionaires come to covet, and his stubborn refusal to pretend that he was missing the old country – Rod Stewart became that person. He took on that role just in time to get it in the neck from the new puritanism which was starting to brew around rock from 1976 on. In May of that year Charles Shaar Murray used a review of an Ian Hunter album in the *NME* to point out that there was a difference between a tax exile and an expatriate. John Lennon, he said, was an example of the latter whereas Rod Stewart, having lost touch with his background, was a tax exile and as such he was 'artistically as well as politically and geographically in limbo'. The following year even *Rolling Stone* pronounced that 'a lot of kids in England don't care what kind of fashionable gauche trinkets decorate Rod Stewart's high-class Hollywood home' or how much money he wound up paying Britt Ekland. Something was changing in the water. Where the wealth of the tax exile rock star had once excited envy, it now seemed to excite a kind of pity. Which is the way it has been ever since.

Rod Stewart is now, in common with the rest of the handful of British superstars, a knight of the realm, though his took the longest time to arrive. He received his honour wearing tartan trousers because clearly he didn't quite have the nerve for the kilt. His attitude to his home country, England, is somewhat complicated by the fact that his primary identification is with Scotland, the country of his father's birth, and he is, along with Sean Connery, one of a small group of highly paid entertainment folk who celebrate their Scottishness by visiting there occasionally while not actually living there. He flies in whenever Celtic have a significant match. This only seems to add to the poignancy of his gilded plight. Ever since 1975, Rod Stewart has been effectively the first stateless superstar. When punk came along in 1977 it seemed that he, more than any of his peers, had a target on his back.

19

'I'm so bored with the USA'

If you were brought up in England in the couple of decades following the war, dental treatment was something you went to considerable lengths to avoid. The technology employed was crude, the hygienist not yet invented, at least some of the men wearing white coats had learned their trade in the armed forces and had the manners that went with it, and it was not unknown for even a seven-year-old's mother to be sunnily asked, 'Does he want cocaine?'

Hence British teenagers who could avoid going to the dentist entirely in those days tended to do so, and thus by the time they were in their twenties the results of all this neglect were evident in teeth that were discoloured, uneven and sometimes not present at all. Keith Richards is just one of this generation; in his autobiography *Life* he devotes two paragraphs to his terror of dentistry and the lengths he would go to avoid it. He wasn't the only one. Even as a star David Bowie worked very hard on every aspect of his external appearance but whenever he opened his mouth it was like being vouchsafed the first glimpse into an Egyptian burial chamber. It wasn't until the late 1990s, after some time living in the United States, that Bowie's teeth were considered sufficiently presentable to be featured on the cover of one of his LPs. Before that he kept them sheathed whenever the camera was around.

Queen singer Freddie Mercury was said to have extra teeth at the back of his mouth. These pushed the ones at the front forward, which is what caused his pronounced overbite. Mercury similarly shied away from having anything done about them, arguing that corrective surgery might change the way he sang. At that time anyway, a British rock star who was prepared to consider any permanent change to his appearance would have been risking the scorn of his peers. Messing around with what providence had given you seemed like a form of cheating. This is why they often seemed determined to beat their detractors to it by heaping the scorn on themselves before anyone else could get a chance. Three of the most prominent English front men of the 1970s, Rod Stewart, Freddie Mercury and Elton John, were so open about their physical shortcomings that they facetiously considered launching themselves as a group called Nose, Teeth and Hair.

It so happened that in December 1976 Queen pulled out of a booking to appear on a TV magazine show because Freddie Mercury was, for the first time in fifteen years, visiting a dentist. The newly signed band EMI offered in their place made more of an impact on the programme than Queen could possibly have made. Teeth were a big part of that impact.

The Sex Pistols had been formed a year earlier from the rascals who hung around Sex, Malcolm McLaren's provocative clothes shop on Chelsea's King's Road. The singer had 'auditioned' by miming to Alice Cooper's 'I'm Eighteen' on the shop's jukebox. He came from Finsbury Park. It was decreed that he needed a more charismatic name than John Lydon. Looking at his teeth, which had evidently avoided dentistry for as long as Keith Richards', somebody suggested he could be called Johnny Rotten.

The name was perfectly emblematic of how the Sex Pistols not only embraced notoriety but also set themselves up in direct opposition to everything that pop music had come to hold so dear. They were, quite self-consciously, in the tradition of the Marlon Brando character in *The Wild One* who, on being asked what he's rebelling against, enquires, 'What have you got?' They followed through on the logic of the old yippie saying 'we are the people our parents warned us against'. Dismissal was the Sex Pistols' art form. They were against everything. Sex was just a few minutes of squelching. Even fun was no fun. They were against all standard notions of popularity. They were in open revolt against their record company, whichever one that happened to be at the time. They had no time for anyone who had gone before. They hated the press. They despised the broadcast media, particularly those arms of the latter, such as Bill Grundy's magazine programme, which had made the mistake of booking them and then dared them to swear, which they duly did. Overnight the Sex Pistols became more famous in Britain than any pop group since the Beatles and more notorious than all the other notorious pop groups put together.

One of the things the Sex Pistols were most against was America. One of the things they disliked most openly were Yanks. In that way there was something profoundly English about punk rock. So much of it was built upon the standard English resentments which spiked any conversation with a London cab driver. When Russ Meyer, the American film director who came to London in 1977 supposedly to direct a film about them, started on a riff about how America 'saved your asses in 1944', the Sex Pistols reacted to him much as their fathers might have done. The subsequent exchange was reported in *Rolling Stone*:

'Like fuck you did . . .' Rotten trails off, suddenly realizing he's put himself in the position of defending his country. 'You can slag off England all you want. There's no such thing as patriotism any more. I don't care if it blows up. There's more tourists in London than Londoners. You never know what accent you're going to get when you ask directions.'

The Sex Pistols tried to drum up reasons for their antipathy to anything American but in truth they were merely being open about a resentment most of their countrymen preferred to keep under wraps. In this they were just displaying their Englishness. There is a classic scene in the British sitcom *Whatever Happened to the Likely Lads?* where the heroes, two young men in the north-east of England, run through a litany of their prejudices about the outside world. They begin with hairdressers, progress through Italians, Germans and the French, then the Scots, the Welsh and Londoners before being forced to admit that they don't actually have much time for the people living down the same street. The punk rock brouhaha, which was obsessing a section of the British media at the time, was all about marking out a small area of territory and then making sure you were on the inside of it. In the spirit of that, the Sex Pistols' antagonistic attitude towards America was a convenient way of flagging up how different they were from all the groups who had gone before. Unlike them, they weren't going to be falling over themselves in an unseemly rush to curry the favour of the United States.

The Sex Pistols' contemporaries the Clash even had a song called 'I'm So Bored With The USA', a sentiment which in the music business milieu was more radical than anything in the Sex Pistols' 'God Save The Queen', which was contending for the number one spot during the week in the summer of 1977 when the nation celebrated the twenty-fifth anniversary of Queen Elizabeth II's accession to the throne. This was really going against the tide. Ever since the Beatles arrived at JFK in 1964 English rock music had been stepping westward, often without thinking about it. It seemed that everyone in this damp island hankered after the same wide open spaces, the same life of ease, the same greenback dollars, the same air conditioning, the same twenty-four-hour TV. There had been an assumption underpinning everyone from the Dave Clark Five to Genesis that bigger was better and that America was an unavoidable component of 'bigger'. One of the first questions the Sex Pistols were asked after it was clear that they were going to make records was 'Are you going to go to America?'

The people keenest to know the answer were those people in the States who had been batting for some sort of return of the insurrectionary spirit in pop music, had seen the likes of the New York Dolls come and go, and were now watching the skies over London for a star in the east that they might go there and worship. Punk rock was all about the energy of two cities, New York and London, both of which seemed to be on the point of falling apart in the mid-seventies. In both cases urban decay had the happy effect of providing living and rehearsal space to bands who drew their members from outside the usual musicians' circles, often from the performing arts and other unlikely places. Malcolm McLaren ended up managing the New York Dolls because he had met Sylvain Sylvain years earlier when the latter had come to London to sell his retro clothing at the Wembley Rock and Roll Festival of 1972, an occasion key to the development of an international brotherhood of people who felt that pop music had gone wrong since the mid-sixties.

Each city kept a close eye on each other's hotspots, on Max's Kansas City or CBGB in New York, on the Roxy and the Vortex in London. There was a brisk traffic in outrage between the two of them, a traffic that was vigorously stirred by print media such as the

NME and *New York Rocker*, all of which were enjoying circulation figures they would never enjoy again. American punk acts like the Ramones and Patti Smith were celebrities in London when they were still a joke in their own town. On the Fourth of July weekend in 1976 the Ramones played the Roundhouse in London and everyone who considered themselves punk came out to see them. The Sex Pistols thought the Ramones were a genuine street gang. The Ramones knew they weren't. For their part they found the Sex Pistols genuinely intimidating and were surprised to find themselves being looked up to. American punk rock chronicler Legs McNeil remembers Joey Ramone coming back changed utterly by the experience. Previously they had been preaching to the same hundred people in the Bowery, most of whom were middle-class pretenders, but now there were signs of the kind of popularity they had never considered before. 'Legs, you wouldn't believe it! They love it!'

A year later the kids who had laid siege to the Ramones' dressing room were now bigger stars and it was time for them to repay the compliment. In the middle of 1977, as 'God Save The Queen' was poised to enter the British charts at number one, despite being banned from the airwaves, British journalist Kris Needs talked to the Sex Pistols in a Wimpy bar in Oxford Street for *New York Rocker* and asked if they wanted to go to America. 'Not really,' said Rotten. 'I did once but after seeing all the Americans that come over here and their attitude . . . They're all so old and like has-beens.'

If this was intended to cool America's interest in this new sound from England it didn't work. There was still a tacit assumption that if something was causing excitement in England it would eventually cause excitement in the United States, and consequently there was a scramble to be one of the conduits for this excitement. American TV networks sent their camera crews on to the streets of London in search of people with safety pins through their cheeks. American magazines gorged themselves on stories about what this all meant for attitudes to the Crown. American record companies abased themselves before Malcolm McLaren, if they could only find him. CBS boss Walter Yetnikoff sang 'Anarchy In The UK' to McLaren to prove that he had actually heard it.

Eventually Warner Bros signed the band for a lot of money and were determined they were going to make an impression. There was always a lot of confusion about whether they were motivated by a genuine belief in the group or a pre-digital form of FOMO. Warner executive Bob Krasnow claims he was sent to London by label boss Mo Ostin with press boss Bob Regehr to run the rule over the group. They went and watched them rehearse in some Dickensian catacomb whereupon Krasnow sent a message to Mo saying this was the worst group he'd ever seen in his life. It arrived at the same time as the one from Regehr urging him to sign them because they were bound to be huge.

In 1977 the American record business was riding high. Fleetwood Mac, a British group that had gone native and prospered, were hitting their peak. Disco was proving massively popular. But disco didn't produce any stars, and besides, the audience who had made Led Zeppelin and Rod Stewart big stars wanted no part of it. On the other hand punk bands like the Ramones and Talking Heads were more popular with the taste-makers than the general public. The last Brit on the cover of *Rolling Stone* that year had been Peter Frampton in February. On that occasion publisher Jann Wenner, omniscient on cocaine, had stopped the magazine's presses at ridiculous expense to replace the standard shot of the guitarist with a shirtless cheesecake pic which Frampton blamed for ending his career. It sold well so Wenner didn't mind.

At the same time *Rolling Stone* sent writer Charles M. Young to London to write about this Sex Pistols phenomenon and to prepare the way for their first US tour, which would start just after Christmas. Punk rock may have feigned a lofty lack of interest in the

United States but it really couldn't wait to get there. The resulting two-part piece appeared in October 1977. The cover was made up of a montage of two images of Johnny Rotten and Sid Vicious on stage with the line 'Rock is sick and living in London'. Young went to see them play the Lafayette in Wolverhampton and called it 'the most amazing show I've ever seen'.

Having set themselves up as the champions of the rejected, the Sex Pistols had to find a way to deal with being sought-after. They never did. Malcolm McLaren and the band behaved exactly opposite to the way any English act would have acted in the past when they were being lined up for their big break. They made it clear that they didn't want to cooperate in any publicity. So why, Young asked McLaren, were they doing it? 'My man in America told me to. If we do *Rolling Stone*, we might not have to do another interview for two years. This band hates you. It hates your culture. Why can't you lethargic, complacent hippies understand that? You need to be smashed . . . This is a very horrible country, England. We invented the mackintosh, you know.'

The anti-American rhetoric was a recognition of the fact that no matter what they might say the Sex Pistols had to go to the US. There was no escaping America or its judgement. No matter who they are, bands are like sharks in that they require perpetual motion to survive, and in 1977 the proportion of the globe a rock and roll band could go and entertain was a lot smaller than it is now. Therefore America it had to be. America, what's more, was rolling out the red carpet. McLaren was in the enviable position of being able to avail himself of the advice and counsel of some of the wisest heads in the American business. Warner Brothers head Mo Ostin, agent Frank Barsalona, promoter Bill Graham and even Sid Bernstein, the man who had put the Beatles in Shea Stadium and Carnegie Hall, all had their ideas of what would be the most appropriate way for the Sex Pistols to enter the United States. McLaren had his own idea. He wanted them to do a tour of Texas. That was all. Just Texas. This obsession dated from when he had been involved with the New York Dolls in 1975 and he had taken them on a tour of South Carolina and Florida. Thereafter he remained interested in the idea of taking a band to a place where that band, on the face of it, had no business to be.

This was the Sex Pistols' American dilemma. In Britain it had been a smash and grab. It could never be the same in the United States. Caught between the desire to maintain his maverick image and his fear of exposing them to the summary judgement of the taste-makers on the coasts, McLaren had decided they would enter the States via the South, possibly in the hope that this would provoke them into making a comparable splash. He was similarly ambivalent about TV. Lorne Michaels had booked them to appear on *Saturday Night Live* before the tour began, but McLaren didn't apply for visas in time and also booked them into some UK dates. When the Sex Pistols pulled out of *Saturday Night Live*, to the entirely understandable consternation of Warner Bros, the slot was offered to the Ramones, who turned it down, and then Elvis Costello, who didn't.

Elvis decided he was going to make a mark by planning his own stunt. This involved breaking off the number they had rehearsed as if the idea had just occurred to him and instead launching into 'Radio Radio', his scorching condemnation of the people who ran radio and how they were trying to 'anaesthetize the way that you feel'. This was the first of a number of occasions when visiting British acts tried to use their brief window of prominence as a bully pulpit. They somehow thought this kind of gesture stood a chance of shaming a business as scientific and set in its ways as American pop radio. They had a touching belief that America cared about what the rest of the world thought.

When the Beatles had arrived in 1964 American radio had been a thing of wonder for them. The acts that spearheaded the British Invasion of the late 1970s, by contrast, considered American music radio an abomination. Having been raised initially as children of Radio One and then exposed to the most gentle of commercial alternatives, they were shocked to find that in America the decisions about what might or might not be played on the radio were a question not of taste but of hard-nosed business.

As they traversed the unusually long distances between shows on their early tours they punched the buttons on their car radios and, hearing Led Zeppelin's 'Stairway To Heaven' on almost every channel, deduced that the American public must be as conservative as their radio stations sounded. They thought they must be listening to a form of radio that was mired in the past. What they didn't realize was that this kind of music mix, data-driven and auditorium-tested to within an inch of its life, would be the future of most radio in their own country as well as overseas. America wasn't behind. It was ahead.

In America, where there was massive competition between radio stations, the questions of what to play and in what order had long been a science. In the late seventies in American radio the senior scientist was consultant Lee Abrams. Abrams took the lead in devising radio formats such as AOR ('Album Oriented Rock') and then, with increasing specificity, the Superstars format and then the Soft Superstars format. Whereas in England the radio market was still at the stage of its development where it was mainly concentrating on enthusing its audience, American radio was keen at all costs to avoid alienating them. Therefore Superstars was Classic Rock with the emphasis on the obvious marquee tracks and Soft Superstars was the same thing with the noisy stuff removed. If the listener had many choices at the push of a button the one thing the program director was keenest to do was to discourage them from trying any of them. Abrams was such a success that he started working directly with British acts like Yes and Foghat to tell them how they could make their music more appealing to a wider audience, even to the extent of advising them what key to play in.

American radio was not going to play punk rock records unless it could be guaranteed they would appeal to enough of the right kind of people. Nobody in American radio was going to get on board until they had some degree of certainty that everybody else was going to do so as well. In the trade papers immediately before the Sex Pistols' visit Abrams was interviewed about punk's commercial prospects. He was keen, as was everyone else in the business, to rebrand it as 'new wave', to point out that in Britain it was all 'very political' and that the jury was out as to whether it was going to be a commercial phenomenon along the lines of the British Invasion thirteen years earlier. In fact most of the people in the United States who were familiar with punk rock as a musical phenomenon thought it was something that had begun with the Stooges in the late sixties and was, if anything, rather passé. Taste-makers who'd been banging the drum for it as a precursor of indie music were resentful of what they had seen as music for purists being hijacked by a bunch of English yobs who had more in common with Chaucer than with William Burroughs. When Charles Young had taken in the Slits when they were supporting the Sex Pistols in Wolverhampton, he primly provided translations for those American readers who were unfamiliar with the argot. 'When the audience becomes restless, she [Ari Up] calls them wankers (masturbators).'

McLaren, who had no patience for the baby-sitting which is 50 per cent of band management, didn't go with the Sex Pistols when they flew out. He surely knew that they probably wouldn't last the distance. On the eve of their departure to the United States just after Christmas in 1977 they were refused visas on the grounds of the many convictions for theft they had accumulated between them. It took a Warner Bros lawyer and a record company guarantee of good behaviour backed by a million-dollar surety to put the tour back on. The Pittsburgh show, which was supposed to be their American debut, had to be cancelled because of the delay and so they wound up playing their first American show in Atlanta, Georgia. As soon as they got to JFK they were delivered into the hands of the tour manager, Noel Monk, whom Warner Brothers had hired, then flown to Atlanta. Once at the hotel, John and Sid decided to visit the strip club across the way and were turned back by police for the crime of being foreign pedestrians. If McLaren had hoped that by booking them into the South he would avoid trial by media he was mistaken. The audience at the Great South-East Music Hall was full of members of the New York media.

People on the tour recall a band who were actually quite professional and competent but they were fatally weighed down by Sid Vicious, a bass player who was neither and kept wandering off in search of his true love, which was heroin. It soon turned ugly. Warner Bros had hired muscle on the tour to protect their investment and they were not above setting about Vicious whenever he got out of line, which was often. Rotten was losing interest in the band and was not speaking to McLaren when he joined them. At crisis points like this all bands traditionally look to the one glass-half-full member who can encourage them to make a fresh start. The problem was the Sex Pistols didn't have any such member. At a time when they needed the traditional arm around the shoulder, that's what they didn't get. They were playing venues like Randy's Rodeo in San Antonio, the Kingfish Club in Baton Rouge and the Longhorn Ballroom in Dallas, Texas; support acts included Rockin' Dopsie and the Cajun Twisters. They were pursued by local media looking for some exhibition of outrage, which they were often happy to supply. And then the audience didn't turn out quite the way that McLaren had anticipated when he fantasized about a tour of Texas.

There are two types of American. There are those who have either travelled overseas or would like to. Then there are the other Americans. Not only have they never travelled overseas, not only do they never wish to travel overseas, but they also sometimes give the impression of not being entirely convinced that overseas actually exists. McLaren's plan to introduce the Sex Pistols via Texas may have hinged on the expectation that he could bring them face to face with this inward-looking America and, by doing so, create the same kind of sparks he had created in the UK. It didn't work out that way. The people who were interested in the Sex Pistols belonged to the cohort of the outward-looking. In every town there was a knot of people who knew more about them than they were expecting – people who had been to Britain or happened to keep tabs on what was happening via weeks-old copies of the *NME* or *Sounds*. In San Antonio there was even one Kathy Valentine whose mother was English, who had briefly been a member of Girlschool and would later go on to form the Go-Gos. There were people there who thought the Ramones were old hat. Everybody who turned up had some kind of preconception. The Sex Pistols could never again be unexpected.

Sometimes they played well. Sometimes they didn't. Some people thought it was a thrilling reinvention of rock and roll. Some thought it was a thrilling burial of rock and roll. The one thing that was never going to go down with any American audience was their open rejection of American hospitality, exemplified by Johnny Rotten's incessant ragging on the crowd. 'I'm not here to entertain you,' he said. 'You're here to entertain me.' It was the same Old World condescension, albeit with a different accent. 'How does it feel to have no taste?' And then finally, at Winterland in San Francisco, where they played to 5,000 people who were expecting a rock show and found a group who weren't going to deliver one and wouldn't have been able to hurl one beyond the first five rows even if they had wanted to, 'Ever get the feeling you've been cheated?' It was their last show. *Never Mind The Bollocks* peaked at number 106 in the *Billboard* charts on 21 January 1978. Warner Bros got their million-dollar bond back but never recouped the record deal. If anybody got the cash from the chaos it was, as usual, the lawyers. The first quote the Pistols had ever given the *NME* in 1976 was 'We're into chaos.' Their American tour was true to that.

Every single British band that was signed up by a British record company in the great punk gold rush made their visit to America. In most cases they had been signed by British record companies in the hope that their American uncles would find them appealing and they would be rewarded in cash or in kudos for providing them with the next Pink Floyd or Fleetwood Mac. Nobody thought all of them would be big successes in the United States but hardly anyone suspected the carnage that would ensue. Most of them had the same experience as Glasgow's Simple Minds. There would be an opening at Hurrah or somewhere comparable in New York, where the likes of Iggy Pop or Lou Reed would be in the audience, and then the following night they would be somewhere hundreds of miles upstate where they would find that nobody had heard of them and slightly fewer cared.

British bands who didn't make it in the USA, which was most of them, always came back with a story. They invented these stories to make themselves feel better. The story was usually about how they would have made it had it not been for one thing. The one thing varied. It might be a TV show they refused to do. It could be a promoter they offended. It could have been the union who black-listed them. It might have been the unfortunate thing they said in an interview. It could have been the outstanding drug conviction that prevented them getting a visa. Maybe it was the superstar act who didn't want to have them as their support act. All too often it was, in their telling at least, because they were just simply too red hot for any of those squares in the States to be able to handle.

Even an Irish band like the Boomtown Rats, who arrived in 1978 off the back of a string of big singles in the UK, had their excuse. In their case it was the rats. Many terrible things were done by Americans trying to speak the language of punk rock and the rats were one of them. These rats were dead ones. They were ordered by Mike Bone of Mercury Records in Chicago. It was Bone's bright idea to send them out to radio stations and other outlets who might need reminding to 'get behind' the Boomtown Rats' new album *A Tonic For The Troops*. According to Bone, 'the rats were double-bagged in formaldehyde but they still had a sort of laboratory smell about them'. Bone's bosses thought it was a terrible idea but apparently Bob Geldof and his manager didn't. By the time Geldof had become a knight and written his autobiography the rat stunt had become the one thing that made it impossible for the Boomtown Rats to make it in the USA.

More likely what killed them was the suspicion among the American record-buying public that they had quite enough music of that kind of their own without needing to be shipping it in from across the Atlantic. What didn't help in the case of the Rats and many other bands that went ashore between the arrival of punk rock and the end of the decade is there was no way they could curb an overpowering desire to tell America where it seemed to be going wrong. Geldof was a classic example of this syndrome, introducing his song 'Rat Trap' at the band's New York debut with the words 'Bruce Springsteen couldn't write a song as good as this' – a sentiment guaranteed to recommend him to precisely nobody. He further harangued a convention of radio programmers with a comprehensive listing of their shortcomings.

The UK's class of 1977/78 was spearheaded by people like Geldof, Elvis Costello, Joe Strummer, Johnny Rotten and Paul Weller, some of the most voluble characters ever to sing with pop groups, people from whom you would never expect to hear sentiments along the lines of 'let the music speak for itself'. Consequently their rhetoric was out of balance with their music. They talked a good fight that in many cases they simply couldn't engage in. Geldof later confessed, 'We came in on the back of five hit singles and a number one and thought that America was going to fall prostrate at our feet. In fact America didn't give a fuck about us.'

Pete Thomas of the Attractions was present the night in March 1979 in a hotel bar in Columbus, Ohio when Elvis Costello got involved in a confrontation with members of Stephen Stills' touring band. This started with some light joshing about the contrasting styles of the two countries' approach to popular music and quickly ratcheted into the kind of full-blown national chauvinism that might have kiboshed the D-Day landings had it been aired in the pubs of Hampshire in 1944. 'We hate you,' said Costello, referring to the whole nation. 'We just come here for the money. We're the original white boys and you're the colonials.' Stills' band failed to see the obvious funny side. The exchanges got uglier, things turned physical, and Costello ended up having to apologize to the entire nation. 'Everybody had that angry, frustrated English thing,' says Thomas. 'They don't do that so well in America.'

Punk rock couldn't find a way to deal with America. Punk rock's edge came from its anger but the bands themselves couldn't decide how to feel about America. Punk didn't know whether it ought to be looking up to it or looking down on it. Punk couldn't for a minute let the mask of indifference slip and just confess to the truth: most of them were every bit as delighted to be there as Freddie and the Dreamers had been in 1964. American photographer Bob Gruen watched Johnny Rotten leave Winterland after the Sex Pistols' final show. 'He just seemed to be in a bad mood from day one.

You know, everything sucked. That's why I was so surprised when I saw him leave Winterland with a girl on his arm and half a smile on his face. It was the most human thing I ever saw, because it was something so out of character to see him enjoy a moment of life.'

England is proud of things that don't stick around long enough to get stale. The nation's favourite comedy programme is *Fawlty Towers*, which had just twelve episodes. That's why it's good. The Beatles lasted seven years as a recording group. That's why their stock is so high. The Sex Pistols were never going to hang together long enough to make a name in America the slow way, the way the Who had done it, which in the end is the only way anyone ever makes their name in America. They would first have had to make a good name for themselves, which was never going to be their style.

In the long term they were a massive influence on the people who saw them and many who didn't. It took another year for the legend of the Sex Pistols to be communicated to the twelve-year-old Kurt Cobain in Aberdeen, Washington, via an old copy of *Creem* magazine. It took a further decade for his band's album to be called *Nevermind* in some kind of tribute to the Sex Pistols album, and for Nirvana to become far bigger than the Sex Pistols ever were. Cobain said, 'I wanted to be in a punk band before I ever heard any punk music.'

In April 1980 the Clash appeared on the cover of *Rolling Stone*, celebrating the platinum success of their last album *London Calling*, which was in many ways a love letter to American rock and roll. They were no longer bored with the USA and liked nothing more than having their pictures taken with it as a background.

The Jam, who were actually Britain's most popular act by the end of the 1970s, who were presentable enough to be on the TV, who made singles that were bought by everyone from bank clerks to art students, and who ought to have been reassuring enough for rock and roll traditionalists, did six tours of America in all. They

tried it every which way. They tried the clubs. They tried supporting Blue Öyster Cult to see if there was any sense in attempting to
key into a bigger audience. They found an American firm to share
in their management. They didn't make any public statement
which was likely to get them banned.

In his memoirs, Jam drummer Rick Buckler remembers an
occasion when they were playing support in America. There was
one solitary Jam fan dressed in a black suit and skinny tie who was
standing up and dancing, much as they were used to people doing
at home, and the security kept putting him back in his seat. 'The
thing about American audiences is that they behaved themselves,'
said Buckler with regret. It wasn't just their punk style that was
stopping the Jam making any connection with the American kids.
In that case the headliners were Be-Bop Deluxe, who did no better.

The Jam also had to deal with some mild culture shock. Buckler
frequently couldn't afford to buy food and drink in the expensive
hotels they were booked into and so would set forth on foot in the
reasonable expectation that there would be a shop nearby where he
could buy some beer and potato chips to consume in his room.
Buying beer meant producing ID, which meant showing a British
driver's licence to a person who seemed surprised to discover that
there were countries other than the United States, and then a walk
back to the hotel which was likely to be interrupted by a police
patrol car pulling him over on suspicion of being strange.

In May 1982 the Jam played the last of their six American tours.
In December 1982 they broke up. If America wasn't having them it
seemed there were no new worlds to conquer.

20

'In the country of Liberace, I'm hardly revolutionary'

The murder of John Lennon on 8 December 1980 was perpetrated by one of his American fans. It was perpetrated in New York, the city he had been pleased to call home since 1971 – though Lennon had never lost his affection for the daily life of the country in which he had grown up. He would grab any opportunity to catch up with visitors who could provide him with the most fleeting taste of home, whether it was through quizzing the *Melody Maker*'s Los Angeles correspondent about how it went with the royal family, talking to the woman who ran Elton John's office about the comedies that used to be on the wireless in the fifties, or asking the producers of the BBC's *Old Grey Whistle Test* that for a 1975 appearance he be paid in his favourite biscuit, the Bath Oliver. In 1976 he had concluded his running battle with the US government when he got the green card that entitled him to residency. At the time he was told he would be able to apply for US citizenship in 1981 if he so desired. Whether he would have done so is a matter of speculation. All four Beatles had to some extent found their futures in the United States. At the time of Lennon's death Paul McCartney and George Harrison were both already married to Americans, and in 1981 Ringo Starr would join them upon marrying the actress Barbara Bach.

Lennon's death was taken to the heart of America in a way that might never have happened had it occurred in London. In a sense it was America that led the world's mourning. It was America that set the tone. Only America had the nerve to salute the passing of a venerable artist rather than, as would have been the case in Britain, the tragic death of a cheeky pup from Liverpool. In America it reawakened affection for the music of the 1960s in general and the Beatles in particular and reminded many baby boomers of what they owed to John Lennon. New Yorkers would even apologize to visitors from Britain for the fact that this deed had taken place in their city, as though they had been guilty of the ultimate offence against hospitality.

The night following the shooting, Bruce Springsteen, who was just beginning to graduate from the clubs to the arenas with his tour supporting *The River*, took the stage in Philadelphia and began by saying, 'If it wasn't for John Lennon a lot of us would be in some place much different tonight.' Steve Van Zandt, another of that generation for whom exposure to *A Hard Day's Night* had provided the first glimmer of another way of living, had assumed the show would be off that night but was told by the man who had christened himself 'the Boss', because he knew that there were times when you had to act like one, 'This is what John Lennon inspired us to do and now it's our job to do the same thing for these other people.'

In death, John Lennon became a citizen of the world, and in this his Englishness could too easily have been forgotten. It took Jan

Morris, a writer from Wales – a nation that keeps a close eye on Liverpool – writing in the days after his death, to remind those who needed reminding that the original impact of the Beatles had been 'paradoxically nationalistic':

> Before they even began their progress across continents they had to an astonishing degree transformed the condition, the style and the morale of their own country, Britain. Nothing in the history of popular art is more extraordinary than the revolutionary effect of four provincial musicians . . . upon a nation so old, so proud, so tired, so rigid in its attitudes, conventions and beliefs, so obsessed with its own past that it seemed nothing could ever alter it.

Even the Britons who had lived through that time hadn't permitted themselves the luxury of thinking back on how it had changed the nation's self-image. Now they did. And when they did they realized that one of the outcomes of that transformation had been the growth of an unquestioned conviction that in terms of popular culture it was Britain's job to show the rest of the world where it was going wrong. British acts considered it part of their national role to arrive in America at regular intervals to jump-start what was bound to be an enervated music scene. This was the overarching narrative of hundreds of four-page features which ran in the British music press at the time. Journalists by the score were dispatched to the eastern seaboard to spend a few disoriented hours jotting down the reactions of these lads from English towns as they first encountered air conditioning, the Chrysler Building, breakfast in America, TV evangelists, cops with guns and people who didn't consider the cowboy hat an item of fancy dress. Most of these lads found it impossible to take the place entirely seriously, which may explain why so many of them failed to make a dent. The notion that was seeded back in 1964 that the old world needed to step forward to come to the aid of the new started to look a bit shaky in the wake of British punk's abject failure to shake up the American chart as it had done in the UK. As the seventies gave way to the eighties and punk was followed by other new things it began to look even shakier.

It's difficult to convey how unimpressed America continued to be with the majority of the products of the musical movements convulsing the UK at regular intervals in the years following punk. Even genuine grass-roots phenomena like the rise of 2-Tone and the ska revival happened in the UK because the country was small enough for its citizens to sense the excitement before it came over the hill from the next town. By the time this reached America it was just a bunch of records that clearly undersold whatever excitement might have been there in the first place. Much of it was 'you had to be there' music. Greil Marcus, the kind of American critic who could have been expected to embrace the political agenda of a group like the Specials, said that the essential problem was that they weren't very good. He added that Madness weren't even as good as the Blues Brothers. There were clearly certain frequencies on which British pop music operated that were effectively inaudible to American ears, and certain programmes the Americans would never get with.

The reason so many of these acts failed to land in the United States is that over there there was no propaganda wing of the music business that was anything like as powerful as the weekly music press was in the UK. These four papers – *NME*, *Melody Maker*, *Sounds* and *Record Mirror* – would have been loath to admit it but the fact remained that they performed the invaluable service for the British music industry of pretending middling talents were exciting. Much as Pavlov's dogs began salivating when they heard the footsteps of the attendants who brought their food, there were a few hundred thousand people in the UK in the late seventies and early eighties who were prepared to believe that every few months a new act was going to rise from English obscurity to challenge the established order and galvanize America. This applied to everything from 2-Tone through the advent of Frankie Goes to Hollywood to the jazz revivalists in a couple of Soho clubs. It was always announced as 'the most exciting times since punk'. Not surprising that so often this set up expectations that were bound to be dashed as soon as the actual record arrived in Cleveland.

On the other hand, in the same 1981 issue of *Rolling Stone* in which Greil Marcus questioned the credentials of the Specials, a group on which the London cognoscenti of the time had confidently hung its hat, a new band was being unveiled, a band that was perfectly placed both to restore the appeal of idealism and to lift the siege on rock's dignity that had begun with punk rock. This group, who came from the British Isles but not from Britain, were just about to begin the first of what would be many visits to the United States. Their singer was quoted in the magazine saying, 'It's my ambition to travel to America and give it what it considers it wants and needs.' Clearly the speaker was not English because he was not talking about giving America what was good for America regardless of what America wanted. Unlike so many of the British bands who made their American debut during this time, this band was not going to condescend to the world's biggest and most economically consequential country. Instead they were going to work with the grain of that country. That's why the speaker was probably the first rock musician to make such a bold statement and not be forced in time to recant it.

The speaker was of course Bono of U2. U2 were soon to become America's new sweethearts. U2 were the real inheritors of the legacy of the British Invasion and in this they enjoyed the massive advantage of speaking the same tongue while not actually being British. They happened to have the nationality that all Americans for some reason believe they have. This was far better than having the nationality that most Americans like to feel they have outgrown.

What Bono couldn't have known at the time he made that bold claim about giving America what it wanted was how the delivery of same would be facilitated and dramatically accelerated by a television revolution which began in the same year. In *Rolling Stone*'s last issue of 1981 they finally got round to running a short feature on a TV service that had been launched with very little fanfare in August of that year, which was already giving U2's tune 'Gloria' the exposure radio had been so slow to provide. This service was Music Television – MTV for short. The feature explained this alien concept for any who might not have grasped its essence from its name. The output of this revolutionary new service was made up of videos of the latest pop hits, all ideally linked by an attractive young woman. 'If MTV's creators are right – still a very sizeable if – this channel will soon wield more power over American pop music tastes than any television shows since *American Bandstand* in the fifties,' said the feature, going out on a limb.

It turned out to be a lot bigger and more significant than that. The first beneficiaries of it were British acts. Hilariously, when *Rolling Stone*'s reporter first dropped in on the new service the video they were playing was 'We Don't Talk Anymore' by Cliff Richard, one of his rare American hits. The fact that Britain was far ahead of the United States at the time in producing video clips is what made 1983 into the year of the second British Invasion, which came along almost twenty years after the first. In its early days MTV's biggest problem was it didn't have enough clips to play. American record companies were not in the habit of shooting footage to support new singles by their acts and some of them certainly weren't inclined to let this new TV service, which was owned by Warner Brothers, have the ones that they did shoot without paying for them. The one place MTV could look to for a seemingly endless supply of novelty videos was Britain. The British singles market was driven by the weekly *Top of the Pops*, which used videos when it couldn't persuade the act to come on and mime in person, and by Saturday morning children's shows, on which all manner of acts would turn up, act the fool and then introduce their video in the hope that the young viewers would, immediately afterwards, make their way to Woolworths and purchase their new favourite. As a consequence of this bands in Britain did videos as a matter of course – and, no matter who they were, they rather enjoyed the process.

Most British bands, particularly the younger, thinner ones, saw the video process as a giant lark. Here they could indulge their fantasies at the record company's expense. Adam Ant had shown the way, using the medium to transfigure himself into a wide range of pantomime types. He was the first pop star who was at his most powerful when acting out his pop star fantasies for the video camera. Where he went, many followed. Video exposure quickly started to make a difference even to the English bands that had set out to follow in the footsteps of the Who by touring all of America's highways and byways. In 1982 the manager of Def Leppard began to notice that his band's album was starting to be listed as a best-seller in stores in American cities the band had never visited. When he investigated further he noticed that these same towns had just been added to the cable network and therefore the local kids suddenly had access to MTV, and that meant they had access to Def Leppard. It made a huge difference.

While many American bands were still trying to decide whether shooting a video would somehow betray their principles, the bands from Britain were getting busy. America was suddenly treated to the sight of Dexy's Midnight Runners, decked out as tinkers, miming to 'Come On Eileen' and the Clash performing 'Rock The Casbah' in a Texas oilfield while a Muslim hitchhiker and Hasidic taxi driver bonded over burgers and beer. By then U2 were going as far as Sweden just in order to be shot by one of Ingmar Bergman's cameramen and then finding he was too ill to do the job. They then crossed over to Norway in search of more dramatic mountains. They then wanted to have the band riding horses but the insurance company wouldn't cover them so they ended up hiring local girls to pretend to be them riding horses. The video revolution was all about the effect and damn the authenticity. Bands from the British Isles loved the idea of let's pretend. They put as much thought into their looks as their sound. This was a generation of musicians who stayed close to their hairdressers. In the case of A Flock of Seagulls, the members of the band actually were hairdressers. The hair was as important to this British Invasion as it had been to the Beatles and the Stones two decades earlier. Bono's mullet. Sting's peroxide. Annie Lennox's severe crop. Whatever they called that thing on Mike Score's head.

By 16 July 1983 there were eighteen British-originated singles in the American Top 40. The Police, the band that had come to America thanks to Freddie Laker's budget airline Skytrain rather than the subsidy of a record company, and had ever since that time cut their cloth accordingly, were at number one with 'Every Breath You Take'. Immediately behind them was Guyanese-British writer/producer Eddy Grant with 'Electric Avenue', a song about a shopping street in Brixton and the most London-specific song to do well in the American charts since the Kinks' 'Waterloo Sunset'. The Kinks were still in business and in the top ten with 'Come Dancing', a song they had written in the hope that it would reconnect with their British audience but which turned out to be far more popular in the US. The entire second half of the top ten was British with Madness, Kajagoogoo, Duran Duran and Culture Club all going as high as they would ever go in America.

These eighteen, which also included Elton John, the Human League and even the Hollies, was more than the previous high, which had been fourteen back in the week ending 19 June 1965. In the light of all this the American publications were starting to dust off the old headlines such as 'the Redcoats are coming'. Most of these records got played on the radio for the same reasons that many of the American new wave bands didn't. They got played because they didn't have guitars on them at all, or if they did they were far from prominent. Even the Kinks hit had been composed on a Casio keyboard in the course of a transatlantic flight. What mattered was the tune. Then the beat, which was designed for dancing rather than throwing yourself around. Dance built a bridge between the British bands and the people that all the nights at New York's Hurrah would never have achieved.

In the years immediately following the punk rock scare in the UK, as the American-owned record companies found that they had on their books a glut of young British bands that had been signed at not a great deal of expense and were eager to come to America, there was an oversupply of not overly humble imported talent which was coming straight from JFK to a couple of nights at Hurrah. Here they would find themselves playing to an audience of metropolitan taste-makers, occasionally sprinkled with big names, which would make them think they had already broken America – an impression that remained as long as it took them to travel the few hundred miles upstate where they would take to the stage in front of half a dozen members of the public most of whom were directly related to the promoter. The size of the place was still something that most visiting bands never got their heads around. They expected Arizona to be a long way from New York. What they couldn't believe was how far it was possible to drive in a straight line away from New York while still being in New York State.

In fact the one thing these bands didn't do was disperse themselves out into the middle of America. They clung to the coasts as closely as American tourists cling to London and Oxford. The promoters, always in the market for some imported novelty, particularly if it was backed by some record company interest, booked these bands. This meant that home-grown acts often had trouble getting a look-in. The bands that this edged out reacted like the jobbing builders of East Anglia did to the arrival, twenty years later, of Polish plumbers. A flier for a San Francisco punk club in 1979 was headed 'We don't need the English!' By 1983 the Los Angeles punk band X, who had just put out their fourth album but had yet to start a riot of their own, sang a number called 'I Must Not Think Bad Thoughts' which directly pleaded, 'Will the last American band to get played on the radio please bring the flag?'

Of course the bigger truth was that this was no longer about bands. It was about songs. And it was no longer about performance. It was about music you could dance to. The real winner in the battle between punk rock and heritage rock was disco. All the 'disco sucks' buttons in the world, all the pyres on which people piled their Donna Summer or Chic records, never dented the desire of Americans of all kinds to dance. The Ritz and Danceteria replaced Hurrah as the places to go to hear music in New York. Playing in the smart clubs of New York and Los Angeles was what ultimately brought Spandau Ballet, ABC, the Thompson Twins, Human League and even Joy Division to a wider audience and encouraged the radio to loosen its stays. Even Lee Abrams, the man who had taught American radio how to subsist on a diet of 'Stairway To Heaven', embraced this new wave, saying, 'All my favourite bands are English. It's a more artistic place. Experimentation thrives there. Everything over here is more like McDonald's.'

The reason experimentation thrived in England was less to do with the restless curiosity of the natives than the fact that the market was driven by hit singles. Record companies were prepared to back the most unlikely acts for as long as it took them to put out a couple of singles. If the singles connected they might move on to an album. If they didn't they went back to their day jobs. Nobody's career had been consumed by the trouble and expense. The same could happen for American artists in the UK. Even Laurie Anderson's 'O Superman', the kind of art music that would normally have very limited exposure, got to the number two spot in the UK singles charts in 1981. In America it wasn't even released.

Records continued to find their way from America to Britain and back again much as they had done in the days when the Beatles learned 'Twist And Shout' from the Isley Brothers. Sometimes this process could take years. The Cincinnati singer Gloria Jones had first recorded 'Tainted Love' in 1964. At the time it flopped in the United States. Twelve years later it became popular on the Northern Soul circuit where British fans in the cities of the north continued to fly the flag for Motown-style dance music even when it had fallen from favour elsewhere. It was here that the Leeds student Marc Almond heard it while working as a cloakroom attendant. He asked the DJ to make him a tape of it. He subsequently cut his own moody electronic version of it with his partner in Soft Cell. 'Tainted Love' was the biggest UK hit of 1982. What was more surprising is that it went on to spend forty-three weeks in the *Billboard* Hot 100. This is the longest time any record has spent on the American chart, Beatles and Elvis Presley included.

Just as the American TV comics of 1964 had been able to bank a weak laugh by the simple act of putting a Beatles wig on their heads, the TV comics of 1984 could guarantee something similar by going before the cameras in some species of Hasidic head gear with dreadlocks attached. In 1983 a great deal was made of the fact that Culture Club was the first act since the Beatles to have three top ten hits in the United States from their debut album.

In Britain, Boy George fitted into two well-established traditions. The first was drag, which had been a feature of mainstream entertainment since long before television. The second was the experience of viewing *Top of the Pops*. This was always watched *en famille* and rarely would a week go by without one of the parent figures in the room posing the question 'Is that a boy or a girl?' This was a question that no longer made anyone feel uncomfortable in the UK. Things were not the same in the United States.

In the US it was widely believed that sexual deviancy was a Trojan horse smuggled into the American living room by MTV, the first but not the last pop indulgence to be entirely financed from the credit cards of parents, and it was going to separate their children from the American way. In a very short time this would result in Tipper Gore's campaign to introduce stickering on records that had any controversial content. In July 1984 it produced the curious sight of Boy George on an edition of the American current affairs show *Face the Nation* debating with Gore Vidal and the televangelist Jerry Falwell as to whether the viewers should worry about the trend that was said to be 'feminizing America'.

Throughout that year the American media appeared to have Boy George on speed dial as he was shuttled from studio to studio, from sofa to sofa and from one excessively concerned audience to another, answering the same questions with his characteristic responses. When host Phil Donahue asked how he felt about Falwell's criticism and his theory that this was poisoning the young of the 1980s as surely as communism was said to have threatened the kids of the 1950s, he said, 'If he thinks we can make children homosexual, he's wrong. There's nothing immoral about enjoying yourself.' To Johnny Carson he remarked, 'In the country of Liberace, I'm hardly revolutionary, am I?' In January 1984 he appeared on the cover of *Newsweek* with Annie Lennox and her scarcely less provocative hairstyle. In April, *Mad* magazine depicted their goofball cover star Alfred E. Neuman as Boy George. The same month George was in every middle-class home in the country on the cover of *People* magazine, which assured its readers that 'kids are getting his message'.

At the time Culture Club were on a tour of large venues. When they fetched up at the Richfield Coliseum, not far from Chrissie Hynde's Akron, the local news station sent a reporter down there who was perplexed to discover that the kids turning up to see them were a bunch of regular kids who were growing up in a new era where it was expected that when you went to see an act you dressed up for the occasion. It appeared George had particularly magnetized all those kids who felt alienated by the aggressive sectionality of American high school culture with its iron divisions of young people into jocks, nerds and beauty queens.

By December 1984 George had achieved the signal honour of being the first man on the cover of US *Cosmopolitan*. By then it was pretty much over. The hits were drying up. The last thing he did that year was get Concorde back from New York to sing his part on the Band Aid record 'Do They Know It's Christmas?'. 1984 had been so much his year on both sides of the Atlantic that it was inconceivable they could have done it without him. He had been overworked throughout that period and, although it wasn't known at the time, he had responded to the strain by indulging in the one thing he had always maintained he would never gravitate to: hard drugs. He had been on the cover of the 1983 issue of *Rolling Stone*, which announced 'England Swings'. The next time he appeared was in 1986, when the story was 'Boy George's Tragic Fall'.

Interviewed in November 1983, one record exec said that in his experience, by the time people get round to writing about phenomena they tended to be over. 'I think the British invasion has already taken place and that we will launch an American counter invasion,' he said. He was absolutely right about that. Most of the British groups who had been on the US charts in 1984 would never bother it again. By the middle of 1985 Culture Club singles were not even breaking the Hot 100. The Human League, Kajagoogoo, Spandau Ballet and the rest would have to settle for cult status.

The record that was number one in the United States for the first month of 1985 was, you can't help but suspect, being bought by a lot of the same mousy girls who had dressed up in dreadlocks to go and see Boy George. It was a record by somebody who would usher in the real future; someone who had come up as a dancer rather than a singer; somebody who had learned from the video revolution; somebody who was, by virtue of their nationality and sexuality, far less apologetic and ambiguous than Boy George. The person who brought to an end the twenty-year summer that had followed the first British Invasion was Madonna. Two things qualified her to begin that next era: she was a girl, and she was American. The future would belong to both.

OUTRO

In September 1984 I interviewed Bruce Springsteen for British TV backstage at the Spectrum in Philadelphia. At the time his British record company weren't absolutely confident that it would ever be possible to make somebody who seemed so specifically, incurably American into a household name in Britain. His following in the United Kingdom was restricted in the main to deep-end fans of American guitar music, the kind of people who preferred to have import copies of anything, the kind of people who prided themselves on being able to put their fingers on the places of which he sang on a map of the United States, the kind of people who preferred to watch American films, the kind of English people who, if given a choice, would probably prefer a bottle of Budweiser to the traditional pint of warm beer.

The record Springsteen was touring in support of at the time was *Born In The USA*. The subject matter of this record seemed on the face of it only to increase the difficulty of his getting a success overseas. The songs were either about or touched upon people and places with which there was little reason to expect the average

British listener to be able to connect: there were songs dealing with the wound of the Vietnam War, the meaning of the Fourth of July, lives spent working on a travelling road gang or hoping not to get laid off at the lumber yard; songs describing the feeling of being with a girl in a hot car at night or sharing a bench seat during a drive with your father, the pangs from memories of what did or didn't happen in high school, the significance of the vacant stores on Main Street, and the melancholy feeling of lying awake at night listening to the whistle of a long, long train. There seemed as much chance of this view of the world connecting with the record-buying public of Britain as there was of a major American TV network making a late bid for *Last of the Summer Wine*.

It turned out to be a lot more successful than anyone had dared predict. Partly owing to the resulting TV film and the increasingly sophisticated videos that Springsteen used to promote the singles that came from it, that record became by far his biggest-selling album in the UK and Europe. The following year he toured Europe in what became the most conspicuously successful case of an American artist exporting an essentially American story to the rest of the world. People from Glasgow to Gothenburg sang along to songs about Vietnam, about two-lane blacktops, about hometowns in the USA they had never heard of and about people whose lives were very different from their own. They cheerfully submitted to Springsteen's imaginative rock operas about the American condition. They punched the air. They whooped in an American style whenever he mentioned New Jersey. They even borrowed from American audiences the characteristic moo of approval that the untrained ear could easily confuse with booing. A few even went so far as to wear a bandana, an item of attire with little history at their chilly latitudes. It was a triumph for the American way of looking at the world. Springsteen abjured all things fancy. His music might have been made according to the prescription urged on George

Washington by the Founding Fathers who wanted everything in the new country to be 'substantially good and majestically plain'. Tickets for Springsteen's show at London's Wembley Stadium on 4 July 1985 changed hands at prices you would have thought would only be paid by the most patriotic Americans. It was the most dramatic case of one country's music apparently taking over another's since the Beatles had arrived in America twenty-one years earlier.

Like the Beatles back in 1964, Springsteen seemed the only game in town. Bob Geldof, then at the peak of his powers of persuasion, laid siege to him following his show in Newcastle, begging him to finish the tour by appearing a week later at his planned Live Aid concert at Wembley Stadium. It was felt that the show needed the benediction that only somebody like Springsteen could provide. Without Springsteen's involvement too much of the show's weight would fall on acts from earlier decades like Elton John, the Who and Queen, all of whom were around the dangerous age of forty and therefore couldn't possibly be expected to take the strain. He had no more luck than Sid Bernstein had in February 1964 when he tried to persuade Brian Epstein that the Beatles should stay another week and play Madison Square Garden. What nobody predicted was that the sixties and seventies acts would emerge from the exposure granted them at the Wembley end of Live Aid with an entirely new lease of life and with their charisma banks magically recharged.

It didn't happen the same way in Philadelphia. Bob Dylan was the headliner at the American end of Live Aid, with a performance that was received with some derision by the British performers watching the broadcast at the after-show party. Mick Jagger and Tina Turner fancied that they would cause the most interest. In fact they were all upstaged by a relatively new artist. Madonna came on in the middle of the afternoon and played 'Holiday' and 'Into The Groove', the songs that by that time all the world was dancing to. 'I ain't taking shit off today,' she said. This was a reference to the fact that both *Penthouse* and *Playboy* had responded to her sudden ubiquity by buying up and republishing nude pictures she had posed for a few years earlier when she was a struggling dancer in New York.

1985 was the year of Madonna's breakthrough. In that year she co-starred in a well-received film *Desperately Seeking Susan*, contracted one of those marriages – to the film actor Sean Penn – which massively increases an artist's fame, and undertook a tour of the United States, the so-called 'Like a Virgin' tour, which seemed to be attended by every teenage girl in the country who could manage to cobble together their version of her outfits, any girl who could leave home respectably dressed and then be transformed into a strumpet by the time she arrived at the venue, every girl who had ever sought permission to act like a bad girl in public. Appearing on the cover of *Time* magazine that summer, Madonna told her story, a story of grandparents who came on the boat from Italy and never in their lives learned a word of English, of saving her money for a one-way ticket to New York, about modelling herself on American icons like Carole Lombard and Nancy Sinatra and also, in darker moments, about the shades of anorexia and suicide that are the flip side of the teenage life. Like Springsteen's, hers was a most American story.

Madonna and Bruce Springsteen, along with Prince and Michael Jackson, would turn out to be the leading lights of the rest of the 1980s. As a consequence it was an era every bit as American as the 1960s had been British. This meant a shift away from the collective and towards the individual. The biggest acts of the 1950s – Elvis, Little Richard, Jerry Lee Lewis and Fats Domino – had all been American and they were solo acts. The 1960s had belonged to the groups, and most of the groups came from the UK. The key part of their sixties dream was that you were going to make it to the top and take your mates with you, which would clearly be by far the most satisfying way of doing it.

In the 1980s it seemed that the line of Elvis Presley had been restored once more. Performing solo seems to suit American individualism. Even Bruce Springsteen, who learned more than most from the collegiate vibe of the Beatles, the Stones, the Animals and all the other British groups of the 1960s which he admired, even he had called himself 'the Boss' during the band's early games of Monopoly in order to stress the fact that, when all the joshing was said and done, that was indeed what he was and the other musicians would not for a second question it. You could never have an English musician referred to as 'the Boss'. The rest would simply never stand for it.

The group, on the other hand, was invented by the English. Its initial inspiration may have been drawn from Texas, from Buddy Holly and the Crickets, but it seemed to better suit the English temperament. It may turn out to be the nation's most significant contribution to the way pop music thinks. Forming into groups appeals to the nation's preferred mode of social organization, which is essentially to defer without appearing to do so. The Beatles did it first and did it best. They are the group which all the groups who came afterwards measured themselves against. The Beatles' unpolished fraternity, their untutored knack of pulling together when threatened and indulging each other when possible, the happy way they lived up to Epstein's description of them as 'the boys', the unbothered familial rudeness to which the critics referred, the way they looked at each other as they played: this was the enchanting mutuality that recommended them to America and the wider world. They appeared to be a magic circle to which you could never belong. Although it was never doubted by the three other Beatles that it had been John's band first and the other three had joined and that he could be expected to feel more proprietorial about it than anyone else, still the price of his being accorded that respect was his never seeking to mention it openly. The English deal with any feeling of inferiority they may momentarily experience in the presence of a superior by never mentioning the fact that they are the superior ones. The whole point about bands is they never openly concede that anyone is the leader.

I once sat on the board of a French-English company and the French half of the meeting would never enter the room until they could be sure that their precise counterpart in terms of rank was already there. On the other hand, bosses of English companies will go out of their way to avoid giving the impression that they can only get the meeting's respect because of the stripes they have on their sleeve. For years Britain's most popular businessman was Richard Branson for the simple reason that he wore pullovers, which is not what most businessmen do. Britain's most popular sitcom character is Sergeant Wilson in the TV series *Dad's Army* because he is well born but goes to some lengths to conceal the fact. Even Her Majesty the Queen observes the same simple rule on entering a room. She never says hello and she never says goodbye because saying either would involve everybody in the room openly admitting that a very important person had either arrived or departed.

England is the country of Cabinet government, of team meetings, of parish councils, of complaints which always begin with the complainer using the word 'sorry', where the established Church finds it wiser to stay off the subject of religion and the preferred topic of conversation is the weather because clearly it would be unreasonable to expect anyone to do anything about that. It is the only country in the world where the expression 'rubbing along' means something because it describes the imperfect business of not mentioning your differences because differences are surely what make us what we are. In this country you get few points for dragging difficult questions into the open.

Two of the key characteristics of all bands is that they contain within them some unresolved tension, some buried resentment, some hard truth withheld, something that someone has always wanted to say but never will. The second characteristic is that they find it best to deal with such problems by never talking about them. I once asked a producer who had spent time making records with the Rolling Stones whether they ever openly discussed what kind of music they should make and how they should go about making it. He assured me that this was something they would never do. They found it best not to speak of such things for fear they would cause bigger arguments. On the other hand, David Cameron may go down in British history as the least popular Prime Minister of all time because he made the mistake of calling a referendum over something the overwhelming majority of Britons never thought about and the small minority who did were quite happy grousing about. At the height of social media madness the most widely adopted piece of communication in twenty-first-century Britain was a poster designed during the Second World War which simply said 'Keep Calm and Carry On'.

Even David Bowie, the most prominent British solo artist of his time, seemed to work with the grain of English modesty, whenever possible shunning the spotlight and presenting himself as a member of a group, whether the Spiders from Mars or Tin Machine. He could never be seen to take himself quite as seriously as Madonna or Bruce Springsteen took themselves and their work. It was not in his English blood to call that much attention to himself, to be seen to rise that far above his station, to go around playing the big I am. A big part of Bowie's act was the way he liked to position himself as the regular south London bloke. Nobody could ever call him the Boss. Indeed the British music press liked to refer to him as the Dame, which was the perfect way of bringing him under control.

The English compulsion to signal acceptance within a social group by giving people nicknames can also be a way of cutting the high and mighty down to size. No surprise, then, that it is particularly popular when it can be applied to a rock god. Hence in England, people know who you're talking about when you refer to Keef, Macca, Moz and Madge. The nicknaming suggests that while other countries and cultures may bend the knee and give these people the honour of their full titles, here at home there's an expectation that they should still take their allotted role in the Carry On film that is the nation's life. Only in Britain would somebody christened Roger Barrett decide that if he were going to be in a group he was better off being Syd. Only here could Quentin Cook realize he would find it easier to flourish in the music business if he changed his name to Norman.

In her book *Watching the English*, Kate Fox identifies an in-built tendency to be ill at ease as the besetting problem of all English people and points out that the way the English deal with this is with humour. She says that while in most countries it's accepted that there is a time and a place for humour, with the English it's a constant. 'Virtually all English conversations and social interactions involve at least some degree of banter, teasing, ironic wit, mockery, wordplay, satire, understatement, humorous self-deprecation, sarcasm, pomposity pricking or just silliness. Humour is our default mode, particularly when we are feeling uncomfortable or awkward. When in doubt, joke.'

Music draws on that same sense of playfulness in the English. The English have a natural tendency to push the envelope just to see if anybody stops them. This being a small island on which nobody wishes to be seen as the wet blanket, people rarely do. Hence it's difficult to imagine the Who's *Tommy* or the Beatles' *Sgt Pepper* being produced by any American acts. Another feature of this being a small island is that there is a real hunger for excitement from overseas and a real knack for tuning in to those distant frequencies. This could be why when white English bands like the

Rolling Stones and Manfred Mann copied rhythm and blues they did it better and more interestingly than white American bands. Sometimes they did it better than the originators did. Because they grew up with only two radio stations – the first run by the BBC, which hardly played any records at all, and the other, Radio Luxembourg, which could only ever be discerned through a blizzard of static – they listened with a rare hunger and consigned what they heard to their secret hearts. Because nobody ever told them what they were supposed to not like or not listen to they grew up taking in everything, which is why Led Zeppelin and David Bowie and Queen came from the UK and could never have come out of the United States. And because they came from a country that venerates the underdog and seeks to take the hero down a peg, star figures as unlikely as Elton John, as prickly as Rod Stewart and as downright strange as Freddie Mercury emerged. Finally, because they came from a small country where the worst that could happen would be unlikely to amount to more than a storm in a teacup, they grew up oddly fearless.

For twenty years America danced to their tune. Will we ever see the like again? In 1964, 15 per cent of all the hit records in the USA were British. In 1983 the proportion of American hits that were British was even higher. In fact in July 1983 over 50 per cent of the *Billboard* Hot 100 were by foreign artists. After this high-water mark the popularity of British acts in the USA steadily dwindled until at one point in May 2002 there were no British artists in the US singles chart for the first time since 1963. Statistics alone don't tell the story of America's love affair with British music, which began in 1964, plateaued in the early seventies, hit a distinctly rocky patch at the end of that decade and then came back for what Jimi Hendrix would have called a slight return in 1983. During the 1960s forty-one British-made records went to the number one position in the *Billboard* Hot 100. In the following decade there were forty-nine. In the 1980s there were over sixty but, because charts were beginning to behave differently, they tended to stay in the top spot for a shorter period of time. Since then the number of British acts getting to the number one position in America has been in steady decline. In the whole of the 1990s there were only ten, and in the first decade of the current century there were a mere four. The British bands most expected to make it in America, such as Oasis, don't; the ones nobody would have predicted, such as Depeche Mode, do. The words Pete Townshend wrote in 1971 still hold good: 'Americans are famous for their lavish spending on European goods, but they always insist on seeing what it is they are buying. They want to inspect the merchandise.'

Music from England continues to be influential in the United States, though it may take as long for that influence to soak through as it took the sound of punk rock to reach Kurt Cobain and re-emerge in the early 1990s as the sound of Nirvana. Nile Rodgers says that there would have been no Chic without Roxy Music. Electronic music has passed back and forth across the Atlantic for almost forty years now, re-emerging on one side or the other under a different name, most recently in the United States as Electronic Dance Music or EDM.

What's most surprising is that as this book is being completed a remarkable proportion of the young men who spearheaded the British Invasion back in 1964 are still active. The knighthoods they are given by monarchs, the honours with which they are showered by Presidents, the munificent deals for their memoirs, the hit feature films in which they are depicted in their flaming youth by better-looking young actors, the awe in which they are still held by generations of young musicians on both sides of the Atlantic, none of this has encouraged any of them to disappear into retirement after the manner of the returning sons of an earlier Empire who similarly made their fortunes overseas. They are still out there playing, partly because they enjoy it but also because they can command sums of money they have never previously been able to command. On their short 2019 tour of the United States the Rolling Stones grossed $10 million a night. That would be $10 million. Every night. This in itself is not surprising when the tickets are going for an average of $159. In that year the Stones were the top earners at the American box office with Elton John, Fleetwood Mac and Paul McCartney not far behind them. The only competition these acts have is each other. The rest of the mere mortals in the list can't really compete with the pulling power of these quasi-mystical figures who made their bones in the British Invasion.

Will we ever see the equal of the impact of the events in the years depicted in these pages? We will not, if only for the simple reason that the revolution in communications has brought Europe and America far too close together for anything to flourish in obscurity for long. This has had the effect of ensuring that any interested party can, with a few clicks, easily hear and see any band on the surface of the Earth.

In the American charts today there are far more records by women, far more by people of colour and far more by people who have come to prominence via TV talent shows. The ascendancy of hip hop has further restored American hegemony in music. There are still some very popular acts who are British, such as Adele, Ed Sheeran and Sam Smith, but they don't seem to bring much Englishness with them any more.

America continues to be the world's leading exporter of Americanness, a product for which there is still a demand both overseas and at home. One of the qualities its big solo stars most embody is the country itself. It's also inevitably part of their subject matter. It's expected of them that they should sing songs about America. 'An American Trilogy' by Elvis Presley, 'America' by Paul Simon, 'American Life' by Madonna, 'Born In The USA' by Bruce

Springsteen, 'Living In America' by James Brown, 'American Girl' by Tom Petty and any number of other examples testify to the way in which they have responded. Much as half of the shelf space in American bookshops is taken up by volumes with the word 'American' in their title, so all American musical performers of any stature at all are obliged at some point in their careers to write a song about their country. Because America is not only a big country but also a big concept, these tend to be big songs with big ambitions.

Ray Davies aside, English performers on the other hand hardly ever write songs which are directly about England or the UK. On the rare occasions they do, the last impression they can afford to give is that they are in any way attached to the place. This is partly because the market for songs openly about England would be confined to England. It's also because the country's songwriting classes, who are after all a subdivision of the country's chattering classes, have grown up with a sense of shame about the place that is difficult to distinguish from the permanent state of embarrassment which is their birthright. But while they don't write many songs that are about England they write quite a few which have Englishness running right through them, even if often the only people who fully appreciate this are the English themselves.

When the whole world in general and America in particular were falling at the feet of English stars like the Beatles, the Rolling Stones, the Who, Elton John and David Bowie, faking their accents, copying their clothes and seeing in them some qualities which were apparently impossible to find in their own culture, we English rarely talked about how good this made us feel. An Irish acquaintance recently told me how his father, who used to rail about the racket his young son made in his bedroom in the early days of U2, was mollified by the sight of them on the cover of *Time* magazine. Here was a band, an Irish band, and suddenly America was taking them seriously. He still thought they were a racket but as an Irishman he was not afraid to say he felt massively validated by their popularity. I know what he meant.

In June 2010, back in the vanished world when performers still received such invitations and were honoured to accept them, Paul McCartney – or Sir Paul McCartney as he was repeatedly referred to by most of the republicans in the room – was presented with the Gershwin Prize for Popular Song by President Barack Obama in a ceremony at the White House. A succession of performers from different genres was wheeled out, supposedly to demonstrate how McCartney's songs are endlessly adaptable across those genres. The best performance, however, was turned in by fellow English pop traditionalist Elvis Costello. No artist better understands the value of McCartney's songs than Costello and therefore what he offered was a straight-up version of 'Penny Lane' with McCartney's band in support. It was a telling choice.

George Gershwin wrote songs like 'Summertime' and 'I Got Rhythm', songs that were completely imbued with American culture, language and values. They were designed to take their place in the highly engineered musical comedies of Broadway. He and his songs were American to the tips of their shiny shoes. What Gershwin would have made of something so slight in its conception, so bracing in its delivery and so uncompromising in its foreignness as 'Penny Lane' is anyone's guess.

Costello began by pointing out how the song meant a lot to his family because it was about a place half a mile away from where his mother grew up. Then he played the song, a song that was inspired, like many of the Beatles' songs at the time, by the marijuana-derived desire to call back the fast-fading memories of their childhood among the streets and avenues of post-war Liverpool. Hence it's replete with references to things which to an American audience are either unfamiliar, such as that monument to English deference the traffic roundabout, or entirely unknown, such as the poppies sold every year in memory of the millions of Common-wealth war dead, or wrapped in opaque smut, such as the sexual stimulation of the vagina known in Liverpool as the 'finger pie', which could presumably be secured or provided in the shelter in the middle of the roundabout long after the last bus had departed. Unmediated by producers or spinners, springing straight from the head of a twenty-four-year-old Liverpudlian-turned-Londoner and then straight to the top of the charts all over the world, 'Penny Lane' was a rare beast in its time and in the present day it's extinct. It may well be the most English piece of art ever to be placed before and enthusiastically taken up by the American public, who are normally kept safe from anything as specifically foreign.

'Penny Lane' is a perfect illustration of the enduring English belief that charm trumps everything, that there is beauty in the most prosaic features of daily life and there will always be an England as long as we are permitted to celebrate its small pleasures. 'Penny Lane' is, as Viv Stanshall might have agreed, 'English as tuppence', and yet there it was, in all its dappled, mustn't-grumble, turned-out-nice-again splendour, being played with affectionate disrespect in the East Room of the White House in front of the President of the United States, his family and the entire American political establishment, further graced near the end by the spit and polish of a piccolo trumpet solo provided by a master sergeant of the US Marines in full dress uniform. This ceremony was taking place not merely to pay tribute to the man who wrote that song, but also by extension to the era that brought it to prominence in the United States and the reverse lend-lease arrangement that brought all these riches from the UK to the USA during the time of the Brit-ish Invasion. If you're English, it's impossible to watch the recording of this performance without experiencing a small bump of what can only be called national pride at this most benign conquest.

This, 'Penny Lane' seems to say, this is us, and we were here.

POSTSCRIPT: AN ANGLO-AMERICAN PLAYLIST

Twenty-five long-playing records that may enhance your enjoyment of the book.

The Crickets: *The 'Chirping' Crickets*

The first LP by Buddy Holly's group came out in the USA in 1957, which was a year before it was permitted to appear in the UK. When it did it was its cover picture, the star of which was not so much the musicians as Buddy's guitar, the Fender Stratocaster, which inspired many young Englishmen to form groups.

Chuck Berry: *Rockin' At The Hops*

In October 1961 Mick Jagger and Keith Richards, who had been to primary school together when younger, met again on Dartford station. Keith was carrying a guitar, Mick this imported Chess album. The group they formed would go on to cover no fewer than five of the songs from it.

Bob Dylan: *Bob Dylan*

Not a lot of people in Britain got to hear Bob Dylan's first LP, which came out in early 1962, but many of those who did were fascinated by the way this charismatic unknown sounded like an old man inside a young man. The record led to his first trip to Britain to play a folk singer in a TV play, to the Animals recording one of its selections, 'The House Of The Rising Sun', and to John Lennon (among many others) adopting the 'Dylan cap' modelled on the cover.

The Rolling Stones: *The Rolling Stones*

Recorded in an eggbox-insulated one-room studio in Denmark Street and predominantly comprising their callow, indescribably horny versions of songs that had been recently playing on jukeboxes in the black sections of American cities, this is still by some distance the greatest debut album ever made.

The Beatles: *A Hard Day's Night*

This may be the most consequential LP in the history of pop. Here's where the idea of bands writing their own songs, projecting their own vision into the world, the whole idea of bands as auteurs on which the edifice of rock was built, actually begins. The music from the film changed everything. In the USA they had to make do with instrumental music on the second side. UK fans got another six no less brilliant songs.

Bob Dylan: *Bringing It All Back Home*

It was the British Invasion that gave Bob Dylan the nerve to make the jump into electric music on the first side of this, his farewell to folk music. He knew that bands like the Animals had done something he should have done himself, so here's where he belatedly got

284

to it with 'Subterranean Homesick Blues', 'Maggie's Farm' and 'She Belongs To Me'. The title referred to his determination to wrest back the leadership of rock and roll on behalf of the country that had invented it.

The Byrds: *Turn! Turn! Turn!*

The sleeve notes of the second Byrds album were penned by Derek Taylor, formerly the PR man for the Beatles, who assured everyone that George and Paul had dropped in on a session to give it their blessing. The Byrds had been formed in direct response to *A Hard Day's Night*. The next record the Beatles made, *Revolver*, would have some of the flavour of the American groups like the Byrds they had inspired.

Simon & Garfunkel: *Sounds Of Silence*

'The Sound Of Silence' had come out in the USA in 1964 and flopped. Garfunkel went to university and Simon came to the UK. He was here when he heard that his record company, inspired by the success of 'Mr Tambourine Man', had overdubbed a rock band on it and the resulting record was headed for number one. The album of the same name nods to his British experience. 'Kathy's Song' was inspired by his Essex girlfriend. Davy Graham's 'Anji' was the standard test piece every British folk guitarist had to master. And of course 'Homeward Bound' was written on Widnes station.

Rolling Stones: *Aftermath*

Released in 1966 in different versions either side of the Atlantic, this was the first Stones album to feature all their own compositions. It was clearly the product of the same prematurely jaded outlook that brought forth 'Satisfaction' and 'Get Off Of My Cloud'. Recorded between tours in Hollywood and bristling with Anglo attitude towards everything from old girlfriends in 'Stupid Girl' and American consumerism in 'Mother's Little Helper' to those who couldn't keep up in 'Out Of Time', this record marked the perfection of a key strain of rock cool.

Blues Breakers with Eric Clapton

The cult of the guitar hero begins here with Eric Clapton, newly sprung from the Yardbirds and appearing as the featured player with John Mayall's band, copying the licks of Otis Rush on 'All Your Love' and Freddie King on 'Hideaway' yet managing to inject some element of additional excitement that was appealing to a younger audience than would ever have heard either of those names. This is still the best blues album ever to be recorded within hailing distance of West Hampstead tube station.

The Jimi Hendrix Experience: *Are You Experienced*

Of all the American unknowns who came to the UK in the middle years of the decade in the hope of starting their lives again in Swinging London, Jimi Hendrix was the one who benefited most. London's many gunslingers were happy to defer to his skills as a guitarist. He in turn made a record that was playful, loose and adventurous, an album he could never have made in New York.

The Kinks: *Something Else*

The Kinks didn't have the smoothest rise in the USA but they always had a following of people who were as fascinated by their Englishness as English fans had been by the imaginative landscape of the blues. From the head boy figure in 'David Watts' and the rhyming slang of 'Harry Rag' to Terry and Julie crossing the river for refuge in 'Waterloo Sunset', there's no doubt which country Ray Davies was writing about, and his American fans were glad he didn't compromise that vision.

Cream: *Disraeli Gears*

Posterity has them down as the ultimate jam band but Cream's name was made by this American-directed LP which condensed their appeal into highly disciplined songs like 'Sunshine Of Your Love' and 'Strange Brew', which sounded just as good on jukeboxes as they did on free-form radio. And, believe it or not, people danced to it.

Led Zeppelin: *II*

This was no longer just rock. This was rock on steroids. It was a noise so high you couldn't get over it, so low you couldn't get under it, so thick you couldn't get round it, and so dedicated to the articulation of emotional extremity and unquenchable sexual desire that you were torn between surrendering to it, laughing at it and telling it to go and stand on a square of cold lino. It was music that didn't make sense at all when played in a small venue. It was music made for the Big Country.

The Who: *Live At Leeds*

The standard line-up of the new decade would be the four-piece with lead singer, playing very, very loud, and nobody did it better than the Who. They had little truck with solos, dealing instead in a kind of rolling thunder that they had been able to develop in the psychedelic ballrooms of the United States, and they knew better than anyone else did how to marry the old rock and roll favourites with their chart hits and their rock opera material. This is still the best ever live rock album and it couldn't have happened without America.

Elton John: *Tumbleweed Connection*

This fulsome tribute to the passing of the way of life of the American frontier was composed in Pinner. It was recorded in a studio just off Wardour Street in London's Soho, only a few yards away from the import shops where the young Elton John and Bernie Taupin had pored over the covers of the Band and Leon Russell albums that had provided its inspiration. Its huge success on both sides of the Atlantic is one of the great mysteries of popular music.

Black Sabbath: *Master Of Reality*

The story goes that Tony Iommi had to play strings with very low tension because he had lost the tip of his finger in an industrial accident. The bass was slackened to match him and Ozzy Osbourne's vocals went down in pitch at the same time. The result was the slurred sound of downer rock, music that appealed very strongly to shirtless American youth who were too young for the Vietnam War and wanted most of all to get thoroughly out of it.

Eagles: *Eagles*

It's worth noting that the record that invented country rock as a category was recorded by an Englishman just across the bridge from the Hammersmith roundabout.

David Bowie: *Aladdin Sane*

The experience of touring America gave English bands the licence to write songs in an American idiom, to sing about dollars, drive-ins and Detroit, to couch their lyrics in a kind of rock and roll that was guaranteed to go down in Des Moines and Duluth, and to project a prematurely jaded attitude to life which was the mark of those who had gone to the other side and survived. If the record had been captured on the run in American studios then so much the better. (See also T. Rex's *Electric Warrior*.)

Rod Stewart: *Atlantic Crossing*

In the middle of the seventies the realization set in among British artists that if you wanted to get played on American radio you had to present them with a product that had been manufactured in America using local labour. *Atlantic Crossing* set down the template.

Ramones: *Ramones*

In America they were a joke. In Britain they were an inspiration. They proved that enthusiastic coverage in the British music papers and a few British TV programme appearances could, once taken back to the United States, be parlayed into the beginnings of a career. (See also Tom Petty and the Heartbreakers, Patti Smith, Devo and others.)

Television: *Marquee Moon*

In 1969, under the spell of American psychedelia, Fairport Convention had given an old English ballad, 'A Sailor's Life', a rock spin. Eight years later the same sound came echoing back across the Atlantic in the first album by Television.

The Clash: *London Calling*

First the record company put them together with an American producer to make the unlovable *Give 'Em Enough Rope*. Then they left them alone with Brit Guy Stevens, and what came out of it was the record that would best represent them in the USA. It reflected what they had learned about pleasing crowds, what American vernacular music had rubbed off on them and to what extent the 'I'm so bored with the USA' pose was exactly that.

Human League: *Dare*

Martin Rushent, who produced this record, said that he'd also worked with Keith Emerson and considered the League's Phil Oakey the better musician for the simple reason that he was capable of making his mind up. Whereas the first British Invasion had been led by bands who were road-hardened and versatile, the second was headed up by people who were neither but had instead the incalculable advantage of single-mindedness and a belief that there was no substitute for a good tune that you could also dance to.

Dire Straits: *Brothers In Arms*

No record better captures that moment in the early to mid 1980s when video took over the music business and America found itself dealing with dressing up as a key element of pop music than 'Money For Nothing', a wry reflection on the changing of the guard which was all the more pointed for coming from a group who had nothing to recommend them apart from the sound they made.

BIBLIOGRAPHY

Albertine, Viv, *Clothes, Clothes, Clothes, Music, Music, Music, Boys, Boys, Boys* (Faber & Faber, 2013)

Avery, Kevin, *Everything Is an Afterthought: The Life and Writings of Paul Nelson* (Fantagraphics, 2011)

Barrow, Tony, *John, Paul, George, Ringo & Me* (Andre Deutsch, 2011)

Birch, Will, *Cruel To Be Kind* (Constable, 2019)

Blake, Mark, *Pigs Might Fly* (Aurum, 2007)

——*Bring It On Home* (Little Brown, 2018)

Blauner, Andrew, *In Their Lives: Great Writers on Great Beatles Songs* (Blue Rider, 2017)

Bowie, Angie, *Free Spirit* (Mushroom, 1981)

Bowles, Jerry G., *A Thousand Sundays* (Putnam, 1980)

Boyd, Joe, *White Bicycles* (Serpent's Tail, 2006)

Boyd, Pattie, *Wonderful Today* (Headline, 2007)

Bracewell, Michael, *Roxy* (Faber & Faber, 2007)

Braun, Michael, *Love Me Do!* (Penguin, 1964)

Bronson, Harold, *Rock Explosion* (Cassell, 1986)

Brown, Peter, *The Love You Make* (Pan, 1984)

Burdon, Eric, *I Used to Be an Animal But I'm All Right Now* (Faber & Faber, 1986)

Burks, John and Hopkins, Jerry, *Groupies and Other Girls* (*Rolling Stone* special report, 1970)

Cartwright, Garth, *Going for a Song* (Flood Gallery, 2018)

Cavendish, Leslie, *The Cutting Edge* (Alma Books, 2017)

Cornyn, Stan, *Exploding* (Harper Entertainment, 2002)

Costello, Elvis, *Unfaithful Music & Disappearing Ink* (Viking, 2015)

Dannen, Fredric, *Hit Men* (Muller, 1990)

Davis, Clive, *Clive: Inside the Record Business* (William Morrow, 1975)

Des Barres, Pamela, *Take Another Little Piece of My Heart* (William Morrow, 1992)

——*I'm With the Band* (Omnibus, 2018)

Doggett, Peter, *Crosby, Stills, Nash & Young* (Bodley Head, 2019)

Egan, Sean, *Fleetwood Mac on Fleetwood Mac* (Omnibus, 2016)

Ekland, Britt, *True Britt* (Sphere, 1980)

Ellis, Geoffrey, *I Should Have Known Better* (Thorogood, 2004)

Fagen, Donald, *Eminent Hipsters* (Cape, 2013)

Faithfull, Marianne, *Faithfull* (Penguin, 1994)

Fisher, Marc, *Something in the Air* (Random House, 2007)

Fleetwood, Mick, *Play On* (Hodder & Stoughton, 2014)

Fox, Kate, *Watching the English* (Hodder & Stoughton, 2004)

Goldsmith, Martin, *The Beatles Come to America* (Wiley, 2004)

Goodman, Fred, *Allen Klein* (Eamon Dolan, 2015)

Gottlieb, Annie, *Do You Believe in Magic?* (Times Books, 1987)

Graham, Bill, *Bill Graham Presents* (Doubleday, 1992)

Hagan, Joe, *Sticky Fingers* (Canongate, 2017)

Holder, Noddy, *Who's Crazee Now?* (Ebury, 1999)

Holzman, Jac, *Follow the Music* (First Media, 2000)

Hoskyns, Barney, *Waiting for the Sun* (Viking, 1996)

——*Trampled Under Foot* (Faber & Faber, 2012)

Houghton, Mick, *Becoming Elektra* (Jawbone, 2016)

Houghton, Richard, *The Beatles: 'I Was There'* (Red Planet, 2016)

Hunter, Ian, *Diary of a Rock'n'roll Star* (Panther, 1974)

Hynde, Chrissie, *Reckless* (Ebury, 2016)

John, Elton, *Me* (Macmillan, 2019)

Johns, Glyn, *Sound Man* (Plume, 2015)

Jones, Kenney, *Let the Good Times Roll* (Blink, 2018)

Kastin, David, *Song of the South* (Turntable Publishing, 2014)

Kooper, Al, *Backstage Passes & Backstabbing Bastards* (Backbeat, 1998)

Kramer, Billy J., *Do You Want to Know a Secret?* (Equinox Publishing, 2016)

Kynaston, David, *Modernity Britain* (Bloomsbury, 2014)

Lewisohn, Mark, *Tune In* (Little, Brown, 2013)

Loog Oldham, Andrew, *Rolling Stoned* (Gegensatz, 2018)

Marsh, Dave, *Before I Get Old* (Plexus, 1983)

Mason, Nick, *Inside Out* (Weidenfeld & Nicolson, 2004)

McNeil, Legs, *Please Kill Me* (Abacus, 1996)

Millard, A. J., *Beatlemania* (Johns Hopkins University Press, 2012)

Miller, James, *Flowers in the Dustbin* (Simon & Schuster, 1999)

Nash, Graham, *Wild Tales* (Penguin, 2013)

Nelson, Paul, *Rod Stewart* (Sidgwick & Jackson, 1982)

O'Shea, Mick, *The Sex Pistols Invade America* (McFarland, 2018)

O'Sullivan, Sibbie, *My Private Lennon* (Mad Creek, 2020)

Osbourne, Ozzy, *I Am Ozzy* (Sphere, 2009)

Paytress, Mark, *Bolan* (Omnibus Press, 2002)

——*The Rolling Stones Off the Record* (Omnibus Press, 2003)

Peel, John, *Margrave of the Marshes* (Bantam, 2005)

Philo, Simon, *British Invasion* (Rowman & Littlefield, 2014)

Pynchon, Thomas, *The Crying of Lot 49* (Bantam Books, 1967)

Reynolds, Simon, *Shock and Awe* (Faber & Faber, 2016)

Rice, Tim, *Oh, What a Circus* (Hodder & Stoughton, 1999)

Richards, Keith, *Life* (Weidenfeld & Nicolson, 2010)

Robinson, Lisa, *There Goes Gravity* (Riverhead, 2014)

Rogan, Johnny, *Byrds: Requiem for the Timeless* (Rogan House, 2011)

Sander, Ellen, *Trips* (Charles Scribner's Sons, 1973)

Savage, Jon, *England's Dreaming* (Faber & Faber, 1992)

Schaffner, Nicholas, *The Beatles Forever* (McGraw Hill, 1978)

——*British Invasion* (McGraw Hill, 1982)

Scher, Paula, *Make It Bigger* (Princeton Architectural Press, 2005)

Bibliography

Searle, Elizabeth, *Idol Talk* (McFarland, 2018)

Shipton, Alyn, *Nilsson* (OUP, 2013)

Spitz, Bob, *Yeah! Yeah! Yeah!* (Little, Brown, 2007)

Springsteen, Bruce, *Born to Run* (Simon & Schuster, 2016)

Stafford, David and Caroline, *Fings Ain't Wot They Used t' Be: The Lionel Bart Story* (Omnibus, 2011)

Stewart, Rod, *Rod: The Autobiography* (Arrow, 2013)

Tannenbaum, Rob, and Marks, Craig, *I Want My MTV* (Penguin, 2011)

Taylor, Derek, *As Time Goes By* (Davis Poynter, 1973)

Thomson, Graeme, *George Harrison: Behind the Locked Door* (Omnibus, 2013)

——*Cowboy Song* (Constable, 2016)

Townshend, Pete, *Who I Am* (HarperCollins, 2012)

Trucks, Rob, *Fleetwood Mac's Tusk* (Continuum, 2011)

Turner, Steve, *Beatles '66* (Ecco, 2016)

Walsh, Ryan, *Astral Weeks: A Secret History of 1968* (Penguin, 2019)

Webb, Jimmy, *The Cake and the Rain* (Omnibus, 2014)

Weller, Sheila, *Girls Like Us* (Ebury, 2008)

Womack, Kenneth, *Sound Pictures* (Orphans, 2018)

Wright, Lawrence, *In the New World* (Vintage, 1988)

Wyman, Bill, *Stone Alone* (Viking, 1990)

Zanes, Warren, *Petty: The Biography* (Henry Holt, 2015)

ACKNOWLEDGEMENTS

Thanks to: Daniel Balado, who copy-edited this as well as my earlier books and really should have been thanked sooner; the British Library and the London Library; Mark Ellen and Mark Cooper, invaluable sounding boards; Bill Scott-Kerr, Sally Wray, Eloisa Clegg and Richard Shailer of Transworld and my agent Charlie Viney.

SONG CREDITS

Lyrics on p 17 from 'Camelot' (Reprise) from the musical *Camelot*, music written by Frederick Loewe and lyrics by Alan Jay Lerner

Lyrics on pp 23 and 33 from 'All My Loving' written by Paul McCartney, performed by the Beatles

Lyrics on p 41 from 'The Times They Are a-Changin'' written and performed by Bob Dylan

Lyrics on pp 85 and 89 from 'England Swings' written by Roger Miller

Lyrics on p 90 from 'Eight Miles High' written by Gene Clark, Jim McGuinn and David Crosby, performed by the Byrds

Lyrics on p 92 from 'I Got You Babe' written by Sonny Bono, performed by Sonny & Cher

Lyrics on p 92 from 'Laugh At Me' written by Sonny Bono

Lyrics on p 135 from 'Good Times' written by Eric Burdon, Vic Briggs, John Weider, Barry Jenkins and Danny McCulloch, performed by Eric Burdon and the Animals

Lyrics on p 138 from 'Jennifer Eccles' written by Graham Nash and Allan Clarke, performed by the Hollies

Lyrics on p 146 from 'Letter To A Cactus Tree' written and performed by Graham Nash

Song Credits

Lyrics on p 150 from 'The Lemon Song' written by John Bonham, Chester Burnett a.k.a. Howlin' Wolf, John Paul Jones, Jimmy Page and Robert Plant, performed by Led Zeppelin

Lyrics on pp 168 and 182 from 'Tiny Dancer' written by Elton John and Bernie Taupin, performed by Elton John

Lyrics on p 184 from 'Suffragette City' written and performed by David Bowie

Lyrics on p 245 from 'Radio Radio' written and performed by Elvis Costello

Lyrics on p 264 from 'I Must Not Think Bad Thoughts' written by John Doe (X) and Exene Cervenka, performed by X

INDEX

Index

301

Index

Index

Index

Index

Index

Index

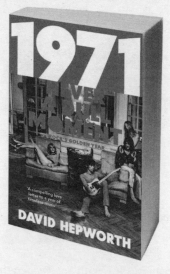

The Sixties ended a year late – on New Year's Eve 1970, when Paul McCartney initiated proceedings to wind up The Beatles. Music would never be the same again.

The next day began a new era. 1971 saw the release of more monumental albums than any year before or since and the establishment of a pantheon of stars to dominate the next forty years – Led Zeppelin, David Bowie, the Rolling Stones, Pink Floyd, Marvin Gaye, Carole King, Joni Mitchell, Rod Stewart, the solo Beatles and more.

January that year fired the gun on an unrepeatable surge of creativity, technological innovation, blissful ignorance, naked ambition and outrageous good fortune. By December rock had exploded into the mainstream. How did it happen? This book tells you. It's the story of 1971, rock's golden year.

'Thoroughly absorbing and appropriately rollicking,
expertly guiding us through one miraculous year
in all its breathless tumble of creation'
DANNY BAKER

'A clever and entertaining book . . . Hepworth
proves a refreshingly independent thinker'
DAILY TELEGRAPH

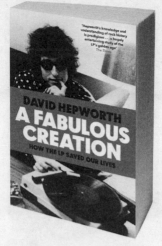

The era of the LP began in 1967, with *Sgt. Pepper*; the Beatles didn't just collect together a bunch of songs, they Made An Album. Henceforth, everybody else wanted to Make An Album.

The end came only fifteen years later, coinciding with the release of Michael Jackson's *Thriller*. By then the Walkman had taken music out of the home and into the streets, and the record business had begun trying to reverse-engineer the creative process in order to make big money. Nobody would play music or listen to it in quite the same way ever again.

It was a short but transformative time. Musicians became 'artists' and we, the people, patrons of the arts. The LP itself had been a mark of sophistication, a measure of wealth, an instrument of education, a poster saying things you dare not say yourself, a means of attracting the opposite sex, and, for many, the single most desirable object in their lives.

This is the story of that time; it takes us from recording studios where musicians were doing things that had never been done before to the sparsely furnished apartments where their efforts would be received like visitations from a higher power. This is the story of how LPs saved our lives.

> 'A joyous and nostalgic celebration
> of the golden age of the LP'
> *DAILY MIRROR*